A Very
Wealthy
Man

A Very Wealthy Man

Marian Denman King

HILLSBORO PRESS
Franklin, Tennessee

Printed in the United States of America

04   03   02   01   00   1   2   3   4   5

Library of Congress Catalog Card Number: 00-102058

ISBN: 1-57736-182-2

Cover design by Gary Bozeman

Published by
HILLSBORO PRESS
an imprint of
PROVIDENCE HOUSE PUBLISHERS
238 Seaboard Lane • Franklin, Tennessee 37067
800-321-5692
www.providencehouse.com

This book is dedicated to my high school English teacher, Mrs. Mildred Flege. And to Mrs. Flege, I could say this book is my gift to you, except for the fact that it is the other way around! This is your gift to me, for you gave me the longing to write and I thank you for this.

Preface and Acknowledgments

I would like to sincerely thank my sister, Frances, for the encouragement she has given me. Without it, I might have given up on this endeavor (and the first book). She has given me encouragement not only with writing, but all my life she has been my sail.

Again, I want to thank Mildred and Teresa Dutton for their reading and correcting the first half of the manuscript, and my thanks and appreciation to Royce and Martha Currie for their help with the second half. Also, Rev. Ray Bobo was always willing when I yelled "Help!" I want to thank Dr. Arthur Butterfield for his medical information when my characters needed help.

My sincere thanks goes out to my son, Scott Goza, Darlene Chastain, and Grover Lunsford for their help with my computer woes. This is one area where I could not pass "Go." One of these three could usually be found when I ran into trouble. My computer had a way of making the manuscript disappear. In desperation, Grover made an extra disk and carried it home with him. This, he said, I could not touch.

And, of course, I want to thank all you dear readers!

PART ONE

Chapter One

CYNTHIA'S DISCOVERIES IN THE GROUND, WHERE JOYCE Kelly's flower garden once sent an abundance of beauties shooting above the warm rich earth in early spring, astounded her.

The first Saturday spring morning that the new bride stepped out to explore and plan a flower bed, she spied a piece of roofing that had been carelessly left lying after the new house was finished. When she picked the roofing up there was a shoot of a crocus struggling for breath. Stooping, Cynthia felt the delicate bloom between her fingers and thought, with a pang of sadness, about Miss Joyce, who had planted the bulb. Then turning, she saw other shoots about ready to unfold, announcing that spring had arrived for certain, and a smile played about the corners of her mouth. Joyce Kelly would be happy to know that Cynthia cared about her precious flower garden where she had spent so many hours on her knees pruning and weeding. Everything had been left in disarray when the builders finished, as the yard was not any of their concern. The house had been built just as it was before and if anyone had not known that there had been a fire, they might expect Miss Joyce to appear at any given moment through the door with her garden hat, gloves, and yard tools. Cynthia Russell felt like an intruder here. When she was a child visiting the house it was like a glimpse of heaven to her, and now actually living here with her husband still seemed like a hazy dream. What would Miss Joyce expect her to do with this or with that? And where should she place this piece of furniture? Should it be here or there, or in another room even? Alyn left all this completely to her discretion. She and Kate Harris looked through furniture stores and old shops for months in search of just the right pieces for each room. Now that job was completed to the bride and groom's satisfaction, yet the hum and life of the previous house was

1

lacking. A house may be built in a few months, but it takes years of hard work to make it a home.

Those who entered the new house walked almost on tiptoe and spoke in low, reverent tones, like there might be a danger of waking the dead. Although Joyce Kelly was gone, it was still her house. Everyone could feel her presence. To Alyn, it was a comfort to feel Aunt Joyce's presence, but just how long would it take to again hear Lizzie Mae singing in the kitchen? Her own family missed her joyful laughter and bossiness, her rapid-fire orders and commands. From the first day that Lizzie was ushered inside the new house, her whole being felt a cold emptiness that was transferred to the family. Where was her old iron skillet and the blue speckled kettle that sang before the water boiled? Looking in a cabinet over the new cook table, she found all new bowls, dishes, cups. Not one item was the same. As tears formed in the corners of her eyes, Lizzie lifted the tail of her apron, and wiping the tears away, she turned to Alyn and with child-like curiosity asked, "Misser Alyn-baby, whut we's gonna do now?"

He placed an arm around her stout shoulders and replied, "We'll do just as before, Lizzie, even though it won't seem the same." Behind them Adam stood silently with hat in hand and agreed with a nod of his gray head. Time marches on as it always has. Buildings may grow old and rot away; people may pass away and go to their own reward; but those left behind must keep plodding along doing the things they have to do the best they know how.

Alyn Russell had learned so much during his lifetime up to now. His growing-up years here on Kendell Mountain were the best. He learned a lot about living from Aunt Joyce, Uncle Anson, the school, and the mountain itself. He learned a lot about dying during the First World War in France, and now he was learning about love from all the people who were hurting most from the loss of the two dearest people in his life. Together, he and Cynthia would build a new life. He would carry on Knollwood Orchards and the Kendell Mountain School and, together, they would make the new house a home.

Chapter Two

THIS YEAR OF 1929 WOULD BE A JOYOUS YEAR FOR THE YOUNG couple who were now looking forward to a new beginning. They were both strong in body and in mind and the only thing they could do was to look to the future. What had happened in their lives before was a tragedy . . . the hanging of Cynthia's father, Hugh Tanner, and the fire that took the lives of Anson and Joyce Kelly. Known as Aunt Joyce and Uncle Anson to Alyn, they were the two dear people who had adopted him. But now, with the help of God and each other, the couple would build their own lives and be happy once again here at Knollwood Orchards.

Being happy after all Alyn and Cynthia had been through would take work for both of them. They could do it; they were not the only ones to lose someone and find a new life. This was a part of living . . . being born, loving and being loved, losing someone dear to the heart. Alyn told Cynthia that he'd heard Aunt Joyce say that "Life is what you make it."

Each year since the end of the First World War, the country suffered an economic crisis. In the little backwoodsy town of Union Gap, Georgia, the crisis was not felt as harshly as in large cities where unemployment was a major factor. Most people here in the little town grew their own food. Up on Kendell Mountain, some had cleared land and had gardens, made their own clothes, bartered for some items, and did a great deal of trading. They also hunted game and wild turkeys.

From the sale of Alyn's house in Boston (left to him by his mother's relative), he had rebuilt Knollwood after the fire. In addition, with his Aunt Joyce's Atlanta Bank, he could carry out the desires from her will for him and keep the Kendell Mountain School in operation.

Up on the north ridge of the mountain, Alyn's stepsister, Kate, and her husband, Dr. David Harris, lived comfortably with their sons

Matthew and Daniel. The boys' first names were actually Jeff and Josh.
When they turned eight, they decided to use their middle names so they
would not sound enough alike to be confusing. It took some getting
used to by family and friends and was more confusing to their teachers
than the sounding alike had been. They attended Kendell Mountain
School, which was nestled back in the woods below Knollwood, where
Kate still taught since the school's founding in 1913. Cynthia had been
teaching there since 1920. Alyn felt a fond attachment to Kate, David,
and the eleven-year-old twins. The boys' lively antics brought back fond
memories of when he was that age roaming the woods with his dog,
Beans, and his friend, Luther. Kate's father, Anson Kelly, had been more
than proud of his grandsons, who looked up to their grandfather with
worshipful eyes.

Now, as Cynthia stood on the ground where Joyce's old flower
beds had been, she looked up and saw Joyce's lavender rose growing
by the chimney beside the kitchen window. It had survived the fire,
growing at the time on an arch at the entrance to the flower garden.
The arch was damaged by the builders as it was in the way, but Adam
rescued the beautiful rose from the ground where it grew. Now it
clambered gallantly up the stone chimney with its buds raising their
heads and opening into a kingly lavender velvet. Cynthia decided to
start at once on the project of resurrecting the flower garden and went
to find Adam to request his assistance. Adam knew all there was to
know about growing things. He would be the one to teach her and tell
her the names of the flowers that Joyce Kelly preferred in her flower
garden. Adam was still able and willing, but as Lizzie put it, "a mite
slower 'dan useter." Miss Joyce never allowed him to help her unless
it was just to supply her with rich woods dirt and pine straw, because
she preferred to work the garden herself. She told him that she loved
the feel of the brown earth and the satisfaction that the planting gave
her. She even loved the smell of the musty dank soil.

Cynthia found Lizzie out on the back porch hanging some wet
towels across the line to dry. Taking a clothes pin out of her mouth, the
stout colored woman told her, "Oh, he ain' chere, Miz Cynthee, honey.
He went 'long wit Will down tu town."

"Oh, well. Actually what I wanted with him can wait. No bother,
Lizzie. Where's Ophelia?"

"She be cleanin' up her house an' a-washin' close. Her and Cora
always does dat on Saddays. Is der sumpin' I can do, Miz Cynthee?"

"Ah, no, Lizzie. There's a little project I'd like to get Adam to help
me with but it can wait . . . no hurry about it. I'll just go in and grade

some of the children's school work." She turned to go back inside, feeling alone and needless at the moment. What was she supposed to do in this house? The colored women did everything and made the decisions about what needed to be done. Would she ever get used to living in this house? "No," she said all at once changing her mind. "I think I will take a stroll down to my old cabin. Do you want to come along with me, Lizzie?"

Lizzie pinned the last wet towel up on the line and, smiling, turned to the young woman. "Oh, dat be too much a walk fer me, honeychile. Dese ole bones wone like it much iffen I put dem true dat. You jes' go ahead and enjoy yo walk, but you be kerful now off all by yo sef, now you hear?"

"I will," Cynthia said with a wave and turned to go inside for a sweater. The more she thought about it, the more she wanted to see the cabin. She had not been there since she started teaching and was living at the school. Her mother, Amy Tanner, and her grandmother, Miss Maudie, both died during the flu epidemic of 1918, and it was then that Ella Fullman took care of her and saw to it that she went away to college. Cynthia had thought of the log house, where she was raised, many times, some fond memories and some not. She remembered how Alyn walked home from school with her when they were small and attending the little one-room school. Sometimes Amy Tanner had freshly baked tea cakes for them, still warm from the oven, and goat's milk to wash them down. She remembered the baby doll that sat on her bed. Alyn brought it to her from a trip to Atlanta with his Aunt Joyce. And she thought of how she and Alyn would sit on the ground for hours and watch the construction men build the new school house. So many other thoughts rushed through her mind, but she tried not to think about the hanging and how her mother was so sick after that with a deep, deep depression.

Yes, Cynthia would go back today and face these old troubling thoughts in her head. Now, maybe they would go away. She had Alyn Russell to replace them, and how she loved him! Now, she could deal with these thoughts. Many times at night while trying to sleep, her mind walked through the rooms and she heard her mother or her granny calling to her.

Now, she was walking down the path where Miss Joyce used to walk and admire the wild flowers along the way. Once, the fine lady brought a big bouquet of them to Miss Maudie. "I just don't know the names of all of them," she told herself, "and they are all so pretty that they look like an angel just touched them."

Voices were heard around the curve from the pathway behind her. There were two young people creating a whirlwind of happy laughter with a hoop rolling along prodded by a stick. When they came into Cynthia's sight she saw that it was none other than Kate and Doc's sons. The pathway became more slanted causing the hoop to roll faster until it struck the young woman on the leg. She grabbed the spot where it hit and began rubbing the pain away. "Ooh, Miss Tanner, I mean, Aunt Cynthee, are you hurt? I'm so sorry. The blamed ole thing jus' got away!"

"Did it cut your leg?" the other boy asked.

"No, Matt, it will be fine in a minute or two. I was just surprised and should have jumped out of the way. Where are you two going in such a rush? How about coming along with me? I could use the company of two jolly young men."

"Can't," Dan answered. "We are on an errand for Mama down to the school and she said to hurry back."

"See you later," Matt answered as they dashed on down the road and left Cynthia standing where the pathway to the Tanner cabin separated from the road. She shook her head in amazement as the thought hit her that someday she might be the mother of two like that. Out loud she said, "Heaven forbid!" and continued on down the path in a lighter mood brought on by the lively twins. Except for being mischievous, they were good and bright students in school, no doubt due to Kate's demands and watchful eyes.

As Cynthia neared the cabin, she discerned its roof; the rest of the house was hidden from sight by bushes, weeds, straggling wild flowers, and deserted rubble here and there. But up above, spring was in the air. Birds twittered and trilled their songs among the tall trees and bushes. Evergreens laced with bright green of spring swayed slightly in the cool morning breeze that caused a piece of rope hanging from a tree to move back and forth. It was hanging where her swing was but now reminded her of another tree and another rope, so she turned her head, brushing a lock of light brown hair from her eyes, and surveyed the disarray caused by years of neglect.

As she stepped forward toward the door, partially ajar and hanging by one hinge, apprehension took over causing a slight chill down her spine. Half expecting to hear her grandmother's shrill voice calling out to her, she took hold of the door and picked up on it to push it open. A flurry of birds flapped past sending her sprawling on the floor. "For the love of Pete! What next?" Brushing her soiled dress, she stood and looked at a dust-filled room. Amazingly, the furniture was still in place. There was the potbellied iron stove that had heated the house, with Miss Maudie's cane-bottomed chair still in front of it. A pillow on the chair, its stuffing poking out all around, looked as though some little animal slept on it. Cynthia walked through the other two rooms, reminiscing about good times as well as bad ones, and decided that the place could be fixed up with not as much repair as the cleaning would take. Maybe someday she would feel up to tackling the job but not anytime soon. What would be the use? Satisfied, she turned to leave.

While Cynthia was in the melancholy mood, she decided to stop by the cemetery and wished that she had brought along a rake and hoe to do a bit of cleaning and weeding. Maybe Kate and the boys would accompany her soon to do this job. She always liked to look over from the clearing down upon Everitt Lake where one could see beautiful reflections of the sky if it happened to be a clear, sunny day. This was a favorite spot where she and Alyn liked to come and remember times passed—not that they would dwell on the past. It would take time to clear their clouded minds of some incidents.

The cemetery had several new graves since she had last been there. "Let's see," she thought, "Of course that isn't counting the recent time we were here for Joyce and Anson's funeral and at that time no one could or would want to look at the other graves." She deliberately walked first to the grave of James Neal Sprayberry, her first husband who had been killed in a logging accident after they had been married for only six months. Then she stopped at her Father and Mother's graves. Hugh Tanner, unmercifully hanged without a trial . . . such a terrible, terrible thing. Her mother died in 1918 of influenza and her grandmother, Miss Maudie, of the same thing; their deaths were only a few days apart. There were graves of several other people who had met with this same fate that held the nation in the same grip. Kendell Mountain did not escape it. She walked on to the place were Joyce and Anson Kelly lay side by side. "Such a beautiful love story they had," Cynthia thought. "It would make a lovely story." She let out a sigh as if to rid herself of her sorrows and turned to leave for home. "Home. As of yet, I can't get used to calling it 'home.'"

Chapter Three

ON THE MORNING BEFORE THE HARRIS TWINS HAD MET Cynthia on the pathway below the big new house, they decided when they woke up early to go exploring as they were prone to do on any given Saturday morning. Sometimes on these excursions they opted to go fishing but this morning it was agreed (between the boys and without parental consent) to climb up to the cave where they had been many times before. One time, they smoked rabbit tobacco in the cave and with that experience done, it was to be the last time for that. The stuff tasted terrible! "Let's take a lantern so we can see to write on the walls like the cave men used to do and then we can take that sissy Joel Thacher up there and tell him it was cave men who did it and we found it there." This was Dan's suggestion. Matt wholeheartedly agreed with a squeal of laughter and they took off with Dan carrying the lantern.

The same as Cynthia, the boys were thankful for a beautiful morning as they breathed in the cool, pine-scented air, although not caring one iota for any wild flowers or bushes. They both were endowed with endless energy and after a few commanded chores, Kate felt more than happy to have them out of her way. David left early with his satchel on the seat beside him as the car chugged down the rocky road. He was going to make a few needed visits with various patients. Now there would be no instructions from their father either so the boys could dawdle to their hearts' content. They pushed and shoved one another up the path with the lantern haphazardly swinging along.

"You got matches?"

"Yep," came a short reply.

"Let me do the drawing."

"No! Not all of it. You'd make all automobiles."

"No, I won't 'cause nobody'd believe cave men could draw an automobile."

"Well, you can't draw anything else."

"Can, too!"

"Cannot."

They came to the place where a large outcropping of rock made a perfect resting place (if one were tired), but Dan sat the lantern on a rock and searched his pockets for his Barlow knife. "I've got mine," Matt said.

"Well, here's mine, too. Thought I'd gone off and left it on the dresser."

"Wouldn't it have been fun to 'uv been along when Uncle Alyn and Luther found all that money?"

"Boy! I'll say it would've! That would've been somethin' else! Do you know how much money was in that bag?"

"Which one? The one that was all counterfeit or the one with the real money that they found underneath the car?"

"The real money, dummy. How much was in that bag?"

"Don't know, let's ask 'im. I'd like to know."

"Why do you need to know? So's you can just drool and wish you had it?"

"Somethin' like that I guess, but anyway, they sure was honest to turn it all in."

"Don't you think folks would know or else they'd a' thought that they'd stole the stuff they bought with the money? Don't you ever think of anything?"

"Aw, shut up and go on. Here, you take the lantern . . . I'm tired of toting it."

"No, you'll just want me to hold it while you do all the drawing."

Then that boy ran off without the lantern. Amid shoving, pushing and punching, they soon came to the place where the cave was. Located behind bushes, it was hidden from view. From so many trips to this place, Dan and Matt knew that this was their destination. When Matt parted the bushes, Dan said in a low voice, "Wait, Matt, let me light the lantern first. There might be an animal in there." Matt gave a low whistle and knew that he would not like to meet face-to-face with a bear in the dark, and then he thought that he would not like to meet up with one by the light of the lantern either.

Now inside, Dan held the lantern up high to disperse the flickering light. They stood there transfixed as usual and then Matt whispered, "Hold the light down, look here." There in the dirt, plain as day, they saw footprints that pointed back toward the darkness. They looked at one another, both feeling prickly goose bumps down their backs.

"Let's get out of here quick!" Matt exclaimed, forgetting to whisper. As they both turned to leave, Matt, the first one in, felt an arm around his throat. "Dan!" he screamed in a choking voice, coughing and struggling. "Help me! . . . Don't leave me!" Then Matt started biting the arm and kicking at an ankle.

The arm was released from around the boy's throat and as he began to run behind Dan, they heard a deep, strange voice say, "Stop. Me no hurt. Stop."

Feeling curiosity stronger than fear, both boys stopped and turned to see who the person was, with Dan holding the light up high. They both gave out with a frightened gasp when they saw a tall Indian standing with his hands contritely down by his sides. The man looked humble and harmless. "No hurt boys," he repeated. "Me *o gi na li* [friend]." One arm went up in a peace sign.

"Dan, I ain't believing." Matt rubbed his eyes as though he could rub the mirage away.

"Me, neither. But he's real for sure."

The boys went outside into the daylight, walking backwards with the Indian following. He was dressed in a sleeveless shirt made from animal hide and long pants tied with a cord. His feet were bare, and his white hair hung long down his back. Outside, the man spoke first. "Not talk people in many moons. Not talk good." Then he reached in a shirt pocket (that had been sewn on crooked) and retrieved two arrowheads, giving them as a peace offering to the two astounded boys. "We must be dreaming," one of them said.

"Thank you," the other said. "We be friends. I be Matt. My brother be Dan." Matt told the Indian in the simple speech he had used.

"Sit," they were ordered as the man sat on the ground and crossed his legs. Dan and Matt did the same. They placed the arrowheads into their pockets.

"Name 'Little Bear.'"

"You no little," Dan said.

"Was. Grew up."

"Yea," Matt said and added, "Everbody does, 'les they die."

"How come they name you Little Bear?"

"Would be change when grow, then be 'Brave.'"

"Why you here? We've never seen you here before."

"Me see boys. Much time. Little Bear hide. Boys tell." Little Bear tilted his head and looked sadly to the ground without really answering their question.

"If we going be friends, I call you 'Chief.' That okay?"

"'Chief' okay. Me like."

"Well, how do you live, Chief? How do you get clothes and food and stuff that you need?" Matthew asked this question and then Dan replied, "Yeah, how?"

Chief looked at them blankly, wondering just how these lads got by without any knowledge of living off the land. This is something an Indian learned from very early childhood, and anyone who lived around these parts, as surely they did, must know something about living off the land. "Creatures in woods. Kill for food, fur make clothes. Eat berries, nuts, acorns. *A ni tsu tsa* not know much."

"Huh?" Matt asked? He shrugged his shoulders.

"We not know Cherokee words."

"Boys," Little Bear told them. "Boys not know much."

Matt scratched the dirt with a stick, wondering why he was so dumb; then Dan spread his arms out and said, "Oh, we know lots of things but our parents buy us clothes and there are too many trees to have a garden and grow things up here so they buy food. Our father is a medicine man and our mother teaches school."

"People cut down forest, plant apple trees. Much apples. Is good." Little Bear was thinking how he had eaten the apples from the time of the first harvest there on Kendell Mountain. He looked wise, and the boys figured he must know many, many things. They sat on the ground with legs crossed, elbows on them, and chins resting in their hands, listening intently to all Chief had to tell. This was better than any book they had ever read. The kids in school would be so envious of the brothers.

"You no tell parents, no people Little Bear here." Chief had a worried look on his face. He wondered if these boys could be trusted. Would he finally be found out after all these years? Granted, he had been lonely for companionship, but after this long he had become accustomed to being alone, being one with the forest and the animals. Letting these boys find him was the first slip he'd ever made. It only takes one slip to change a person's life forever!

"Why we no tell, Chief? The people we know would be so happy to have you living up here in this cave."

"Yea," his brother chimed in. "We've been in this cave many times, but our folks don't know it. Parents think kids are dumb and will always get hurt."

Dan nodded his head up and down in agreement. "They sure do, but our Uncle Alyn told us that he and Luther found a case full of money in this cave when they were close to our age."

The Indian pursed his lips in thought and agreed with a slight nod. "Me saw man. Stood back in dark cave. Saw man put *a de la* [money] there. Me no touch. Not mine. Saw boys come. Saw *gi li* [dog]. Me run. *Gi li* bite."

Matt stood up then, stooped to pick up a small stone, tossed it down the hill, and watched it hit a tree. "What would be the harm if we tell about you? You could come live with us maybe."

"No! Soldiers come! Take Chief far, far away over mountains and plains to far land. Not be penned up like cows, horses. Chief home be here." He spread his hands around. Soldiers took my people many moons ago. All family gone. *E do da* [father], *e tsi* [mother] run like deer. Run many moons. Find cave here. They stay. Many moons, they get papoose, Little Bear. Now Little Bear hair like snow. Father, Mother go be with Great Spirit."

Dan and Matt both had studied in their history class about how the Cherokees were removed from their land in 1838. Families were taken from their homes with only the clothes on their backs, and the men who had been out hunting came home to find their families gone, some of them never seen again. As soon as the Cherokees were marched away, their homes were looted and burned. That summer was hot with drought conditions and steaming heat that only added to the misery of these people who were pinned up in forts that had been built along the way in preparation for their arrival. The forts had stagnant water, irregular meals, and a lack of adequate sanitation resulting in disease and many deaths. The Indian shamans did what they could, mostly in vain. This was known as the summer of the *Nunna-da-ul-tsun-yi*, "The Place Where They Cried." History calls it "The Trail of Tears."

Many Cherokees escaped and hid away in the crevasses and caves of the north Georgia mountains, banding together in groups. During the Civil War, many of them joined forces with the South. Little Bear's parents had found this cave on Kendell Mountain and stayed to themselves. Once again they escaped the wrath of soldiers, this time the Yankee soldiers, who snaked their way south missing Kendell Mountain by only a few miles.

This Cherokee couple had been married only a week when they fled from the area where their people were marched away. Running Wolf and Red Bud had a number of children die in infancy with Little Bear the only one to survive. They had taught Little Bear the Cherokee way of life and spoke mostly the Cherokee language to him. They knew English and could write and speak it well. However, it was evident that they did not speak much English after they fled to the cave because Little Bear was not fluent in this language.

DAN STOOD UP, EXCLAIMING A FEW CUSS WORDS IN amazement. Before he could say anything further, the Indian man with a perplexed look on his face asked, "What strange words mean?"

Matt answered for his brother. "They are bad words and I'm going to tell on him. Our father would beat him to a pulp if he knew he talked like that and our mother would drop dead!"

Chief turned to Dan and asked, "You want mother drop dead?"

"Oh, heck no!"

"Why say?"

"Just because the soldiers were bad and it makes me spittin' mad, that's why! We like you and we don't want that to happen to you, Chief, but you need to know that there are not any soldiers doing that anymore. You would not have to go anywhere else. Our Uncle Alyn owns this land, and he would like for you to stay here as long as you want to."

"Yes, and our father and mother would like it, too. They all will like you and want to help you anyway they can. What if you were to get sick or somethin'? Our father helps everyone who gets sick, and our Uncle Bob is a preacher man who tells people about God . . . The Great White Spirit . . . and he would like to talk to you, too. You have to let them come to see you, Chief. We promise . . . [he started to say 'Honest Injun' but caught himself just in time] . . . honest, no one will harm you."

The old Indian bowed his head, thinking. He had loved this land all of his life. With each day, he wondered if this would be the day that the soldiers would find him here. There had been numerous occasions when he came close to being sighted by some of the residents on the mountain. He had seen the dark man and the boys many times as they hunted for rabbits, always fearful that the dog would smell his presence. He had seen the nice lady and man walking through the woods admiring the beautiful scenery and the waterfall. They posed no danger for they had eyes only for each other. But he feared the men who had a strange-looking machine that belched smoke. They looked mean. Only did the mean expressions change as they held jars under a spout and filled them with liquid. Then they smiled. Little Bear could smell a pungent odor and wondered just what the men had made that pleased them so much. As he thought, he decided that these boys were honest, and if they said there were no more soldiers, then he would believe them. He had been very lonely through the years. Now, he would have friends. Up to now, he had only observed people from hiding places, wishing he could walk up to them and have them speak directly to him. He remembered the nice man and lady who took walks through the woods and sometimes sat beside the waterfall. They looked perfectly peaceful. He would like to have had a nice wife like her, someone to love him. Then, there was the fire that he observed from afar and never saw the man and woman anymore. Little Bear saw the sadness on people's faces, and he saw that joy had been taken away. Yes! He needed to be around people. He was now a very old man.

THIS WAS THE DAY THAT LITTLE BEAR WOULD BE INTRODUCED to civilization. What would it do to him? Would it change him any at all—his ways or his thinking? Perhaps he was not too old to accept a world so benign, so different from anything he had long ago accepted as the only way of life.

Chapter Four

"FRANKLY, I THINK THAT THE SCHOOL BOARD SHOULD decide whether or not that Indian can live at the school."

"School will be out in another month so what could he possibly hurt anyway? And look how old the man is! I know he can't do much work, but the room in the basement isn't used for anything so what would be the harm in having him live there?"

"Oh, maybe you're right. I suppose it won't hurt to give it a try and see how it works out. I heard he's fairly agile so it might be that he could use a rake and a broom."

The two women were talking while waiting for Ezra Cronon to come over to the counter and sack up their purchases and put them on their bill. "Good afternoon, Miz Kirby . . . Miz Pedegree," Ezra said as he started placing the groceries in a bag. "That Indian could become a problem for the community alright," he said, taking up the subject of their conversation. "Then agin, he might jes' be a docile ole man. It wouldn't be human to jes' let 'im live on up there in that there cave and have 'im die all alone."

"A person never knows, but we can't be too careful around the children, you know," Mrs. Pedegree chimed in. Then she added, "Well, I declare, would you look at that!"

They all went to the large window to look out and see Alyn Russell and Adam Jones riding by in the Knollwood truck, with a man, woman, and two children in the back. Several suitcases could be seen stacked one upon the other beside supplies the men had bought earlier from Ezra.

"Now, who in the world could they be?"

"Could've come in on thu train," Ezra offered. The truck moved on out of town leaving the general store occupants to wonder.

Billy O'Shields, Union Gap stationmaster, had caught Alyn as he drove past the railroad station and asked his opinion as to what he should do with this family he'd found stowed away on a freight car. The man said that he'd lost his job in Atlanta and was unable to find any other work after walking the streets for several months in search of a job. They could have made a slim living doing some odd jobs, he'd explained to Billy, and his wife would be willing to take in washing and ironing, except for the fact that their house was repossessed by the bank. They had nowhere to go but to some relatives in Kentucky who might possibly be unhappy to see them move in on them. Alyn asked and was told that they had no way of contacting them since they were without a cent to their name.

"Billy, I'll just take 'em on up to our place until we can decide what is best. Maybe I can contact their relatives."

"Sure, Alyn, I'd be much obliged if you'd do that," Billy replied, relieved that the responsibility would be out of his hands.

The man looked honest enough and capable of hard work even though the wife had a haggard look as if she were worn to a frazzle. She sat crowded between Alyn and her husband with their little girl on the man's lap. Adam had volunteered to ride in the back of the truck, with himself and the boy dangling their legs down off the back of the truck, suitcases piled behind them with the supplies. The Knollwood truck disappeared around the bend of the road out of town and traveled on up toward the road that led to Knollwood Orchards.

This family had been displaced overnight, like so many now. News reports held listeners spellbound with grave announcements that the economy was in serious trouble, prices falling, and businesses closing. Money became scarce to the middle-class workers as their jobs disappeared when factories and companies closed down. This was not a time to be living in large cities. Many who had hurried north to work in automobile factories now found themselves idle as machines produced so much that workers were not needed. Shantytowns grew up in vacant lots and dumps.

PRISCILLA LYLES, A PLAIN WOMAN YET STILL ATTRACTIVE AT thirty-eight years of age, ventured a smile, then blinked, trying to see through tears now forming in her eyes. She stood holding a dusty, ragged curtain aside while gazing out, seeing nothing. She contemplated the sudden changes in her life. Life can do strange things to a person if one lets it. Nothing will ever be the way it should be; life is what we make it. Brad, who had run all the way around the house, came dashing in the back door followed by Jamie and exclaimed, "Mama! There's a outhouse in the backyard! Can you feature that? We'd have to go outside to use the toilet!"

"And there's no water faucets or sink in the kitchen," the little girl said softly. "We had electric lights in Atlanta."

"Brad, Jamie, be quiet," their mother urged, dabbing at her eyes with a handkerchief from a pocket. The advice was superfluous and might just as well gone unspoken.

"But, Mama, what about cold nights and there might be bears out there."

"People used outhouses long before bathrooms were invented, and I'm certain there is a well somewhere on the property for water," she answered.

Just then Alyn and Cole Lyles came through the front door where they had been talking about the Tanner log cabin. Alyn had already explained that his wife grew up here and the house had not been occupied since 1918 after her mother and grandmother's deaths. "I know it is in bad shape, Cole," Alyn said, "but we'll have some help come in and give it a thorough cleaning. You folks are welcome to it for as long as you like. And now is the time to plant a garden so Sam and Will can come down and plow up some ground to get it ready . . . maybe take down a few more trees out back."

After looking in the two bedrooms, Cynthia came back to Priscilla and placed a hand on her arm for a reassuring touch. "It will be beautiful. With clean windows and new curtains and all the other homey things, you'll see. I know it looks rough now, but don't worry. Why, in no time you'll have a home here."

Brad still worried and tugged at his mother again asking, "But how will we get food, Mama? We can't wait for a garden to grow."

It was Cynthia who answered first, and Alyn interspersed suggestions. They could supply a laying hen, several young fryers, and loan them a fresh cow. That would get them started, along with a supply of whatever else was needed from the general store. The Russells had many unused wedding gifts packed away that this unfortunate family was welcome to have. To Cole and Priscilla, the generosity offered them seemed unbelievable.

Priscilla actually smiled, feeling grateful for these gracious people who had come to their rescue. If her grandmother could raise a family of eight children without running water, or an inside bathroom, then she could manage also.

"We'll need to check for roof leaks and clean out the chimney," Alyn added.

"Oh, Jamie, we'll be living like pioneers," Brad told his little sister. "It will be fun."

"Good thing you were a Boy Scout," Jamie answered in her low, calm voice.

Priscilla was thinking of the Russell's beautiful house where they had spent last night and had the whole upstairs all to themselves. When her family was huddled on the floor of that boxcar, all hope had flown away and a curtain of fear grasped her body causing her to shiver, not from the cold so much as from the unknown. People can become so complacent in their warm, secure lives, feeling they have done well in preparing themselves for the future. Then all of a sudden . . . it is snatched away. Now, here was this Russell couple so secure, their lives in order, and seemingly with no worries. Priscilla was thinking, "How do some have it all when our world just suddenly falls apart? We have tried to live right and have done no one any harm. We have worked hard, but evidently none of this mattered." These thoughts ran rapidly through her mind like the freight train that tossed them about around each curve, leaving bumps and bruises.

With the offer of this place to live and help to start over, Priscilla saw a fragile thread of hope. Cole came to her, placed an arm around her waist, and said softly, "We can do it, 'Pris'; we can start over. Somehow, I'll find work." Then he kissed her lightly on the cheek. Turning to Alyn and Cynthia, Cole said, "We thank you people for your graciousness. You are like angels to us. Surely God has used you to help us and we will do our best here and take good care of your place."

"Thank you," Priscilla said softly, failing to find the right words to say more.

THEIR WALK BACK UP TO KNOLLWOOD WAS INVIGORATING. Just to be able to relax, smell the fragrant spring air, hear mockingbirds calling to one another from a sumac bush, and the jays up high in pines giving worried answers . . . it was nothing short of a miracle for the Lyles family. Brad and Jamie skipped along investigating with curiosity all the wonders that were so foreign to what they had known in the city. Soon, an automobile was heard before it came into sight. When it rounded the bend, Alyn said, "Over to the side, children. Here comes Dr. Harris and his wife, Kate."

"Hello," Cynthia called and asked, "Where are the boys?"

"Out and about," Kate answered, swooping a hand towards the woods, meaning they could be anywhere for the forest was their domain. "Probably out with that Indian no doubt."

"Indian!" Brad exclaimed.

His sister ran to her father and grabbed his hand with fear showing in her face. "Are Indians in these woods, Papa!" she exclaimed with tears and then wailed, "I want to go home!"

Cynthia stooped down, patted the child, and assured her that there was only this one Indian here. He was a very old man with white hair and a very nice Indian.

"I still want to go home, now!"

"Shush, Jamie. It's alright," Cole said with a look on his face that begged for an explanation of these people in the car.

It was Alyn who introduced them and explained to Doc and Kate that the Lyles would be living in the Tanner cabin. "We'll be neighbors," Kate smiled. "And I may be your teacher in school," she said to the children.

"School! I thought we wouldn't have to go anymore," Brad protested with a scowl and pursed lips.

"There will always be school, young man. You can't get by without it."

Brad thought that this Mrs. Harris already sounded like a school teacher. She told him that she would send her boys down to make their acquaintance as soon as they showed up. He told his sister later that since they were a school teacher's sons, they would no doubt be sissies. He pictured them wearing extremely clean clothes and little hats with ribbons in the back. "I'd even bet they have lace on their drawers," Brad grinned, hopefully.

Chapter Five

CHIEF LITTLE BEAR LIKED THE COMFORT OF HIS ROOM IN THE basement at Kendell Mountain School. It could be very easy for him to become soft and sluggish with a complacent life of ease since all his life he'd been toughened by the elements. A person without a purpose might easily suffer from boredom.

One day while lying on his cot, he contemplated his new life and decided it was time to go home to the cave where he was born and had lived all his life. He missed hunting. Not using the bow and arrow could make him lose the accuracy of which he'd always been so confident. Little Bear sat up, slipped on his moccasins, and said with assurance, "Me go now," for no one to hear but the walls and himself.

The empty hallways were silent. If a voice spoke, there would have been an echo bouncing off the walls. Summer called all the students to flee on joyful wings, each to parts unknown. A few years ago Little Bear would have been stealthily darting among the woods here and there stalking deer or fishing in a favorite spot. Now, his movements were slowed but still accurate; his eyesight dimmer. "Little Bear much work. Be ready when snows come," he said as he slipped silently out the door and faded through the dense forest as a vapor.

Bob Russell asked his wife, Tiss, if she had encountered Little Bear in the last few days. No, she had not seen him either, and Ty Western, the agriculture department teacher, said he had not shown up to help him as he had been doing. With the boys all now gone home, he needed help. At the old Indian's age, he was not much help but better than nothing. "I feel sure he's gone back to the only home he's ever known—his cave," Bob told Tiss. Taking down his old beat-up hat that he'd always used for fishing or hiking, Bob said he would see if Alyn would accompany him up to the cave.

"WHERE'S TAD THESE DAYS?" BOB ASKED HIS NEPHEW. HE and Alyn were going up the steep pathway behind the big house. They had passed the spot where the huge oak tree (the hanging tree) had been for two hundred years. It had held Alyn and Cynthia's initials as childhood sweethearts. Out of respect for Cynthia's feelings, since her father had been hanged on the lower limb, Alyn had the tree chopped down and sent off to the Dutton sawmill.

Sidestepping the stump, he answered Bob's question. "Tad and Selma took the kids and went up to Murphy to visit his sister Nellie and her family for about ten days. I let them use Jim's old car. It's still in good condition, but I bought new tires for it. Tad said they'd be back soon, but your guess is as good as mine just when that'll be."

Bob answered, "With that Sassy being such a constant talker and singing those crazy songs of hers, I'd be ready to poke a stopper in her mouth by now!" They both smiled and agreed on this. Then Alyn held a barbed-wire fence apart for Bob to pass through.

"Look at this mending job, would you?" Alyn said as Bob stood up on the other side.

"Hmm, looks rather ingenuous if you ask me."

"It's wrapped with leather. That's funny. I'll have to talk with Will about this. He's always finagling with something, but it would've been easier just to put in a new stretch of wire." Then Bob held the wire for Alyn to step through. "You know, Uncle Bob, if Little Bear has come back up here to his cave, I wouldn't blame him one bit. This land once belonged to the Cherokees; it was where they hunted and fished. They must have loved it as much as I did as a kid. When my aunt and uncle kidnapped me and took me away, I felt kind of a kinship to the Cherokees. They were taken away, too, far from here. I could sympathize with them alright!"

Bob stopped. Alyn turned and waited for his uncle who was puffing from climbing the steep grade. "Whew. I haven't had this much exercise in quite awhile. Probably could do without some of those church dinners, too." He took out a handkerchief and, removing the hat, wiped his brow. "You are right, of course. If the Chief wants to stay up here, then he has a perfect right to do what he wants. He's lived here for years without anyone's okay."

"I found an arrowhead once and kept it in a box under my bed. Could've been one of his. There were times as a kid playing in the woods that I felt like I was being watched, so I guess I really was, by Little Bear."

Bob smiled. "Young boys keep all sorts of things. I used to collect marbles," he said, understanding what Alyn was talking about.

They started on. The forest was redolent with the fragrance of mountain laurel and wild azaleas. White dogwoods sprinkled the area with a snow effect. Alyn picked a twig from a laurel bush, twirling it in his fingers, and thought of the many times he had brought a bouquet of them home and Aunt Joyce oo'd and ah'ed over them while she placed them in a vase of water. "I used to wonder how older people could recall so much from the past, and now I know."

The men had started on up the path when Alyn made this statement out of the blue, and Bob turned to look at him wondering just what he meant. "You will have a lot to tell your grandchildren."

"Grandchildren! You'll have me an old man in a matter of minutes." The two chuckled over this, then went on in silence. After a while Bob said that he hoped Alyn would remember where the cave was located.

"We're just about there. When you see a large outcropping of rock then we've arrived. Look!" He was pointing up the steep acclivity to where the rock outcropping was now in sight. "The entrance to the cave used to be covered with bushes, and it must be still but even more so. Oh! We overlooked bringing a lantern along."

"I wonder how Little Bear has managed there in the dark cave?"

"Maybe he has had electric lights installed," Alyn quipped grinning.

"Yeah. We'd all like electricity, wouldn't we? He got so used to them down at the school I suppose he wanted to run them to the cave."

Alyn cupped his hands around his mouth and called "Little Bear, come on out!" as he poked his head inside the dark cave. "Hey, Chief, you have company; come on out."

"It certainly is dark, Alyn. What could he possibly do here in the dark?"

"Beats the life out of me, Uncle Bob."

Then Little Bear appeared silently behind them carrying two dead rabbits. "What want? Little Bear no like people come. Me stay here." The old man passed Alyn and Bob and entered the cave.

"How do you see in here, Chief?" Alyn asked.

"Light lantern," was the simple answer. The men stood in the entrance waiting to see what Little Bear would do. By that time he had struck a match and lit a lantern.

"Well, of all the . . . where did you get a lantern?" Alyn asked.

"And matches and oil?" Bob put in.

"Boys bring . . . Boys good. Bring much."

"What did you do before you got the lantern and matches?"

"Get lantern many moons ago. Make fire with rocks, get oil from bear grease. Now boys bring matches."

With much curiosity, the men looked around. Alyn gazed up at the ledge where he and Luther had found the bag containing $50,000 in currency long ago. Miss Joyce's brother, Jim, hid it there after he found it in the train wreck in Union Gap that took the life of his wife. Evidently Jim knew about the cave (or his cohort, Alonzo Turner, did) and they hid it there until all the excitement caused by the train wreck and the search for the bag had subsided.

"Come," Little Bear beckoned and began walking further back into black darkness, holding the lantern in front of him.

Feeling hesitant, Alyn asked, "Little Bear, aren't you afraid there might be a drop-off somewhere back there?"

"No drop-off. Little Bear know cave. Go way back. Rooms . . . lake . . . door, way back. Come. See."

Alyn and Bob looked at one another in complete astonishment. Light from the lantern danced on their faces and made odd shadows against the dirt walls as they walked, stooped over, down a corridor-like hallway. Soon water could be heard trickling down the walls when they came out into a large room with stalactite hanging down from the ceiling. "This where mother, father, Little Bear lived many moons. Little Bear make graves here," he told them pointing to the two graves of his parents over against a wall. "Go more. Come." He led the way. They came to another natural room where a waterfall gushed from the ceiling, pounding down into the lake below sending its spray onto the observers. The two men stood motionless with mouths gaping open, utterly amazed. The sound of the water held them spellbound for several minutes, then Alyn broke the silence. "All this seems absolutely unreal! I'm seeing but not believing."

"All this and no one has known about it before! How could this be?" Bob said in wonder of God's creation.

Alyn continued in amazement, "Didn't anyone, not even Aunt Joyce or Adam, know this cave existed? I don't know why Luther and

I did not explore further inside. Guess we were probably too afraid of a bear living in here," he added begrudgingly, thinking of the fun they had missed. If the boys had explored more, they surely would have met up with Little Bear way back then.

"Any fish in that pond, Chief?" Bob queried.

"Much fish. Little Bear catch, eat. Is good." Little Bear had never had time to recognize a loss or a longing to feel connected to someone or to know the feeling that someone actually cared whether he was alive or if he was lonely or sad. His days had always been filled with his work for survival or making clothes from animal skins. The deep cave was so far removed from civilization that the Indian never saw anyone unless Adam, Alyn, and Luther ventured that way on hunting outings. Hidden among dense trees, he spied on them unnoticed, watching them grow as they ran through the woods and he, all the time, longing to be their friend. He had seen Miss Joyce's brother, Jim, and his partner in crime, Alonzo Turner, place the bag of money on the ledge. Then he had seen the two boys find it there, and he was glad, for he had no use for it. The men were very mad when they discovered the money was gone and had fought each other, blaming one another for taking it. Now they would not come back and give him a chance to be discovered. "You go. Many moons. Big man now. Where dark skin boy go?"

Alyn touched the old Indian's shoulder as though he'd been a friend for years. "He died a long time ago. I went off up north and then across the water to a bad war."

The old man's eyes widened and showed fear. "You soldier?"

"No. I am not a soldier, Little Bear. You have nothing to fear from me, or anyone else, anymore. You stay here in your cave or you come to our place anytime you like."

"And to the school, too," Bob added. "You don't have to hide from anyone." They recognized relief on the Cherokee's face. Alyn turned, looking all about. He saw an old bucket, a long-handled pick, some glass jars with lids, an axe, hatchet and some rolled-up rope.

"Where did you get all of these things, Little Bear?" Alyn questioned pointing to the different items.

"At house," was the honest reply. "People have much."

"Yes. That is true but taking them is stealing."

"Little Bear no steal!" he indignantly replied. "Father say no steal. Little Bear pay for all."

Bob smiled at this answer. "Just how did you pay?" he asked.

"Bring back lost cow. Mend fences. Many things do. Not steal."

"You are a good man, my friend," Alyn told him. "There are two little boys who think you are their good friend too, and I'm glad they found you here. I wish the dark boy and I had found you long ago." He again pressed the old man's arm affectionately.

Bob had an inspiration that he suddenly exclaimed. "Alyn, wouldn't it be great if Little Bear would be a scout leader for all the boys around here?"

"Why, yes! That's a wonderful suggestion." Then the men took turns explaining to Little Bear just what this meant. For the first time, they detected a faint smile on the Indian's wrinkled old face.

Chapter Six

"JUNE BUG A-SITTIN' IN A SIMMON TREE,
Sings his tunes in thu key of E;
Sits on a twig most all thu day long,
Thinks he's thu bes' when 'e sings this song.

"Tum-de-dum, Tum-de-dum, dum, dum.
Here come, ole frog a-beatin' on 'is drum.
'Dum-de-dum,' said crokey ole frog.
'Come on down an' sit on my log.'

"I sing Tum-de-dum, Tum-de-dum, dum, dum.
Then you go, Tweetel-dee-dee
Tweetel-dee-dee, dee, dee
All de day, jus' you an' me."

Selma turned around to the girl in the backseat. "Sassy! For a-cryin' out loud! Will you please hesh up? You not been quiet since we lef' yo Aunt Nellie's house. All that racket back there makin' my ears plum hurt. Now, be quiet."

"Makin' my ears hurt, too, Mama, and she keep poking me with a pencil or puttin' her hand over my mouf when I try to say sumpin." Joe stuck out his tongue at his sister and crossed his arms in disgust.

"Well, jes' how much longer is it 'fore we be home? I hafa do sumpin. It boring jes' a-goin' an' a-goin' an' a-goin'. How much longer, Pap? An' that not all, I really gotta go. Bad, and right now, too." Sassy sat up and looked all around to see if she could recognize any of the area.

"Girl, I wish we lef' you at home," Tad said to his stepdaughter. "You ain' been nuthin' but trouble." He pulled the car over to the side of the road. "Go up that bank and in them bushes, an' you hurry up, you hear?"

"Look all around first," Selma warned as Sassy tromped down the gulley and up the red clay bank.

"I wish a snake bite 'er on thu rump," Joe said brightly. The boy snickered as he pictured the event in his mind—the girl squatting with her dress up and a snake slithering up and striking the bare area.

"Joe! You don' wish no sech a-thang! Be plum 'shame 'er you-self, a-wishin' bad thangs on yor sister."

"Sassy say she gonna run away an' be a famous singer and folks flock to see her perform on stages everwher."

Tad grinned at Joe's statement. He knew his stepdaughter had a mind of her own; in fact, that's why they called her "Sassy" instead of her real name, Lula Belle. But he knew that she was all talk. She was forever making up songs and twirling around, oblivious to anyone else being within hearing distance. Then she was always talking and answering herself pretending someone was carrying on a conversation with her. "That gal's gonna come to no good end iffen you don' straighten her out, Selma," Tad told his wife.

"Me? What about choo? You always leave the displin' up to me. An' you tolt me when we married you help me wit her."

"Well, go see what's a-keepin' her. She done been too long. Joe's wish may done be come true." Selma got out slamming the car door behind her.

"Or maybe a ole wile cat done gobbled her up," Joe said.

"Boy, you got as big a 'magination as her."

Selma went up the same way Sassy had gone, calling her to come on out of the bushes. "Sassy-girl, you come on here now! We gotta get on home an' you jes' dilly-dallying 'round here. Sassy! I said come on now!" Selma looked all about but did not see any sign of her daughter. "Where you be? Sassy!" Then she screamed loudly to her husband, "Tad! Tad! Get up peer! Sassy ain' nowhere 'round."

"Oh, my gosh. Now what?" Tad hurried out and up the bank followed by Joe hot on his heels. Tad was thinking as his legs went into action, "I'm gonna give that gal a few o' my choice words."

Around a bend in the path came Sassy running toward them screaming, "Run! Run! Here come a man wit' a shotgun!"

"Run, girl!" Selma hollered.

"Don' shoot, Misser! We a-goin' fas' as we can," Sassy yelled to the man who had stopped on the path, firing the shotgun into the air. The blast scared off a flock of squawking blackbirds that before were calling loudly to one another in the tall pines. Tad and Joe were already back in the car with the motor running. Selma came flying down the clay embankment jerking her daughter along by one hand.

"Git in that car, missy, and don' you say 'nuther word, you hear?" She gave Sassy a firm shake of the shoulders and pushed her into the car. Relieved to be out of the woods and out of danger of the shotgun, Sassy breathed deeply as she sat down beside Joe. He was snickering joyfully behind a hand clasped over his mouth.

Choked by tears, Sassy stared down at her feet and for the first time in her life she could not think of an adequate explanation other than, "I seed that ole outhouse an' it looked like a better place tu go 'cause der wuz bees in them bushes."

Tad glanced over at his wife as he steered the car back onto the road. Both of them could not help but grin at one another and chalked this up to just another one of Sassy's shenanigans.

Looking back, Tad told the girl, "See iffen you can be quiet 'til we get home."

She sat rigid and tall in her seat, with an air of one who had received an injustice. The quietness lasted for only a few treasured minutes, then a soft song could be heard from the backseat. Joe nodded, his eyes closed. Sassy could sing all she wanted to for all he cared now that sleep overcame him.

IN THE PAST MONTHS SASSY TOOK ON THE STATURE OF A budding young woman. She felt it herself, turning to and fro to gaze in the looking glass behind her bedroom door. Yes! There were definite signs; signs that she liked. "Mama, I needs me a brassiere! And Mama, Joe has tu sleep on the couch from now on 'cause I needs this room all tu mahsef."

Selma came in from an adjoining room and suddenly discovered that Sassy Belle was absolutely right. "Girl, you thirteen, soon be fourteen, an' you already looks lak you ever bit fifteen. What we gonna do wit choo?"

"Mama, how come am I so light skinned? Ever one of the coloreds around here are dark an' I feels funny, so . . . so different. Why are there so many shades of colored folks anyway?" Sassy looked at her reflection in the mirror with Selma looking over her shoulder. The question that she had put before her mother hung suspended in mid-air while Selma searched for the answer. She had not yet prepared herself for such questions. "I looks pretty good for a light-colored gal." She turned a complete circle as she glanced at herself from all angles.

"It's because your paw was a light-skinned man. His paw was a white man."

Sassy turned a puzzled face to her mother with hands on hips as her mother continued. "You got blue eyes, too, like hizzen."

"I meant to ax about that, too . . . but what's a man got tu do wit it? You said babies come from a woman."

"Girl, you sho is dumb. Why, when I was your age . . . oh, for heaven's sake, jes' forget it for now."

Satisfied with her sudden growth, Sassy looked smug as a cat, happy that her mother agreed with her. "But, Mama, I been havin' belly aches all day long. Is growing up s'pose tu hurt? I sho don't like that part."

"Don' tell me, baby, dat you got dis, too!"

"Got what, Mama?"

Selma sat wearily down on the bed and pulled her daughter down beside her. She explained what happens to women each month with few and simple words and then went to find some old sheets that she could cut up and explain to Sassy how to use them.

Chapter Seven

"CAN WE HAVE A QUARTER, MAMA?" DAN BEGGED. HE WAS in the front seat, his brother Matt, in the back.

"May we have a quarter?" Kate corrected. "What in the world for?"

Matt supplied the answer, as the twins always did when one made a statement that required a reply. "Because Mr. Cronon said the shipment of the new *Boy's World* would arrive today for sure. Can we please have a quarter, Mama?"

"I said, 'May' we have a quarter?" Kate said more emphatically this time. "And I thought the *Boy's World* only cost ten cents."

"Well, they do, but we'd like a jawbreaker, too, and they are two for five cents." Then a stretched-out "Pleeeze" was added.

"If you boys will promise to stay out of trouble maybe I could find a quarter."

"Oh, but what about Brad?"

"Yes, we couldn't leave him out."

Kate was now steering the Model A into the yard of the Tanner cabin. "Only fifteen cents more for one comic and five cents for the jawbreaker."

"But there's only one of him, and he'll get two jawbreakers."

"My! So selfish you are, young man! He may want something else with the nickel." Kate turned the engine off as the car came to a stop. "Hop in the back, Dan. Let Mrs. Lyles sit in the front with Jamie."

The little house looked clean and the yard neat from a recent sweeping. Several chickens that had been pecking in the dirt went flying around the house frightened by the sound of the automobile. The clearing out back looked quite different, no longer the familiar surroundings where Cynthia Russell grew up. Cynthia had given Priscilla some red petunias that now graced flower boxes underneath the two front windows, and the front door painted a bright red lent a festive feature to the little house. Jamie commented that it looked like the Three Bear's house in the woods.

The boys flung open the car doors but before they could bounce out, Brad came racing from the house and hopped in with them. "Hello," Priscilla smiled to Kate.

"Good Morning, Priscilla and Jamie, how sweet you look in that pretty dress. Are we all ready to go?"

"All ready. Come along, Jamie," Priscilla said to the child as she got in and seated herself and held out her hands for Jamie to sit on her lap. So the happy group took off on this lovely June morning for an excursion in Union Gap.

"Kate, this is all still too unbelievable. A month ago I would never believe that we would be living here among such wonderful, generous people." Priscilla was all smiles, completely reconciled to a new life that she'd never dreamed would be hers.

The Lyles had not been back down to town since the day they arrived in the boxcar. There was too much with readying the Tanner house, clearing the land, and planting a garden to think about anything else. Alyn and Cynthia stocked the house with supplies from toothbrushes and soap to food, bed linens, and cooking utensils. Doc and Kate also did as much. Today, the trip to town was more of an outing and an opportunity to get acquainted with the town folks. Cynthia asked Kate to spread the word about a pounding party for the Lyles family, and she was to ask Mayor Marvin Cates, whose father was once mayor in Union Gap, for the use of the town hall for the party. There had not been a party since Alyn and Cynthia's wedding, and this would be a rewarding one.

With the town scoundrels, who had set fire to the Knollwood house, gone, life around town had returned to its complacent nature. Now, here were the Lyles for the town ladies to discuss and also the Cherokee Indian. Yes, a party would be a delightful event.

"Just to live in this fresh mountain air and be away from city life is like heaven," Priscilla said with a sigh. "Cole loves it already as much as I do."

"Look at the pretty creek alongside the road, Mother." Jamie pointed to the rippling water falling in little cascades over rocks. "And the bushes have pretty blooms on them, too."

"Yes, sweet. They are pretty."

The backseat area buzzed with big plans being made by the three boys. The Harris twins had previously told Brad all about Chief, who lived up on the mountain in a cave. Uncle Alyn told them that they had only got a glimpse of the entrance and would be amazed at the rest. Now they were promising to take their new friend up there to see for themselves. They also promised to take Brad to their great fishing hole. On days when the fish were not obliging, the fishing hole became a swimming place. Also, the falls up at the mountain top would be a wonder for the city boy to see. Maybe Chief could show them some more Cherokee "stuff," as they put it. "Chief Little Bear is now a very old man and needs someone to look out for him," Matt said. The boys discussed all this, unanimously deciding that this would be their undertaking. Then, when they had children of their own, they each could tell them how they had had their very own Indian chief.

At the same time, the ladies were carrying on a conversation with Priscilla telling Kate that she grew up in an orphanage and Cole's parents lived in California, too far and too expensive for visits. Things had gone well for the young Lyles couple until recently. "We could see this depression coming on, Kate. There are so many people in the city out of work now. You can pick out the ones you see in town who are walking all over hunting jobs, any kind of job. I never thought that we would be among them! Why, I even put cardboard in my shoes because I wore holes in the soles from walking so much looking for work. When I lost the job that I'd held for a number of years, I did find work finally in a shoe factory. Of course, it was something entirely different than I'd ever done and extremely hard. I worked for fourteen hours a day polishing new shoes as they came off the line."

"It was rather ironic that there you were polishing all these new shoes when your own had holes in them," Kate replied.

"Yes it was, and the pay was a pittance. Cole could find nothing at all and was looking after the children. What I made would not even put food on the table much less pay the house note and other bills."

Kate shook her head and sadly said, "I wonder what it is all coming to. It will probably affect our school here before long. If businesses cut out their support, we may have a teacher's salary problem."

When the car neared town, the children sat up to look around. Dan said, "Oh, there's a friend of mine." Then he hung out a window yelling to the boy through cupped hands, "Hey, Carl, where're you going in such a hurry?"

Carl threw up a hand and hollered some jubilant news. "Hey, Dan! Over at the Blakley pasture! There's a carnival a-settin' up! Ya'll come on over."

Kate exclaimed, "What! In this town? How do they think they will ever make any money here?"

"Hey, wait, Carl!" Dan called.

"Mama, please let us out here," Matthew said as he bounced on the seat. Kate slowed the car and the back doors flung open before the car came to a complete stop.

"Wait just a minute, boys. Come back here, now," their mother demanded. The twins and Brad came back with looks like "times-a-wastin' so hurry up with the orders."

"Now you guys remember, the men are setting up the carnival so stay out of their way or they will run you off."

"Yes, Ma'am," each answered as they ran away with Kate calling after them, "Meet us at the store in one hour, you hear." Walking backwards, Matt supplied the answer. "Yes'um, in one hour."

With the sound of pegs being hammered into the ground, tents were taking shape in the pasture on the north side of the town. The noise was compounded by shouts of orders, trucks loaded with animals and equipment backing into their designated places, and carnival people walking all about. Within a few hours, the town would be transformed into a place of wonder and excitement.

Union Gap's southwest boundaries were Kendell Mountain and Coleman Mountain, making it a small world dominated by a few stores and a railroad station. Streams snaked through the gap in the mountains and emptied into Crooked River. To the east and north, beyond the small town where the land is richer, lay a few farms of plowed fields and fenced-in pastures. On the main road in town, there was the general store, a small café, a rooming house, a filling station, and a clump of frame houses. Dr. Harris's office was upstairs over the general store where it had been since the good doctor set up practice years ago. A number of houses sprung up on the cross streets. At the end of one of these streets was a Baptist church.

In front of the church the three boys caught up with Carl. "Boy! This is gonna be great," he said, "and a man told me that there's gonna be a talent show and people can sign up to do things."

"Well, I can't do much of anything myself," Dan said. Matt answered, "Me neither. Oh, this here is Brad Lyles. He's our friend and is new around here." Carl and Brad acknowledged each other with a "Hi."

They entered the carnival grounds with wide eyes and mounting excitement. "Wow! Would you look at this!"

"I ain't never seen the like."

"Me neither."

"Watch out; here comes a truck."

"Old Mr. Berkley will make a fortune renting his pasture to this carnival."

Just then a man stepped forward into the group of boys. "Hello, fellows. It will take the rest of the day to get set up and you will be in the way, so how about doing us a favor and earning yourselves free admission tickets at the same time?" The man was tall and broad shouldered, with coal-black hair and piercing eyes that demanded attention. Wearing a wide-brimmed black hat, he looked like a villain from a cowboy movie. He moved the hat back with one finger as he looked down at the boys and then tugged at one end of his mustache and queried, "What about it?" He possessed a voice of authority and evidently was the carnival's owner.

"What would we do?" Carl asked in an exuberant voice.

"You could go from door to door around town and up on the mountain areas passing out these posters and flyers. The merchants will surely be happy to display the posters. Nail some on fence posts." Then he spread his arms wide and added, "Use your imagination."

"Okay!" They all chimed up at once.

"Captain Goodtime," the man called himself, told the four boys to scatter, do a good job, and then come back for their passes. They had their work cut out for them for the next hour.

"What about up on the mountain?" Brad turned and asked Dan.

"Aw, we can take them on the way home."

"Let's go. Everyone scatter." Dan told Brad to come along with him, leaving Matt and Carl to do as they pleased. They all ran off with excited chatter to make their deliveries.

KATE STOPPED THE CAR IN FRONT OF EZRA'S GENERAL STORE & Hardware. Old men in faded overalls (who were too old to do much farming and had left the fieldwork to their sons) now congregated on benches, chewing tobacco, whittling, and some playing checkers. When the women and Jamie emerged from the Ford, they all looked down at them and tipped their hats.

"Morning, Miz Harris," and "Morning, Ma'am," to Priscilla. "Them boys gone over to watch thu carnival being set up?" Mr.

Blakely asked smiling, and the smile revealed missing teeth.

"That's the direction they headed in, Mr. Blakely," Kate said pulling on her gloves and patting her hat in place. "Over to your pastureland I heard them say. This is Mrs. Cole Lyles, gentlemen, and their daughter, Jamie." The men stood for a second except for one who held onto a walking cane across his lap. "They are living in the old Tanner house now."

"Pleezed tu meetcha, Ma'am," each mumbled as the three passed by them.

"Well, don't that beat all. Them's thu ones that rode in on a freight train."

"They wuz plenty scroungy-lookin' that day, they wuz."

"Right nice-looking woman all cleaned up."

"How's her man, 'Cole,' was it, a-gonna make a livin', I wonder?"

"How them city folk all gonna do that?"

Then they all went back to their game and whittling.

"Priscilla, would you like to come over to the railroad station and mail a card to Cole's folks? Don't you think they would be pleased to hear from you?"

"Kate, I don't even have any stamp money."

Kate waved a hand. "Oh, bosh. I have two cents, or a postcard is only a penny. Come along. The post office is in there. We could have parked over there first, but we'll walk all over anyway."

"That stationmaster may not be so pleased to see me again," Priscilla worried.

Kate wondered whether or not she should tell her new friend something that would surprise her. She seemed to hesitate, and Priscilla asked, "What is it, Kate?" She was holding onto Jamie's hand as they walked along.

"It's like this, you see . . . my dad, Anson Kelly, owned the railroad, and when he and Joyce died, the railroad was willed to my sister, Joan, and me."

"Well, I do say!" Priscilla was caught off guard. She had never expected Kate to surprise her with this information. To think she and her family had stowed away on Kate's train, and here she was being so kind to them now.

"Yes, God has arranged a lot of things in this town. You'd be shocked to say the least." Kate looked at Priscilla to see both surprise and embarrassment in her expression. "Come along. We have lots to do. I want you to meet a good friend of mine, too, Mrs. Ella Fullman. We all call her 'Miss Ella.' Oh, wait." She took Priscilla by the hand to stop her. "Look," Kate pointed up over the buildings to the hill beyond. "See that large, white house up there?"

"Yes. It is a gorgeous place."

"That's where she lives. Just wait, you'll see. We'll go there today. The house has a Victorian parlor with eleven-foot ceilings. There are handmade lace curtains on every window and imported Tiffany lamps all over, as well as mahogany armoires. Oh, and a wonderful long porch lined with rocking chairs. She usually has Carlotta bring little tea cakes and lemonade out on the porch when visitors come. Miss Ella is an older lady. She's very nice, and she will love you and Jamie to pieces."

Jamie, in her nice new dress that Kate had supplied and with pigtails bouncing, danced down the steps in front of her mother at the end of the board walkway. "Oh, Mother, this is such a nice place. I do like it, but I hope there will be some girls for me to be friends with."

"Well, little lady," Kate said, "there is a nice girl you will like a lot, and she lives up there in that big house with her mother, Carlotta, and her daddy, Smiley."

Jamie clapped her hands, smiling. "What is her name, Mrs. Harris?"

"Her name is Emily Elizabeth Phillips. We call her Emily."

"That's a very pretty name. I like that."

Kate explained that Carlotta worked as housekeeper for Miss Ella and she married Smiley Phillips, who also works for her keeping the house in good repair and the yards in order. He came in on the train one day, said he was tired of being a salesman living out of a suitcase, and would accept any work offered. Miss Ella heard him and latched on immediately. He loved the ornate antebellum house that Senator Fullman's father built for his bride years before. It took only a short time for Smiley and Carlotta to fall in love. "You will not take my Carlotta away from me, sir, so the two of you will have to live here!" Ella had demanded in her usual bossy manner.

The stationmaster, Billy O'Shields, was standing out on the platform talking to another man when the women and child approached. He took off his cap and said, "Good morning, ladies, an' little miss. How are you, Miz Harris?"

"Fine, Billy. You may remember Mrs. Lyles?"

"Well now, can't say as I . . . oh, but you look so different, Ma'am. Hear you folks are staying in the Tanner house. Hope you will like it here." The skinny little man, slightly stooped in the shoulders, adjusted his green-shaded cap while surveying Priscilla.

"Yes, thank you, Mr. O'Shields."

"Billy, Ma'am. Everybody just calls me plain ole Billy. Pretty little lady here," he patted the child on the head. "Your boys have done been in here a whilst ago with this here poster about the carnival. Them's sure excited younguns."

"Yes, they are. Could I get my mail, Billy, and Mrs. Lyles needs a postcard."

"Please come on in." He took out a pocket watch to check the time, knowing that the train was not due in for a while yet. "Soon be time for the 10:52, so no mail yet. Haven't seen Doc lately. He a-doin' alright?"

"Yes. He's okay, just staying busy."

Billy walked over to the cage. "That's good. A body needs to stay busy, but I reckon it's bad for folks to be sick to keep him busy." He handed a postcard through to Priscilla. Kate handed him a nickel, and he passed out the change.

"We will be back later to get the mail. No doubt the boys won't be ready for a long time. If they come back by here, tell them to meet us for dinner over at the boardinghouse, would you, Billy?"

"Yes, Ma'am, sure will but I'd lay a dollar to a dime they'll be eating that carnival food."

"I'm sure they won't be selling any of that today, and besides, they would already have their quarters spent." As they turned to leave, Kate noticed Billy reading the postcard. He knew everyone and everything about them.

"Let's go by the mayor's office first. I'd like to get an evening arranged so we can tell Miss Ella when we go to visit her."

"That's completely up to you, Kate." They were now crossing the road where Kate pointed to the town hall building and explained that Mayor Cates's office was there. The building also housed the large room where entertainment events were held. "This will be a lovely event, I just know. It is always fun to get together and have a square dance and put on the feed bag, as the men always call it. People come from all around no matter what the event is, just so they will have an evening of entertainment. David usually calls the square dances, and we dance to the music by a group who brings their instruments."

"It certainly sounds like fun, doesn't it Jamie?" her mother smiled, and the child answered with excitement in her eyes as well as her voice. "Oh, yes, and I do hope children are allowed to come."

"By all means they are," Kate answered Jamie. "There are lots of girls and boys, and they play outside way after dark." The building sat off by itself under a grove of trees with a small creek trickling by. "Miss

Ella instigated this building being built, and it certainly has been put to good use. She donated a piano, and there isn't an event that she doesn't play. You've heard of the old saying that the opera isn't over until the fat lady sings, I'm sure. She isn't fat by any means, but no party is over until Miss Ella plays."

"She must be an accomplished pianist," Priscilla said.

"No, she isn't at all but she just likes to play fun songs and have a good time. She is quite a card, that lady."

The group went inside to find the place empty. No one was seen anywhere, so Kate just showed Priscilla and Jamie around and said they'd come back by there later. "Let's just go on up and talk with Miss Ella for awhile and let Jamie and Emily meet each other," Kate suggested, and that's what they did. They walked along talking about each place of business or each house they passed. They met a few people who stopped to talk and who, no doubt, were curious about the lady and child with Kate Harris.

They walked past the general store and turned a corner, walking to the end of the road where the steep driveway up to the Fullman house began. It was a long driveway that circled around in front of the house, and then steps led up to the house.

"Mama, I haven't even been in a fine house like this in Atlanta," Jamie whispered to her mother. "Look, that girl on the porch must be Emily."

"Yes, there she is in the swing," Kate told her. "Come on down, Emily," she called to the child. "You have some company." The little girl got out of the swing, holding her doll, and came down to greet them.

"Hello, Miz Harris," the pretty girl with big brown eyes and long dark hair grinned.

"Hello, Emily. This is Jamie Lyles and her mother. They have come to live up on the mountain, and Jamie will be going to school with you."

"Oh? Well, that will be nice. Come on, Jamie, and I will show you my room. We can play if ya'll are going to stay awhile." She took Jamie by the hand, and they disappeared into the house just as Carlotta came out when she heard voices. After a few words of greeting, she showed the two ladies to the parlor and went to tell Miss Ella that she had visitors. They sat in the parlor looking around at all the finery.

"Except for Carlotta and a maid, Miss Ella lived here alone for years," Kate said. I never could understand how she could live in this monstrosity alone. Miss Joyce and I talked her into helping with the school, and you wouldn't believe all the things she did for us.

Remind me to tell you all about it sometime."

Miss Ella came in like a whirlwind, calling to Carlotta at the same time to bring in tea and some refreshment for them. They talked and laughed at Miss Ella's tales for a long time, much longer than Kate had planned on staying. The old lady kept the conversation lively. She said that she felt like she had known Priscilla for a long time and just knew she would fit right in, and, oh, she was sure her husband was a fine man. The party would certainly be in order, and she would spread the word around town about it. "Kate, you don't have to do one thing, now, just leave it all to me, and I will go down and talk with Marvin Cates. We will make the arrangements, and I will get word over to your husband's office about the date." On and on she went until Kate insisted that they must go. "Well, at least leave the child here to play with Emily for awhile. You can pick her up when you start for home. Emily needs some company, and I'm sure your Jamie does, too."

So, the ladies left with their ears full, as Kate had said they would, and they laughed going down the hill with Priscilla agreeing that all Kate had told her about Miss Ella was right. After picking up the mail and making some purchases at the general store, Kate and Priscilla now sat in the dining room of Eva Mae McAdams Boardinghouse. Their table was covered with a sparkling white cloth, and in the center sat an elaborate lamp that looked somewhat out of place in the simply furnished room. Frugality had become a way of life to Priscilla, who felt appalled at the generous portions on their plates. "What a waste! I'll never eat all of this," she exclaimed in astonishment. During the Lyles' hard time in Atlanta, there was nothing to be wasted, or not much that could be wasted. Priscilla had been reluctant to order, knowing that Kate would pay the bill.

"I'm so happy, Kate, that Jamie has Emily to play with. She is a lovely child."

"Yes, she is and such a joy to Ella, who simply dotes on her every whim. She treats her like she is the grandchild she would never have. I'm afraid Emily may learn to be selfish, though, if Ella doesn't stop buying so much for the girl. Tomorrow, I know Smiley will take the girls over to the carnival. He's a nice man and a hard worker, too. Carlotta is lucky that he came to our little town. They will most likely insist that Jamie spend the night so the girls can go to the carnival together. If they do, and you don't mind, Jamie will have a grand time."

"It will be fine with me. Jamie would love it. I just can't get over that large ornate old house and here in this town, for goodness sake!" Priscilla exclaimed.

"Ella's husband was a state senator, and his family before him had untold wealth, which he must have inherited."

"Some people seem to have it all," Priscilla said and at once regretted making that statement. She thought of Kate and her sister, Joan, inheriting their father's railroad. "Oh, I didn't mean . . ."

Kate cut her off with a little wave and said, "Ah, think nothing of it. I understand what you mean."

"Nice to have you folks in our town, Ma'am," the waitress said to Priscilla as she stopped by and filled their iced tea glasses.

"Thank you. I appreciate the welcome." When Kate asked her to go down to town with her, Priscilla had feared that people would not welcome her because of her circumstances. Now, she was glad to be wrong.

The two ladies picked at their food, taking time while enjoying each other's company. The conversation was light and occasionally they laughed at what the other said. Priscilla asked Kate to tell her about her living in Atlanta, where her parents' house was; she just might know the street.

"How in the world did you and your father leave Atlanta to come up here?"

KATE THOUGHT FOR A FEW SECONDS BEFORE SHE ANSWERED. "To make a long story short, my father knew Joyce Abernathy years ago. She asked him to help her organize and build Kendell Mountain School. Her father had left the money in an escrow account for this."

"Just how did he decide that the school would be here on Kendell Mountain?" Priscilla queried.

Kate laid her fork down and took a sip of iced tea. "I mentioned that it was rather involved, but I'll try to shorten the tale. Alyn Russell's parents, John and Virginia Russell, came to this town as missionaries to the mountain people. I don't know exactly how they happened to find out about Kendell Mountain, but, anyway . . ." she leaned forward and almost whispered, "there was a terrible accident that took their lives; oh, but I did not mention that Colonel Abernathy died suddenly before this happened with a massive heart attack. The Russell's carriage careened off the road when it was spooked by another horse and wagon going by. They were thrown down the embankment and killed, but little Alyn was thrown clear only a few feet from the road. He was taken in by the colonel's daughter, Joyce. She loved the boy, who was only five then, and raised him as though he were her own." The waitress, with an iced tea pitcher, came by to refill the ladies' glasses. They declined any more, and the woman left a menu for desserts as she walked away. Kate continued, "I'll tell you another time how Alyn was kidnapped from here when he was thirteen, but as I was saying, when Joyce met Daddy again after many years, she persuaded him to help with the school. I really don't think it took too much persuading with Daddy. He was enthralled with the idea and loved it from the moment it was mentioned to him. Then, he suggested that I come up and teach."

They both took bites and sips. Kate seemed to be resistant to reveal something further. After thinking and taking another bite of food she said, "I may as well tell you, for it isn't a secret. My first husband, Paul Silvers, disappeared. It was like he was obliterated from off the face of the earth. Well, as you could imagine, I was distraught and hurt to the very core. I know Daddy realized that teaching here would pull me out of my depression."

"How could a man do this to you, Kate!" Priscilla exclaimed. "Was he seeing another woman?"

"I feel quite sure he wasn't. That would not be at all like Paul. I believe someone must have killed him. He'd gone on a trip for his firm, and they never even heard a word from him either although he was very stable in his job. No one ever knew what happened to him."

"That had to be devastating! I didn't mean to pry, Kate." Priscilla reached over and touched her friend's arm. "I'm so thankful that you and Cynthia are my friends. I'll never get over all your kindness to my family and me."

"Thank you, and by the way, I haven't seen Cynthia lately, have you?"

"Come to think of it, neither have I. Cole said that Alyn told him she's been sort of sick lately."

Then Kate leaned closer and whispered behind a cupped hand, "Do you think she is pregnant?"

Priscilla raised her shoulders slightly, smiling, "Who knows?"

Kate paid the bill, and they left to do some shopping.

Chapter Eight

SATURDAY, THE DAY AFTER THE CARNIVAL SET UP IN UNION Gap, dawned fresh and new with excitement in the air. Saturday! The day that the carnival would open! A soft haze covered the valley below, giving a ghostly effect. It had rained during the night but not enough to put a damper on big plans for this special day. Never before had a carnival come to this town. In 1910, there had been a murder, a hanging, and a train wreck all within six months' time! But never a carnival. Each fall, the town always had put on a festival. Now a carnival could be added to the annals of events. If a boy or girl had no money to spend, they could just walk through the grounds and look to their hearts' content.

Alyn Russell announced that the children or grandchildren of the people on his place would receive an advance of fifty cents each for chores they would be expected to do later. He included the Lyles children in on this deal. Work always abounded at Knollwood Orchards. The children were expected to carry part of the load; they were not asked. Work was taught. The livestock and chickens needed to be fed, water troughs kept full. Eggs must be gathered each day, rugs hung across clotheslines and beaten, washing hung up to dry, porches swept, kindling chopped and brought in, and on and on. The list was endless. These were only a part of the daily chores, and with carnival money handed out in advance, there would be new jobs added. All chores must be done during the morning hours, and after the noontime dinner, everyone would be ready to go.

The Harris twins came early to help with whatever could be done while Adam went up to get Little Bear. He could have come down on his own, but Alyn said he would not show up unless coaxed.

Since the coming of spring, Lizzie Mae had been ailing to the point of relinquishing her kitchen domain to her daughter, Ophelia. Actually, this happened more gradually than all at once, for back in the winter Lizzie took to a corner in the kitchen where she peeled potatoes, strung beans, or whatever could be done from that place. Ophelia made it seem that she was taking orders from her mama, even when her strong voice could be heard calling to one of the children out back.

"Who a-goin' wit dem chullun?" Lizzie questioned without looking up from her bean stringing.

"I heard Pap say he gwine to," Ophelia answered with her head nearly in the oven checking on her prize pound cake. "He say ole Injun Chief a-coming down to go wit' 'em, too."

"Law, law. How he gits up and down dat mountin beyond me. He lak a sixty year old. We 'bout thu same age and here I set whilst he run around out dare everwher. Dat carnival may take 'im off when dey goes. He better be kerful. Tell yore Pap tu look affer him good."

"Misser Alyn done tolt 'im."

"Wher Miss Cynthee? She be a-goin', too?"

"No'm, Mama. She say she don' feels too good dis mawnin'. Misser Alyn an' Misser Cole gone over tu Clayton. I's seed Doc an' Miss Kate let dem boys out as dey went by. Dem boys wen' screamin' out back fer Pap."

"Well, dey better take Sassy an' Joe, too. Go on out dare and tell yore Pap whut I said."

Ophelia dried her hands on her apron tail. Going out the kitchen door to the hallway, she pushed open the screen door and yelled out to Adam just as he drove up with Little Bear sitting tall and straight beside him on the wagon seat. Matt and Dan were running along the pathway toward them with Joe and Sassy trailing behind.

"Sassy, girl, you behave yo'sef now, you hear? An' stay wifs de res'. Is ya'll gonna git dem Lyles chilluns?"

"Yass'um, Grammaw, to everthang yo jes' said. Does ah look pretty 'nuff, Grammaw?" She patted her hair and smoothed her dress, turning all the way around for Ophelia to have a full view.

"Yo looks lak you jes' stepped outten a pitchur book, chile." She gave Sassy a quick pat on the rump as the girl turned toward the wagon smiling a wide, toothy smile.

"Come on, here, gal," Adam called. "Dese chere mules eben be in a hurry today."

The children all piled in, Sassy on the back with her legs hanging over the side and Joe beside her. As they pulled out of the yard, Ophelia heard her stepgranddaughter singing.

"Camp town ladies sing dis song, do dah, do dah. Camp town race-track five miles long, oh, do dah day," until they were out of hearing distance, the wagon's wheels bumping over the deep ruts in the road.

This was the first time Chief Little Bear had left the mountain since he was born. There had been no need for it. The mountain gave him everything he needed to sustain life. He was going to the Gap now merely out of curiosity rather than desire. He felt some trepidation, but when he tried to back out Adam dispelled his fears by explaining all about the people and businesses in town. He would see a train that takes people to other places, if they want to go; it wouldn't take them by force. And, no, there were no soldiers there. Today, he would also see a carnival where people take a day off from their work to have fun. There would be a big wheel with seats on it, and he could ride on it way up in the air. "Why did they do this?"

"Because it would be fun. Children love it, and the ride makes them squeal with laughter." He would see a man swallow fire, a mirror that makes people look tall or short and in all kinds of shapes. Also, there may be a man that could throw knives at a woman standing next to a board and never even hit her.

"Hum, Little Bear do that easy!" the Indian replied with assurance.

So now Little Bear was anxious to see all these wonderful things that make people happy. The wagon was passing by Kendell Mountain School when the children started booing, hollering "yuck" and the like, but Little Bear quietly said, "Me no like." Then the children all fell backwards and across one another with laughter.

Joe and Sassy said nothing at all. They just looked at the structure, wondering what it would be like to go to school. Then Sassy said, "I would not lak to sit in a room all day an' read books."

"Dat be boring," Joe added with a frown. "I lak to go fishing. Catch me a big ole bass an' watch 'im fight." He made like he held a rod with a fish jerking the line from off the back of the wagon.

"Miz Harris teach me 'nuff," Sassy went on as though Joe had not spoken. "She tell me 'bout everthang an' she say I real smart, yes she does. It jes' takes two afternoons a week, too. Ya'll know whut she says? She says people gets on airyplanes an goes all over everwhur. Some day I gonna do dat. Yessir. I a-gonna go somewhere an' be a movie star."

"Aw, Sassy, be quiet," Joe said. "You cane nebber do dat."

"I can, too. Miz Harris, she say I can do anythang I wants. Dat whut she say."

"Wait 'till you hear whut Mama say!"

"She won' know 'cause I won' tell 'er."

"You gonna be in big trouble, you is."

"Ain't."

"Is."

"Ain't."

"Oh, hush up."

Before long the wagon rolled into town. Chief Little Bear gazed at each building and all the people walking about. And the people stopped in their tracks and gazed back. Adam pulled on the reins guiding "Buck" and "Buster" down the road where the carnival would be in the pasture at the dead end. Music was blaring well before their arrival; other wagons were already parked in places specified, their mules grazing on the abundance of tall grass. The excited arrivals took orders from Adam before dashing off to parts unknown. Sassy chose to go alone; Joe went along with Adam and Little Bear.

Sassy wanted to look for the place where someone said there would be a show of dancers, singers, and a talent contest. Her money would rest in her purse until she got this information, for she did not want to spend it all before obtaining a ticket for the show that was to change her life forever. Everything was so foreign to her, so different from anything she'd ever seen in her lifetime, so simply out of this world. The blaring music was marvelous to her ears! It made her dizzy with excitement, thrilled her soul. She made several spins as she walked along, kind of in a dance. People walking by saw her delight and smiled. She saw no one; she only hugged her arms around her torso as she turned with surges of delight. This would be the day she would win the talent contest, she just felt it in her soul. What were they offering for the prize? Money maybe, or perhaps a chance to work with the carnival. Everyone would believe her when they saw that she was a big star with her name up in lights!

"Let's see now, whut will my name be? Certainly not 'Sassy'! Hum, well . . . they put 'Belle' in my middle name so I'll be jes' 'Belle.' But 'Belle' whut? Oh, I recollects that fancy movie star named LaMont. Aunt Nellie took me tu see that movie show when we visited her, and I knew right den I'll be lak Miss LaMont one fine day! Yessirree bobtail, I now be 'Miss Belle LaMont.'"

She saw the big tent before she got there. It loomed tall above the others—a bright green with yellow stripes. Dodging people, she noticed the ticket booth out front and a lady sitting inside. Sassy's heart did a few leapfrogs. She swallowed hard and ran the rest of the way.

"Hello, honey," the ticket lady in a carnival costume said with a raspy course voice. "We are not ready yet to sell tickets. The show doesn't start until two o'clock."

"But, Ma'am, I jes' wanted to sign up for what that there sign say," Sassy told her as she pointed to the large sign in red letters advertising a talent show.

"I see. Just what is it that you do as a performance?"

"Oh, Ma'am, I sing like a angel." Sassy put one hand to her chest and with eyes closed said in a voice of childlike gratitude, "Why, when I sings eben birds hesh up."

"Oh, do they now? Just ain't that nice." The woman surveyed the girl before her from head to toe. "You look kinda different, honey. Where did you come from?"

Sassy thought of the place across the ocean that Mrs. Harris had studied with her. The people had olive skin and dark hair and they spoke a funny language. "I comes from France and my name 'Belle LaMont.' You can jes' call me plain ole 'Belle.'"

"French, huh? Yes, you do look French. Where are your folks? Did you come to the carnival alone?"

"Nome. Dey be all scattered 'bout I reckons."

"Say something in French. I do love to hear French people talk. One time we performed down in New Orleans and there were a lot of them there."

Sassy rolled her eyes in thought for a few seconds. "Well, you see, Ma'am, I come here a long time 'go and now I plum forgot all dat French jabber an' jes' talk lak peoples 'round these parts."

"Don't your parents ever speak French to you?"

"Nome. Dey bes too busy."

"You must have been adopted from France."

"Yass'um. Dat bes it. Whut choo jes' said. I 'dopted." Sassy grinned brightly, pleased with the outcome of this conversation that at first was heading nowhere. "Jes' write down my name on your lis' as 'Miss Belle LaMont' from Paris, France."

So Belle LaMont skipped away to sit in the shade of a willow tree and daydream until two o'clock.

BEHIND THE LARGE TENT WHERE SASSY STOOD IN FRONT waiting to get in, Matt, Dan, and Brad sat on the grass waiting for the show. They had met up with Calvin and, upon agreement, decided that he would make the motion for his friends to slip stealthily under the backside of the tent. Calvin had a ticket for he was to be a contestant in the talent contest. Beforehand, Dan asked Calvin, "Can you whistle like a whippoorwill, Calvin?"

"Sure," the boy answered, pursed his lips, and made the soft, sweet sound like the bird.

"Yesss! That's great! Okay, guys, that will be our sign that the coast is clear and we can go under the tent." So while the three were waiting out back, they pricked their arms with Dan's pin knife and drew blood, making crosses over their hearts with the red ooze, swearing to be blood brothers forever and ever, so help them God.

Out front the crowd was gathering, anticipating a good show. To entice more people, a little stage had been set up outside the ticket booth and now Miss Lola, "The Exotic Dancer," a sign blared in large red letters, was dancing and gyrating to the loud, tinny music of a record player.

Among the sea of upturned faces was Adam, holding on to Joe's hand, and Chief Little Bear. Adam had a pleasant smile on his face, but Chief watched blankly in complete amazement. He had only seen his parents do Indian dances around a fire inside the cave. They taught him to dance and he joined in. Now this . . . so different . . . and to the terrible loud sound.

Captain Goodtime was at one end of the stage clapping and yelling, egging on the watching people to do the same as he. And they did, with some also whistling. Then Captain Goodtime's dark beady eyes caught sight of Little Bear in front of the stage. Chief was dressed in deer-skin pants and shirt and a black hat (that Alyn Russell had presented to him). Alyn had stuck a feather under the band, and Chief Little Bear now would not be parted with his hat for one minute. With his white hair braids hanging long against the shirt, Little Bear was a striking figure. The townspeople all knew about him and now did not consider him an oddity. But not so with the carnival owner. He stared in amazement, not believing what his eyes beheld. What a terrific addition this Indian would be to his carnival. Yes! He had to have him! He'd make up a concoction and bottle it as "Genuine Cherokee Miracle Cure" that cures all! The Indian could stand beside a table full of bottles, his arms folded, while Captain Goodtime himself would be expounding on the medicine, of course, made entirely by this Indian medicine man! After the dance, the captain hurriedly left the stage to find two of his strong-armed men and lay a trap for Little Bear.

At two o'clock, Calvin came running around to the back of the tent yelling, "Dadgummit! I gave the signal five times! I guess folks in line thought I was a-practicing for my act! Go on . . . get under. They're all going in now!" He lifted the tent as the three scampered underneath, with hearts pounding, and found seats close to the stage.

During her lifetime, at least for as long as she could remember, Sassy wondered how it would feel to look down upon a crowd of upturned faces of cheering people, clapping hands—to feel it all rain down upon her! Yessirree bobtail! They would be cheering her. Since the age of eight, she knew that one day she would know this feeling. Sassy had been ushered in early by the ticket woman and presented to Miss Lola to be fitted into a costume and instructed as to how to stand while she sang and how to do her hands. The captain told Miss Lola beforehand that this French girl was to win or her head would roll. Captain Goodtime could be mean as a coot when riled. He had also been known to have a quick trigger finger. When he first saw this girl, he knew she would fit nicely in this show and also into his personal plans.

The excited girl turned around before a long mirror to fully inspect herself. She said that had to be another person that she saw looking back at her. A jaunty hat sporting a blue ostrich feather accentuated her sparkling blue eyes. She looked trim and neat and very satisfied with herself.

"Miz Lola, I got a angel that talks to me all dee time. Yes, I have an' she say, she say 'Belle, gal, yo sho can sing, jes' lak a lil' ole bird' an' she tell me I a-gonna be a movie star, she sho do. Yes, Ma'am, dat what she say."

"You don't say! Well, we've got to work on your speech. I tell you what . . . when you go out, just don't say anything. Not one word, you hear? Just sing."

"Iffen you say so, Ma'am. I jes' sing 'cause I sho can do dat."

"Now come along. It sounds like that whistling boy didn't do so well. You will be next."

"It would pleasure me a whole lot, Ma'am."

They walked to the flap that would lead out on stage and waited until the moment Captain Goodtime would call Belle's name over the speaker. She heard a small ripple of clapping making it evident that Calvin would not be the winner. As he was shown down the steps, he saw that Joe had taken his seat, so, dejected and disgusted, the boy left the tent in a huff.

"And now we have Miss Belle LaMont, straight from France to entertain and thrill you with her singing! Give her a big round of applause," and Captain Goodtime spread out his hand toward the place where Sassy was to enter. The crowd roared. Enamored by their enthusiasm, Sassy walked with short awkward steps on high heeled shoes to the stage center, her eyes wide with slight apprehension. As the captain backed off the stage, Sassy stood there savoring the moment. She twisted a strand of light brown hair, cleared her throat, took a deep steadying breath, and opened her mouth to sing.

The boys all sat up straight. Joe stood and, pointing a finger, said, "Dat mah sister! Hey, Sassy," he waved. Dan jerked him to his seat.

"If that don't beat all," murmured Matt.

"Mama gonna whup her backside," Joe giggled and then exploded with laughter. Joe had spotted the guys down front and an empty seat beside Dan and begged his grandpap to let him sit there.

Belle LaMont sang without any music. She sang an old love song that Aunt Nellie played on her piano and taught her last year. Her voice sounded older than usual. She sang to the audience and each listener felt as though she were singing directly to them. Like a butterfly, always flitting about in her own world searching for the right bush, she now flitted from one side of the stage to the other. The song was a tearjerker, unlike the usual silly songs she sang. She had sung the song for Tissy Russell who picked up on the tune and played it on her guitar. She practiced with the girl over and over and tutored her even before a carnival was thought of. Now Sassy hugged the microphone like it was a lover. She had seen this done in the movie that Aunt Nellie took her to see.

When the song had ended, the audience burst into wild clapping and whistling, and Captain Goodtime practically ran to where the girl stood. He put an arm around her and drew her to him tightly and looked down into her face, winking. With a pink color in her cheeks and stars in her eyes, Sassy stood there with a satisfied smile as if to say, "I told you I could sing like a angel."

"Ladies and Gentlemen, there will be no need for any further contestants; they are cancelled. Shortly our main attraction over in the big tent will begin so you may go directly there in just a moment, but first, I present to you, Miss Belle LaMont, winner of the twenty-five-dollar prize!"

Tears blurred Sassy's vision. She had won! "Miss LaMont, come with me." The captain took her by the hand. Then the clapping started again. Up high on a bench close to the back, Adam grinned and punched Little Bear on the shoulder. "Sassy Belle sho does look difrunt but I'd know dat voice anywhers." They stood to join in the crowd filing out.

Behind the stage was an office enclosed by a small tent. Captain Goodtime led Sassy there, pointing to a chair that sat beside a small makeshift desk. "Sit here, please. . . . Well, you certainly did win that contest without any doubt," he said as he sat down on a chair behind the little desk. He opened a box covered with a cloth that he drew from underneath the desk and took out twenty-five dollars, handing it to the awestruck girl. "Now, Miss LaMont, how would you like to travel with us and perform everywhere?" He rared back in his chair and crossed his arms.

"Mu-mu-me, Suh?"

"Yes, you. We will make you a star, and you will sing to your heart's content."

Enhanced by his words, her eyes looked at him dreamily.

"You won't have too much time to think it over," Captain Good-time implored, adding that she would probably never ever have another chance like this to be a star. He put a hand on his chin beard stroking it. "That is, of course, unless you are performing on my stage and a Hollywood talent scout discovers you."

Those last words set Sassy on fire. Her eyes grew round and large. He gave her a benign smile. There was no point in discussing her coming along any further. He would not take her by force as they would do the Cherokee, for he wanted absolutely nothing to do with the police. This girl, a minor, could be considered a runaway, but the Indian would no doubt be thought to have just gone back home alone.

The captain decided to give Belle LaMont a minute or two alone with her thoughts and told her that he would be right back. Sitting there, a mixture of joy and anxiety overcame her. She thought of her mother and how sad she'd be at her daughter's leaving. Then, she heard a reassuring voice, like an echo . . . or, was it her angel, that whispered, "You can do anything, girl, just do it!" Her look softened as this thought sunk in. Could she? What would her family say? She knew at once exactly what they would say, an emphatic, profound "No!" In her head, her mama, Selma, was saying, "You be too young, baby. You don' know nuthin' 'bout living. You need tu learn from my mistakes and 'sides, whut good you think it do for a colored gal tu go a-traipsin' off tryin'-a be sumpin' she not!"

An odd smile played at Sassy's lips—odd because it was conniving for Sassy, too old, unlike her entirely. The flippant girl, always romanticizing about everything, decided that with another year being added to her age in a few days, she would automatically be grown up in mind as well as body. "Look at Mama," she said out loud to herself, "she had me when she was 'bout my age, and didn't Mama hersef say I had become a woman jes' this week?" she concluded simply. "Dat nice dancer, Miss Sophie, she will help me an' the fortune-teller, Madam Star, an' Miss Lola, she will be lak a mama tu me I jes' knows. I a fass learner, yes I is!"

With all these thoughts, Sassy was trying to convince herself that the decision should be entirely up to her. She felt with certainty that she had found today what she had been dreaming of. All at once she wished to be a part of it. Her skin tingled with excitement. When the man came back to her she said, "Okay, I will come along. When you be a-leaving?"

He winked and replied. "That is wonderful, Miss LaMont."

"You can jes' call me 'Belle.'"

"'Belle,' then. So it is all settled." He made this statement with finality. "We are going to pack up tonight and be on our way at dawn in the morning. It is going to rain so we'd be out of business anyway."

"I'll slip out tonight at midnight and will haffa walk so it will take me a spell. You won' go off an' leave me, will you?"

"Oh, heavens no, my child. We'll wait for you but try to hurry."

"I be's here."

Then Sassy hurried out to see the main attraction, checking her purse to have another look at her money. It was more than she had ever seen at one time . . . and all of it her very own! Over in the large main tent Sassy found her grandpap and Chief Little Bear. The people next to them moved over to make room for the girl.

"Ah won, Grandpap! Lookie here." She opened her purse to show him the money.

"We saw you, baby. You done real good an' ah'm real proud o'you."

"Look," she said turning to Joe and Little Bear on the other side of him. "Look at the funny clowns." They had been doing all kinds of antics and pulling tricks on people on the sidelines. One was a midget who seemed to be the main attraction. He was so mischievous that one clown pretended to make a telephone call for someone to come and take him away and right straight into the ring came a small police car with about ten clowns getting out dressed in policemen's uniforms. After chasing the little guy around the ring several times, they all gave up and piled back in their car and drove away. Then, in burst five horses, with riders dressed in Confederate uniforms. One horseman leaned over and picked up the little guy by the rope around his waist and set him on the horse behind him. The laughter went wild all except for Chief Little Bear, who stood up exclaiming in a loud voice, "Soldiers! Soldiers bad! Me go."

"Wait!" Adam called while Little Bear was busy scampering out in front of the people on the bench. "Dey ain' real soldiers, jes' pretend-like."

But Little Bear paid Adam no attention. "Me go. You stay," he told Adam as he kept going. He was soon dashing up the aisle and outside into the arms of two strong-armed men, henchmen of Captain Good-time.

It was not discovered that the old Indian was missing for many days. Everyone had assumed he was safe in his beloved cave.

NO MATTER HOW SORRY SASSY FELT IN HER HEART, A pervading sense of guilt remained. The guilt was there, but it in no way changed her mind about leaving with the carnival. It was now getting close to midnight, and the girl awoke with a lump in her throat. She drew in a deep breath and swallowed away the lump. A light wind whistled through pine trees outside her window with a regular rhythm, calling the girl to come. Sassy slid out of bed and stood beside the window gazing out into the darkness. She heard the roar of Rushing Creek that was hurrying along to Crooked River. It, too, was calling her name. She breathed deeply of the cool night air blowing gently through the open window fanning the curtain. With resignation, she decided that she would procrastinate no longer. Yes! This is it! It's now or never. Quietly, she dressed, threw a few things into a ragged, worn suitcase, and stole out into the night.

There was a soft rumble of thunder off in the distance, followed by little faint pulsations of lightning. She'd have to hurry for it might rain before she could get down to the Gap, so she quickened her pace. The frightened girl ran for a while, but the cumbersome suitcase slowed her steps. At first she kept to the road down the mountain but then decided it would be much shorter if she cut across by the Lyles' place and take a footpath through the woods.

Everything was going well for a while until the suitcase flew open with clothes spilling all about. Sassy stooped, picked up the clothes, along with pine needles and dirt, and threw them in the suitcase. "Whut else could happen?" she asked herself. On she went through familiar territory until she came to the dense trees. It was incredibly dark. An owl left his limb, flying right in front of the frightened girl's face, making a hooting sound. She let out a low moan, trying hard not to scream. Soon, thorns grabbed at her clothes. She stumbled over protruding roots growing above ground and became only a dark silhouette against the black night. The land became jutting cliffs with overhanging vines that sent their tendrils to the ground. Fearful that she would get lost in the maze of vines, Sassy turned and retraced her steps back to the road.

Now running again to make up for lost time, she startled a deer that was drinking from the trickles of water that splashed out from a bank and then ran directly across the road. Here, there was the dank, pungent heavy scent of moss. The night was ominously quiet. Sassy did not stop nor waver even though her courage began to wane. On and on the girl traveled. "It's a good thing I wore my good shoes," she thought.

Well before dawn, Belle LaMont, revived in spirit, walked onto the carnival grounds, soggy from the soft rain that had started when she was back on the Kendell Mountain road. Her dress clung to her body, water dripping from her hair and running down her face like tears. There were men all about doing final necessities and tying down canvases over truck loads. Sassy slowed her pace when she saw him approaching. Holding a lantern up high, he saw it was Belle and started walking toward her. "We thought perhaps you'd changed your mind," Captain Goodtime said with a great feeling of relief. He saw dollar marks before his eyes instead of her face.

Sassy looked him in the eye and said, "Never."

TAD LET THE DOOR SLAM BEHIND HIM. HE FOUND SELMA standing disconsolately gazing out a window. "I been thinkin' about the past, Tad, and a-wondering jes' wher I went wrong." She had cried a river of tears and now no more would come, just the blank empty feeling. He walked over to her and held her tight.

"Selma, you didn't do nuthin' wrong, hon. Stop thinkin' like that. Kids is a-gittin' plum wile now a-days. Dey gotta fine out thangs for theyselfs. She be back 'fore long. You see. Yes, she will and she come up that road a-runnin'—jes' cane wait tu get back home. She git her belly full o'that carnival life and come back in a hurry. You gotta get a-holt o'yousef, woman. You got Joe to take ker of, remember?"

"Ya'll didn't fine out a single thing, then?" she asked finally.

"No. Nobody seen a thing. It was like a-lookin' fer straws in thu wind. Misser Alyn, he talked to thu sheriff and he a-puttin' out a bulletin. You know, Selma, my Paw, he feel like that girl be his own flesh an' blood. He was madder'n a wile bull an' a-runnin' all over town talkin' tu folks. He kill that man iffen he fin' 'im." Tad smoothed Selma's hair and kissed her on the forehead. "We jes' haffa wait, hon, that's all we kin do."

"We kin pray, Tad. We kin pray."

EARLY THAT SAME MORNING RIGHT AFTER DAWN, THE carnival trucks pulled out of Union Gap even before any rooster crowed. They pulled out with two more people than they had arrived with. Each of the trucks were given their instructions about the way they were to go because each were to travel different routes. If stopped, there would be no sign of Sassy or the Indian. They were in an unmarked truck driven by Tony Howard, also known as "Captain Goodtime." As far as anyone would know, they had gone off into oblivion. This truck would travel north, cut across Tennessee, down through Alabama, and then across the back roads of Mississippi to the coast.

They would all meet up there in Mississippi at the farm that belonged to Tony. He would miss a few bookings through Georgia and Alabama, but to miss them would be inconsequential for he'd make up for the loss and more when the carnival regrouped and traveled in the other direction. Right now, he'd leave behind him no shred of evidence that the carnival ever existed. The smoothness with which his well-thought-out preparations had gone was a good omen, he thought, and did not need Madam Star to tell him this.

Only Tony, Sassy, and Little Bear were riding in the truck that now left Union Gap heading northward. It would be a long, long time before Kendell Mountain people would hear from Sassy and the Chief. The Indian was old. Would he survive this grueling ordeal? Sassy did not think of it in that light, but as an adventure. Tony had previously ground into the Chief's head that he need not try to escape because his soldiers would find him wherever he went. He would protect the old man if he stayed put, and he promised that before long they would return to Kendell Mountain. This, of course, was one of his lies because he knew he would be arrested if he returned there. Little Bear did not know that this man Tony did not have an honest bone in his body, and Sassy did not know that her Cherokee friend was being taken by force.

Sassy had always thought of herself as different from other people. She had imagined herself as a courageous queen of the Nile. Doubtless, she would find an opportunity to prove her courage. The truck crept on like a snake, slithering along on its belly, winding and curving. The countryside took on a new façade as they moved farther and farther from all familiar things the girl had known. At first, she had been wide-eyed; now she felt challenged. These folks who were to be her companions were a strange, different breed of people. Somehow they must be a special people as a whole, yet each possessed a separate kind of talent in his or her own way. Sassy thought that the whole thing carried a hint of romance about it, and she shivered with delight. Her heart beat fast and hard. She was smiling, trying to suppress excitement, and thought that her leaving with the carnival was as unreal as a love scene that she had seen in a movie. She tried to talk with Little Bear and explain to him about how much fun they would have and how she had always longed to see other things and other people's ways.

He would only reply with a grunt or just pretend to be asleep and make no reply at all. The people he knew on Kendell Mountain were his friends, but this man driving the big truck was different. There was something about him that would not let Little Bear like him or feel comfortable with him. This one could not be trusted. If he had stayed in his cave and not gone to see the carnival, he would not be in this situation. Hindsight can be very cruel, and it never did anyone much good. A person recognizes mistakes he made that may have been avoided, all the time thinking, "if only . . ."

Chapter Nine

IT HAD NOW BEEN TWO MONTHS SINCE THE CARNIVAL LEFT town. A great cloud still hung over Knollwood—a cloud of sadness. The number of trips up to the cave by different people without any sight of Little Bear created suspicions in Alyn's mind. He found Adam in the barn and began to question him more about the day at the carnival.

"Lak I said, Misser Alyn, he dun thought dem soldiers be real and he say to me, 'You stay. Me go.' An' I thought he was gonna hi-tail it back to his cave and I couldn't go off affer 'im on account o' thu churrin, so we jes' figgered he could fine his own way back home."

Alyn sat on an overturned barrel, his hands clasped together across his knees. Adam was mending a harness. The barn smelled of hay and the odor of animals. This was a musty smell that he'd always liked. He was sorting over in his mind what Adam was saying. "It just does not add up, Adam. We've all searched the mountain and the cave. He could not disappear into thin air. You know, I just can't help but believe that the carnival took him away by force."

"'Bout thu onliest way they'd get 'im," Adam interjected.

"They got both of them, I just know. Sassy would have gone willingly with just a little bit of encouragement but not the Chief." Alyn leaned over his knees, propping his arms across them. "I've been to see the sheriff a number of times, but he has heard nothing. Seems like that caravan just rode on out into the wild blue yonder."

"Yasser, hit sho do," Adam answered with a shake of his head.

After a few minutes of silence, deep thought, and Alyn rubbing the back of his neck wishing there was something that he could do, he changed the subject. "Adam, remember when I was a kid how you used to tell us stories out yonder on the grass under the Chinaberry tree?"

"He-heh, ah sho do's," the old man chuckled. "All you churrin jes' ate up all dem lies lak soghum syrup on a biscuit!"

"Lies? . . . For crying out loud! I thought your stories were all true."

"Well, some o'hit was fer sho, but my 'magination jes' kept on a-goin' in a whirlwind."

"It would be nice if you would tell some of your stories again because we need to cheer the kids up a mite. How about tomorrow night after supper? We can have cake and ice cream out there like old times."

"Sounds right nice, tu me. Reckon ah could think up somethin' by dat time."

"Okay, then . . . you get your lies all ready, you hear? And let's get Will and Sam and their instruments and I'll tell Tissy to bring her guitar along. And, oh, Adam, . . . don't worry about having a good time while we're sad about losing Sassy and Little Bear. We can talk about them and how much we miss them, but I do believe we'll get them back. And wouldn't Sassy love a singing party!"

"She'd try tu hog all my story-tellin' time," Adam grinned. "Don' forget tu invite the Lyles kids and the Harris boys. Dis'al be plum nice lak we useter."

"That's how you always started off those stories, 'Use to, when I was a chile,'" Alyn smiled and threw up a hand as he turned to leave. There was lots of work to be done and here he was sitting around talking. The extra workers called in to help with the apple harvest were hard at work, and he needed to be also. He had come in to show two men where to find the tables that had been stored in the basement. They were to set them up in the backyard for dinner. Lizzie Mae had complained that they were opening jars of black-eyed peas that she had laboriously shelled for canning only recently, it seemed. As Selma raised up from taking a pie out of the oven, she replied that this is one of the occasions that the peas had been put in jars for in the first place, not just to look pretty on the shelves. Lizzie just said, "Humph, young folks now days sho am sassy." But when the word "sassy" had come out, Lizzie caught what she had said and was sorry for it when her grandson's wife turned with a sad look on her face. "Ah jes' ain' no good fer nuthin' no mo," she mumbled under her breath.

Alyn came through the door calling for Cynthia. Ophelia answered that she had gone up to the Harris' house to help Miss Kate "do somethin' er other 'bout some school plans fer nex' month."

"Well, you ladies are invited to a Singing-Banjo-an'-Guitar-Pickin'-Story-Tellin' party tomorrow night in our backyard, that is if you bring cakes to go with my ice cream."

They all smiled and made nice comments except Selma, who only said, "Without Sassy to sing?"

"Now, Selma, dat girl is not daid and she come back 'fore long. You don' 'spec' everbody to nebber eben smile again, does you?" It was Tad's sister, Pearlie, who answered. Pearlie had come to help with the August harvest work, and the four women were now hard at work in the kitchen. Pearlie's two daughters were cleaning the house.

The next evening produced beautiful weather for a backyard gathering of a crowd of people. It was good to be together, and the tasty food made it even better. After their fill, some of the men got up a game of horseshoes out beside the car shed. Some ladies sat at one of the long tables eating while the children kept in motion the swing that hung under an oak tree nearby. The boys, Matt, Dan, Brad, Joe, and Pearlie's two boys, had a game of marbles going in the dirt. The game became so loud they had to be called down. It ended up with a chase around the house.

Everyone ate the ice cream and cakes and then flopped down in chairs or on the grass to listen first to Adam's tales and then the music and singing. As they had been back in Alyn and Cynthia's childhood, Adam's tales, taken from his own childhood, were still fresh in the old man's memory as though they had happened only recently. The children devoured every word that seemed like ages and ages ago to them, back in the dark past. Adam made the Civil War tales seem more real than their history books recorded them. These all held the children's interest, but they liked it best when he told funny stories. Some were real and some were so ridiculous they could not possibly be true.

For instance, once when he had gone hunting he came upon a possum with his head stuck in a jar. "Dis ole possum foun' a whiskey still and dis jar had a few spoon fulls of the whiskey in it dat thu possum went for. The onliest problem was dat he got 'is haid stuck in the jar. Here come his wife with her churrin a-riding on her back and she took ole Misser possum twix her teeth by du tail and had tu back up a-pullin' him 'long to take 'im home. So she led 'im 'long and 'e turned 'is haid and 'e bumped into a tree trunk and broke dee jar right offen 'is haid." Most of Adam's stories had morals to them, but this one was rather stupid. The only moral that could possibly be found is to watch what you are doing and where you are going and you will keep out of trouble.

Adam had several more stories and, after that, the music proved to be just what everyone needed to help their doldrums subside.

THESE LAST FEW MONTHS, CYNTHIA WAS AMAZED AT HOW much at one she and Alyn were, as though way back when they were children it was meant to be so. There had not been a honeymoon, for neither of them felt it would be respectful to go away and pretend to enjoy a trip, even though it had been months since the fire.

Cynthia would always hold those first days dear, not only for their passionate moments but also the times that they walked quietly hand in hand up to the grassy meadow where they had played as children. Some days the couple carried a lunch basket up to the falls and sat barefoot on the cool grass making clover chains.

It was up on the sloping meadow one day that Alyn told his bride, "I will love you forever, my dearest, and that is a vow. My whole world spins around you."

Cynthia circled his face with her fingers. "And I will love you, my husband, for ever and forever. But I just can't seem to find enough words to explain how much I love you. And even as high up as the sky is, as wide as the whole world is, as deep as the ocean is . . . all of that is not enough to measure my love for you."

Her words brought tears to his eyes, and she kissed them away. "You, an English teacher," he grinned a boyish grin, "and you can't find the right words?" He kissed her upturned face all over, then her sweet, pink lips. She was on her stomach, and he on his back looking up into the sky chock-full of puffy clouds. She picked a blade of grass and tickled his face.

"You are many miles away, sweetheart. Now tell me, where are you?"

"Do you really want to know?"

"I wouldn't have asked if I didn't, silly."

"Okay then." He waited for a minute studying just how he could put his thoughts into words. "I was in a foxhole in France wishing I was right here on Kendell Mountain with you like we are right now."

"Oh, you! Really now, where were you?"

"I swear to you on a stack of Bibles, that's the honest truth. I wished it many times, and now I'm never going to leave this mountain again."

"Can't we make a little bitty trip or two every now and then?" Cynthia teased.

"You know what I mean, Cynthee." He said it the way he'd always pronounced her name. "I've wished a thousand times that I'd jumped out of that carriage when I was kidnapped and had taken off through the woods where they could never have found me. If I had, no doubt I would've gone to the cave and maybe found Little Bear there." He paused to reflect on this time back when he was a boy on this thirteenth birthday.

"Well, Love, you're here now, and I won't ever let you get away again," Cynthia said in a lighter mood to dispel his dismal thoughts. She tickled his ribs, and the spell was broken. There was no need to dwell on things that happened long ago. Besides, nothing could be done now to change the past.

THE NEXT DAY AFTER THEIR PICNIC, ALYN NOTICED THE leaves of September turning their color so suddenly that it reminded him of a fire seen through the trees on Kendell Mountain. The sadness that accompanied this discovery was a haunting reminder that in two months, it would be the anniversary of this tragic fire that took the life of Aunt Joyce and Uncle Anson and destroyed the original Knollwood house. He was standing now in the library, a replica of the original, with the tall windows that Joyce had loved so much. It was here she had stood as Anson Kelly made the announcement to her that he was the same person she had loved when she was a girl of sixteen. He had come to Union Gap to settle a claim after a train wreck. Joyce at first had not recognized the tall attractive man until he told her who he was. Unknown to Anson, they'd had a child that was put up for adoption at the insistence of Joyce's parents. In later years Alyn found their son, Paul Silvers, whose body now lay in a graveyard in France, while his wife, Kate, was distraught as to his whereabouts. Alyn now was the only person who held the secret of what had happened to Paul.

Now gazing down from the window, these events ran through his mind while he stood holding the drapery aside. As he thought, his eyes narrowed. Aunt Joyce, who had taken him in as a child, was no kin although she was mother, father, and aunt to him. She would remain dear to his heart forever.

The problem at hand was brought on by a great heaviness of heart—a guilt for having the secret of Paul bottled up inside him. Kate's father, Anson Kelly, requested that Alyn not reveal this secret. He knew the revelation meant that Paul and Kate were half-brother and half-sister as well as man and wife. But now, Alyn felt compelled to tell Cynthia what had happened to Kate's first husband. Actually, he thought with Kate happily married to David Harris and a family of their own, she also might feel relieved to know about Paul. The information would settle her mind and bury the past. When Alyn and Cynthia gave their vows of undying love, they also vowed to never keep secrets from one another. Yes, he would tell her! He felt a sensation flood through his body as if suddenly a tremendous weight was being removed from his shoulders. That night in bed as he held Cynthia in his arms, he revealed the secret, and his wife was in complete agreement to telling Kate.

Chapter Ten

CYNTHIA WAS STANDING IN HER FLOWER GARDEN A FEW days later when she saw them turn in the drive, and she went out to the car, hailing David and Kate Harris with a wave of her hand. "Where you folks headed?"

"Down to town," Kate said. "Doc has a little office work to do."

"Why don't you just stop off here with me and keep me company. I have a few things to show you," Cynthia suggested to Kate who turned and looked at Doc for his approval. In agreement with Cynthia, he shook his head. "She might as well. I don't think her heart is in working in the office today."

"Ah, I really didn't want to go. Doc's right." She turned to David, saying that she could walk on home if he did not stop back by for her by the time she was ready to go.

"Oh, no," Cynthia exclaimed, "You'll stay for supper tonight. The boys will be showing up sooner or later and Doc, just stop your work by supper time. No burning the midnight oil tonight." So Kate stepped out of the car, waved to her husband as he rolled away, and the two women walked inside with their arms linked, giggling like school girls.

"Let's sit in the parlor, Kate. It rarely gets used." She led the way down the hall to the parlor door. Kate sat on the settee beside the fireplace and Cynthia in a low rocker facing her. That morning Ophelia had put pine branches in the fireplace, and they now gave off a woodsy aroma. Although formal, the room was comfortable and pleasant. When Cynthia and Kate had chosen the furniture, they had kept this in mind. "I intend to see that this room be used," Cynthia insisted at the time. "I don't want it to be closed off until we have a house full of company." The old furniture from Joyce Abernathy's parents' house in Atlanta could never be duplicated no matter how long they searched for it.

"Well, Cynthia, are you all set for school to start next month?" Cynthia smoothed her dress, placed her arms on the chair arms, and started gently rocking.

"As ready as I'll ever be, I suppose. I guess all the crops are in and maybe parents can turn loose of their boys. We may have a few absentees for awhile. It always seems to just creep up and leap upon us, doesn't it, like there'll never be enough time to get everything done. In the city, school starts in September."

"It certainly does come on us in a hurry, and then when it does, we generally aren't ready for all the hustle and bustle. And wouldn't you know it . . . our supplies haven't arrived yet, either. I sent in our order in plenty of time."

"They'd better get off their backsides down there in Atlanta unless they expect us to just play 'Ring-around-the-Roses' with the students."

Kate smiled at her statement and replied, "Isn't it so! I was hoping to go through the material for each grade by this time. The teachers need to have it in their hands as soon as possible or they won't know what they will be teaching. I can't see why the curriculum changes so much from year to year."

"Maybe they think that there have been so many advancements that it has to be updated."

"Well, frankly, I can't see as there has been that much advancement. Anyway, I'll have to phone them down there and see what the trouble is. If they can't hurry it up, then we'll have to delay school opening until we get the material. Oh, dear . . . that's what I was going to do today down at David's office. Oh, well, tomorrow's another day."

"And here I've detained you." They both laughed then Cynthia added, "What about Priscilla and Cole? Don't you think they would make nice additions to our staff this year?"

"We certainly could use them but then that's for the school board to decide. When we have the board meeting, one of us could bring that up. Priscilla should be good in the office because she did office work before her job played out, and Cole seems to be good with repairs. The maintenance man did give his notice after we had the last meeting. I declare, don't things just work out grand for this school!"

"Always have. That's because it was meant to be," Cynthia asserted. "But it is a shame that Mr. Fuller's old mother is ailing, and he has to go to Alabama to be with her."

Selma came in asking if the ladies would like a cup of coffee. "An' I jes' took a apple brown betty outten thu oven. What about a little dish o' that?"

"I smelled the wonderful aroma, Selma, and my stomach was already doing flip flops," Kate told her.

"Yes, Ma'am! Be's right back." Selma went out the door without getting an order from Cynthia.

"I suppose it's okay to indulge since I'm eating for two now," Cynthia said as casual as though she expected Kate to already know.

"What! Oh, Cynthia." She got up and crossed over and stooped to hug her. "That's the best news I could hear. Does anyone else know yet?" She backed up to her seat again.

"No, and I haven't even told Alyn yet, so please don't reveal this until I tell him. I'd rather wait a little longer to announce it. But I'm pretty sure, having morning sickness and all that. Should I go to David or another doctor over in Clayton? I think I would be terribly embarrassed to have David examine me."

"That's completely up to you and Alyn."

Before Selma returned, the two discussed Sassy and how Selma was taking her disappearance. They agreed that the woman was putting up a front, struggling to bear the burden that was hanging heavy on her heart. Everyone was distraught. Sassy had been one of them since she was five years old when Tad and Selma married. The girl, with her happy, talkative, singing, ways, captured their hearts at once.

Until David returned, the ladies spent the rest of the day discussing baby names, having lunch, and walking about the flower garden. They also planned a trip to select furniture for the baby's room.

A BUMPER CROP OF KNOLLWOOD APPLES WAS NOW BEING picked and crated to be trucked down to the Union Gap train station and out to various states. Alyn hired additional workers to help with the picking, culling, and crating. Cole and Priscilla Lyles offered their services in exchange for the use of the Tanner house, and Jamie went on a trip with Ella Fullman and Emily. Brad was expected to work. This was the time when everyone worked long and hard.

In the kitchen, Ophelia bossed Selma and Beth (Will's wife), while Lizzie Mae bossed Ophelia. They made apple butter for canning, apple tarts, apple bread, and the tasty brown betty kept the kitchen redolent with the sweet aroma. All this was done between serving meals.

Alyn needed to sign some freight bills after the crates of apples were loaded in a boxcar. Then with the loading completed, he sent the men off to buy Coca-Colas over at the general store, telling Sam, Will, and Tad he'd be back shortly and they could wait around for him. He wanted to talk with David Harris. The doctor's car was parked out front so that meant he was upstairs in his office. He climbed the outside stairs, tipping his hat to a lady coming down.

"Afternoon, Miz Stewart."

"Good afternoon, Alyn. How's your wife these days?"

"She's fine, thank you. Is the doctor in?"

"Yes. He's up there."

Alyn opened the door that led into an outer office. He knocked on the door of the examining room and called to David. He told Alyn to come on in and greeted him, pointing to a chair as he kept stocking his bag with supplies. "Have a few rounds to make soon. What's up, Alyn?" Then another question, "Did you get 'em all loaded?"

"Yep. That's the last shipment. Now I can rest, and you can buy that new big Packard," Alyn grinned.

"Well, we have to feed the family, you know."

"All joking aside, Doc. Have you got a minute or two?" he asked with a serious expression.

"Sure. You not ailing, are you?" Doc stopped what he was doing, closed a supply cabinet, and zipped up the bag. He sat on the corner of a table wondering why Alyn looked so serious.

"Cynthia and I decided that it is time to put some of the past to rest but want to leave it up to you."

"Why me?"

"Because it has to do with Kate, so what I'm about to suggest should be your decision."

"What in the world? Is something wrong with Kate?"

"No. You could say it is something wrong with me." Then Alyn began the long tale about meeting up with Paul Silvers during World War I in France. Alyn was on a mission with him and saw Paul get shot and killed. This left Alyn in charge of the other men with them, and he insisted that they bury Paul in the little church cemetery there. He could not bear to go off and leave him lying there.

To Doc, the strange story sounded like something straight out of a novel and still baffled, he asked Alyn to continue. The locket that Paul carried in a coat pocket revealed two pictures inside—one of Joyce Abernathy and one of Anson Kelley. Alyn had seen photographs like these in Aunt Joyce's album when he was small and remembered them.

Also, there was a letter in Paul's pocket that was addressed to Anson Kelley with a stamp on it. Paul had no doubt planned on mailing this letter the first chance he got. He could have written the letter from a foxhole, thinking that he might not ever get back home again.

David Harris remembered that Joyce and Anson had hoped to find their long lost son who had been adopted when a baby, and as he realized what this startling discovery meant, he jumped up from where he was sitting and exclaimed, "What! That can't be!" He ran his fingers through his thick hair (now sprinkled with gray), took several steps, then whirled around to face Alyn. "That would mean they were half brother and sister! . . . Then, no wonder he let her believe that he just left her and disappeared. Well! That must have been a terrible decision for him to make because no doubt he was still very much in love with her. And all these years I've hated him for hurting Kate so. He had discovered the secret of his identity."

"Yes," Alyn answered softly. "I'd sure like to know just how he happened to find out. It must have had something to do with that trip he made to Florida to find an old woman who was heir to a will he went to settle." Both men were silent for a short time thinking on this. Then Alyn spoke up. "Uncle Anson asked me not to tell anyone about this and by all means not to tell Kate. I thought at the time that she should know but respected his wishes so that's why I could say nothing. Don't you think she should know now after all this time?"

"By all means! Of course she should know. But, Alyn . . . please, not in front of the boys and I'd rather not be there. You go on and you and Cynthia . . . just . . . just tell her I had to see after someone. She'll know I used that as an excuse, but it would be best this way." Then Doc put an arm around Alyn's shoulders and said, "Thanks for coming to me first."

"I wouldn't have it any other way, David. Come on up in a little while. I could take Kate and the boys home, but she'll want you, I'm sure."

KATE WAS TOLD THE WHOLE STORY THAT AFTERNOON IN the office at Knollwood, the same place where Joyce and Anson had read the letter from Paul when Alyn handed it to them. After her tears subsided, Kate wanted to talk, and they let her say all she needed to.

"A part of me died when Paul left me. My only solace was the school. At night I was tortured with dreams, seeing Paul in a hazy blur. I asked God to give me relief from the despair and pain that I could not openly talk about, even to Joyce. She would have been there for me, to talk and preach and suggest and to give me her love. She would have been a firm shoulder to cry on, but we each have our own personal battles to fight. Joyce had hers when you were kidnapped, Alyn. Still, through everything, I'd go to bed at night with the hope that the dawn of a new day would bring Paul back to me. I never could bring myself to believe he'd left me for someone else. God answered my prayers . . . not with Paul coming back, which he knew could not be, but with my beloved David and our two wonderful little boys.

"Now, I grieve for Paul because he was the victim. Poor Paul, my brother. I'll never understand it, but I must accept it. When I think about Joyce giving up her baby because her parents insisted on it and the agony that Daddy suffered in wanting so very much to find his long-lost son, well, I can see they must have suffered more than I did when he left. But all the time, Daddy knew his son only as a son-in-law; he never even knew that Paul was his son. They had a great comradeship. I always thought they were more like father and son than father-in-law and son-in-law."

Kate wiped her eyes and dabbed at her nose again, pensively. She, too, felt as though a great weight had been lifted. She rubbed her forehead, thinking. "Alyn, do you suppose that there could be a way you and I could go to France and bring Paul home? I'd like to put him beside his parents."

Alyn hugged his adoptive sister and rocked her in his arms. "I'd like that very much. Yes! We'll go soon."

Cynthia chimed in, "The two of you had better go before February." She looked at Kate hoping that she would not reveal that she had learned the news before Alyn.

"What's this?" he asked with a blank look.

"In February you will be a father!"

"What? Me, a father!" He held his wife and kissed her on the cheek and then lightly on her upturned lips.

One minute the little group was sad for Paul and now this wonderful news. "Maybe . . . could I . . . should we leave you to go to France?"

"Oh, stop stammering, love. Of course you will go. After all, David will take good care of me, and I will watch after Matt and Dan. And besides, you need to go before school starts."

"Oh, yes. That would only leave a month! It couldn't be done that quickly," Alyn worried.

"But wait, I know what we could do," Kate spoke up. "Priscilla can take care of the school office in my place. Cynthia, you could show her while I'm gone, and I will start at once to show her as much as I can now." She took a deep breath and turned to Alyn. "Oh, please, Alyn, couldn't you get the legal documents or whatever it will entail and let's get this done at once, or as soon as possible."

DOWN IN MISSISSIPPI, PREPARATIONS WERE BEING MADE FOR the fall carnival season. Tents were still loaded on trucks where they had been stored in a barn for the last four months. The rides had been painted, oiled, and checked for any flaws. New tires for trucks were bought, and all work needed to get the show on the road was done. This included repainting a new name on the trucks. The new name was to throw off any suspicions in the event they were stopped and questioned while on the road. This trip had been set up for Texas. By the time winter blew its icy breath, the group would head back to Mississippi and stay until spring came tripping in.

Tony Howard was extremely pleased with the job that Lola and Sophie were doing with the French girl, Belle LaMont. With their coaching, she had emerged from her cocoon a full-fledged butterfly! After they painted her face and preened her hair, she looked as beautiful as any Hollywood movie star, and in the costumes they selected, she even felt like a star.

Although she felt beautiful outwardly, the old Sassy inwardly felt dirty! Her mother would be appalled if she knew that Tony Howard had been teaching her other things. Sassy was appalled herself to find that she was so ignorant about being a woman and just what men did to them. After several of these episodes, Belle went to Lola crying that Tony had hurt her. Lola put her arms around the perplexed girl.

"Oh, my dear, didn't you know absolutely anything?"

"No'm. He tolt me everybody does that. Did he ever bother you, Miss Lola?"

"Well, . . . you see . . . frankly," she found herself groping for words. "Oh, for heaven's sake, child, he breaks in all the carnival women like that! If they don't like it, then he tells them to hit the road.

I'm not saying that I approve because I don't. It isn't right. You just come to Lola, baby, if you ever need me. I'll give him a warning because I know something that certainly would make it hard on the man, and I'll sure use it."

"But, Ma'am, he done this a lotta times since June and I'm already fed up with him."

"We'll see, honey, we'll see. Just you try not to make him mad because he's got a real mean temper, and we wouldn't want him to mess up that pretty face, now would we?"

"Another thing, Miss Lola," Belle said with worry written on her face. "My mama tolt me I'd be a lady once a month, and I haven't been one now since June. Does that mean I won't be a lady no more? Is it 'cause he done that?"

All of a sudden Lola looked as though she would be sick. She gasped for breath, holding a hand to her chest. "Oh, please! Not that! I'd like to strangle that man!" Lola took her arms from the girl and sat down on the corner of her bed. Her eyes were filled with worry and she feared for Belle when the boss found this out. If she could not perform on the show, Tony Howard may send her packing.

"Sit down here beside me, Belle," Lola said patting the bed cover. "Just let me think for a minute or two." They were in Lola's small room. It had only the bed, chair, a mirror behind a door, and a little stool. Belle backed up to the bed and sat down waiting for a reply to her question. She thought it was a good question and wondered why Miss Lola took so long to answer. Her mama would have answered immediately.

Lola lifted her head and looking Belle straight in the eye, asked, "Did your mama not tell you what causes women to have babies?"

Belle had her hands clasped, hanging between her legs. She just shook her head from side to side in answer to Lola's question.

"I'll have to tell you a few things, my sweet, and I ask that you please stay calm and let's just discuss what we can do." And they did. It was Belle LaMont who had come here but little Sassy who went out the door ashamed and feeling like a whipped dog. This was not what she had anticipated would happen to her. All she wanted was to be a star. He promised her that, but now what would happen to her? She wanted to talk to Little Bear. Would he understand? Did he know where babies came from? Suddenly, Sassy wished with all her heart that she was at home on Kendell Mountain safe in her own room. She'd go and find her Cherokee friend. He would be out back somewhere, maybe in the barn. And with a sick feeling in the pit of her stomach and also in her heart, Sassy went to look for Little Bear.

Chapter Eleven

ALYN WENT DOWN TO THE RAILROAD STATION AND MADE contacts from there to get things rolling for the big trip—things such as applying for passports, booking passage, and making arrangements for the body to be brought into the country. Also, he would ask David about arranging for the body to be transferred from the northern railway system to Kate's own railroad that started service in Richmond, Virginia. Overseas phone calls were made to Paris, France, by the Georgia senator seeking permission for Paul's body to be exhumed. It would travel from the little graveyard beside Saint Abien Church (if the church made it through the war) to the English Channel and there be put on board a ship to America. Alyn and Kate would accompany Paul on this long and tedious journey. Kate was bringing Paul home at last.

OUT OF THEIR RESPECT FOR THE DECEASED, ANSON AND JOYCE Kelly, a large crowd of people stood in the Kendell Mountain Cemetery for the eulogy of their son. Reverend Bob Russell, brother to Alyn's father, John Russell, stood with his Bible in hand and read from the passage of John 5:25–29. Then he began to speak to the people, both white and colored, whom he'd come to love over the years as though they were his earthly family as well as his brothers and sisters in Christ.

"My brothers and sisters, winter is coming on at a rapid pace. The green color of leaves has now lost its supremacy. Winter is only weather resting up for springtime. Winter covers everything with its cold breath until in the springtime when bulbs send their shoots up from the earth, their flowers unfolding colorful petals, and until trees are rested and ready to hold onto their new crop of leaves.

"That's what bodies in the earth are doing . . . resting . . . waiting, until God calls a halt to time as we know it, a halt to war, a halt to sickness and to death. He will call these bodies forth and join them with the spirit that has gone on before. He will change them to a new life, to blossom and bloom forever. Think of this, my friends. Forever is a long time! In fact, there will be no end to time and therefore no more need for the very word 'time.'

"I have been told that our brother who lies here now was a Christian. He had given his heart to the Lord when he was twelve years old. I have also been told what a beautiful singing voice this man had. We have the assurance direct from our Bibles, that our brother has now gone to that place where no mortal can go. And on that last day when God calls the bodies forth from the ground, he will be called forth to meet our Savior in the air and joined with his spirit that has gone on before. We, too, who are his brothers and sisters in Christ will all go together to be forever with Christ and with our loved ones. Think of it, people . . . to be with Him for all eternity! But, let me ask you a question, have you made your preparation? Jesus said, 'He who believes on me, though he die, shall live again.'"

A quiet hush, a quiet serenity fell over the group as though a mist had fallen over them and held them spellbound. Then quietly, Tissy Russell began singing.

"Amazing Grace how sweet the sound
That saved a wretch like me.
I once was lost but now am found,
Was blind, but now I see.

'Twas grace that taught my heart to fear,
And grace my fears relieved;
How precious did that grace appear
The hour I first believed!

Thro' many dangers, toils and snares,
I have already come;
'Tis grace hath bro't me safe thus far,
And grace will lead me home."

With tears streaming down her face, Tissy emphasized the last verse of the song; her words now building so loudly that it echoed down through the valley and across Everitt Lake. Hers was not the only face wet with tears.

"When we've been there ten thousand years,
Bright shining as the sun,
We've no less days to sing God's praise
Than when we first begun."

The silence after she had finished the song lasted for a few moments, then Reverend Russell held up his hand and with bowed head, gave the final prayer.

The long shadows of evening spread its fingers among the trees, and only the faint sound of a whippoorwill in the distance broke the silence. Paul Silvers, known only to a very few here, was buried on this cool October day beside his parents. The tombstone had already been put in place before the casket had been delivered by train, and the name on it read:

"ANSON THEODORE KELLY JR., a fallen soldier, to arise a child of God." Home at last.

No one would know that his name was Paul Silvers, husband of Kate Kelly. David Harris took his wife's hand in his tightly as they turned to go.

Chapter Twelve

THAT AFTERNOON AFTER PAUL'S FUNERAL, SUPPER WAS served at Knollwood for the family and a few friends. It turned out to be a time of remembering, both good times and bad. Ella Fullman announced that she would stay the night and ride down to the Gap with David come morning. Everyone sat joyful and happy on other occasions, but this time it was without the usual banter and laughing. The table's center flower arrangement had been made by Beth and now was being admired by Ella as she named off the flowers in the ornate bowl that Ella had given to Cynthia and Alyn. Ophelia and Selma brought in steaming bowls of food and placed them on the table, greeting the familiar faces with low tones and without their usual smiles, in reverence of the funeral.

After the blessing was said by Bob Russell, the food was passed around, and the women came back in with pitchers of iced tea and filled the glasses. Kate, who had been silent up until now, told about the Christmas dinner party at her father's house in Atlanta where she had the pleasure of sitting next to Joyce. They became fast friends that very evening. Alyn interrupted by saying that things were much more interesting in the children's room when Kate's niece got in a fight with another little girl after she commented that, "Alyn Russell was an ole redneck hick." It turned out to be a free-for-all. This subject made everyone feel more like talking.

Cynthia commented, "Women fighting over my husband even at that age! Well, at least he brought a baby doll home to me for Christmas."

"Speaking of baby dolls," Alyn smiled, "I think my wife has something to tell you." He turned to look at her for a sign of approval for his saying this.

"Okay, folks, this is my official announcement. We are going to have a real live baby doll. How about that!" There was clapping and congratulations offered.

Bob stood and raised his arms out to restore quiet. "People, there is another announcement to be made here. I'll leave that to my beautiful wife, Tissy." He took her hand and drew her to her feet.

"Now, Bob, this may not be the time," she protested. "We shouldn't take any thunder away from Alyn and Cynthia's announcement."

"Go ahead, Tiss, let's have it," David Harris urged. He already knew what she was going to say.

She looked at Cynthia and said with an embarrassed flush. "We are expecting, too."

"Oh, how marvelous, Tiss!" Cynthia stood and went over to hug the young wife of her husband's Uncle Bob. "We can plan and compare our aches and pains with each other."

"So that means I'll have a cousin," Alyn said. "He, or she, will think I'm an uncle, however."

"What's the date, ladies?" Ella asked.

"Tissy in January," Bob spoke up, and Cynthia just said "February for me."

Ella turned to Cynthia on her left. "These two children will grow up together and be so close, but I do hope they will be of the same sex so they will be more company for each other like Matt and Dan."

"Well, if they are both boys, they may beat on each other all the time like our boys do," David grinned. "They'll keep me busy with broken arms and scrapes."

Ophelia came in with desserts after they'd all ignored their plates of food, and accepted no more tea. Selma followed with the coffeepot. "Smells so good," Ella raved. "It doesn't smell like apple whatever like we always seem to get," she smiled.

"No'm. It's pound cake with peaches 'n whipped cream," Ophelia said as she set a plate in front of Ella, who only said, "Oh, well, what's another five pounds?"

Priscilla and Cole felt left out. They had been listening, determined to learn more about these people, and desired to fit in. Someone asked them direct questions every now and then to make them feel more at ease and to join in with the conversation. On the other side of the room, the children had no problem talking to one another.

There was so much that could be said, but in Kate's heart, she only wanted to be alone . . . to sit in solitude, to reminisce about

Paul. It was all she could do to keep tears from forming. David turned to her every few minutes to see if he could detect what was going on in her head. How long would it take for her to put this day behind her? How long would she grieve for the young man who was once her husband? He would do everything in his power to help her forget. If only there was a pill or a shot that could wipe all traces of him from her mind. She must not live in the past! No. He would not let her! A long time ago David had lost his bride-to-be, who was unmercifully murdered, and that nearly caused him to withdraw into a shell. Now, he would not let that happen to Kate, his beloved beautiful wife and mother of his two sons.

The spell was broken when Alyn announced that the school board needed to have a meeting since opening day had taken place without one, and they had to tend to some important issues. It would have been done the month before but because of his and Kate's trip to France, the meeting was postponed. Then, there was the apple-picking season before that.

"I understand that Priscilla did a wonderful job in your absence, Kate," Ella said. Priscilla flushed, still she was happy that she could come through for Kate. Everyone agreed to have the meeting next Thursday night. All of the board members were here at the table now.

Selma came back in with the coffeepot but had no takers. David stood, saying that they had to get on home, and then Cole and Priscilla followed suit, with the children not wanting to leave. "Come on, now, kids. You'll all see one another at school tomorrow, if we can get you up. It's past bedtime," Cole told his two.

When Kate passed behind Tissy's chair, she stooped over and kissed her lightly on the cheek. "Thank you, Tiss, for that lovely song today, and I am so happy for your wonderful news."

Later that night Alyn and Cynthia sat by the fireplace talking after their visitor, Ella, had retired for the evening. Alyn had Tad bring in logs that morning when they got up shivering in a cold house, and now it was comforting to gaze into the fire and watch hot flames lick around the logs causing them to pop and crackle. He stirred the fire with a poker.

"Cynthee, my Love, I've been doing a lot of thinking lately about the economy situation."

"It doesn't look very bright, does it?"

"Not at all. Not at all! What do you think about my disposing of the Atlanta General Bank?"

"Good gracious! That would take some thinking to make a decision like that. Besides, that should be completely your decision. Have
you consulted with anyone on this?"

"No, not really. David and I merely touched on the subject one day
recently. He didn't have any idea I was serious in the least." He turned
his back to the fire, facing his wife on the couch. "You will remember
that Aunt Joyce gave me instructions in her will that the bank funds I
receive are to go to Kendell Mountain School, which we've been doing
all along. The way the economy's going, I was thinking that if I could
sell out, we'd hold the money in escrow for the school so it would be
safe."

Cynthia looked at her husband with loving eyes. "Whatever you
think is best, Alyn. It is your decision. I'm not any help with matters
like this."

Alyn took the morning train to Atlanta. He had always hated the
monthly board meetings down there at the bank and told Cynthia
when he kissed her good-bye that after sleeping on it, he'd decided to
sell out his stock in it completely. They would take up the finances of
the school at the board meeting on Thursday night. He had come up
with some ideas on that also.

Of course, there were the donations that still came in from businesses and individuals, but just how long these donations would
continue, no one could surmise. Alyn had been keeping up with the
business news and stock market reports that now gave a grim picture
of the economy. He was glad that his deceased aunt and uncle in
Boston had had the foresight to dispose of their shipping business.
Those funds now were in stocks and bonds that provided Alyn and
Cynthia a hefty income. Alyn himself had disposed of their house up
there in Boston, those funds going into the rebuilding of Knollwood
after the fire. And now he would dispose of the bank that had been
built by Colonel James Abernathy, Joyce's father, the funds going into
the school account. Alyn decided that he and Cynthia would be okay
here on the mountain. Yes, indeed.

Chapter Thirteen

KENDELL MOUNTAIN SCHOOL BEGAN ITS SIXTEENTH YEAR of operation with two hundred boarding students, fifty-five day students, eight teachers, and three kitchen workers. Each teacher had a full load, some of them teaching two subjects. From the school's inception, Bible was a required subject, as was church on Sunday and Wednesday night prayer meeting. The school's aim was made clear from the start—educating the underprivileged as well as those who could pay. Educating the backwoods' poor was the aim of Alyn's parents, the missionary couple who came up with the idea for the school that was completed by Joyce and Anson Kelly and the board of directors.

Each year advertisements were sent to newspapers about the boarding school, and each year the enrollment increased. During the twelfth year of operation, a larger chapel was added because the seating capacity of the original one had become inadequate. Now, the old chapel was split up into several new classrooms, these too greatly needed.

And now the school board was having its meeting around a table in the school's dining hall. President Alyn Russell asked the recording secretary, Kate Harris, to list in the minutes those who were present. Besides himself, there was Reverend Robert Russell, chaplain (and principal of the school); Kate Harris, recording secretary; Cynthia Russell, treasurer; and Ella Fullman, operating funds enlistment chairman.

After Reverend Russell opened the meeting with prayer, asking God to bless the meeting and equip each member with the wisdom he or she needed to carry on the school's business, Alyn then listed the topics for discussion to be acted upon during this meeting. He leaned forward in his chair and read from a paper that he took from his briefcase.

"Item Number One: The addition of an infirmary for the boarding students for any overnight stays and, of course, the day students for their care on any given day.

Number Two: Discuss funds for medical supplies and also Dr. Harris's services to attend the infirmary.

Number Three: The resignation of Mrs. Ella Fullman.

Number Four: The hiring of Patricia Russell as head of the Music Department, that is if the vote is passed to accept the resignation of Mrs. Ella Fullman.

Number Five: Appoint an assistant principal.

Number Six: The resignation of Kate Harris as school secretary.

Number Seven: Vote on a school secretary, if the resignation is accepted from Kate Harris.

"Now this next subject was not listed with these items because I thought of it later and think it is important that we consider this suggestion." He paused here and glanced toward each member, all sitting motionless, wondering what their president had come up with. "I have heard of other schools requiring their students to work so many hours each week for the school. This seems to be a very good idea because it would not only help the school, but it teaches the students responsibility. Also, they could receive so many credits for the work they do for the school."

"Just what kind of work do you have in mind?" Bob asked.

"The boys would do jobs like helping feed and milk the cows, feeding the pigs, cleaning out their pens, and tending the gardens. This is another thing I didn't mention. If we grow our own food, think of the savings there. In fact, the girls could learn to sew and make crafts to sell, the same for the boys. They could make birdhouses, etc. The jobs for the girls would be serving food at mealtimes, clearing the tables afterwards, and sweeping and cleaning . . . oh, just all kinds of jobs." Alyn leaned back in his chair waiting for their reactions to these suggestions.

Bob's reactions were heard first. "Frankly, this was done when I went to seminary. One job I was required to do for a quarter term was to ring the rising bell and thirty minutes later, the breakfast bell. And then I rang the lights-out bell at bedtime. The jobs changed each quarter to give the students an opportunity to learn different jobs. Yes! I think this is something that is important for Kendell Mountain School to do."

"Okay, let's take each item one by one now," Alyn said, picking up his pencil to check the items off as they discussed and voted on them.

He reached out and moved a flickering lamp closer to his paper, cleared his throat, and looked around at the others, some of them making comments about being there until midnight and hoping there would be plenty of coffee. The meetings were informal compared to the ones led by Anson Kelly when Alyn and Cynthia were children. Now, they were more in the form of discussions as Alyn had suggested. He disliked formal, dull meetings like those he had sat in at the Atlanta bank.

He now looked over his paper toward where his wife was seated and asked, "Sweetheart, would you mind putting on a pot of coffee for us, please?"

"Be happy to, Love. Looks like we will need lots of it." She rose to put the pot on the stove that was still hot from supper only a short while ago.

The task of taking over the Kendell Mountain School Board had been a great strain on Alyn following Joyce and Anson's deaths. His heart was not up to the tremendous task and told the members that he could not possibly do it without each of them teaching him what the job would require. But after the Christmas holidays were over, things fell into place rapidly. It had now been eighteen months since the fire! Could it be possible? In looking back, he wondered just where the time went. He also had had to go over Joyce's books and learn how to deal with the orchard and shipping. When someone mentioned the length of time it had now been, Alyn said that he felt certain Joyce and Anson would approve of the things that the board had done for the school up to now and would continue to do.

He adjusted himself in the chair, wishing that it was his office comfortable one, and glanced at each person present. "Now, folks, you all will remember what an ordeal it has been over the years to work with the sick children without a proper infirmary. We all know that we need one without a doubt but uppermost in our minds will be the funding for such an undertaking. Funding at this particular time when the economy is at an all-time low will be difficult. The funds from the sale of Aunt Joyce's bank are solely for the running of the school and should last for years to come if used wisely." Alyn looked at them each, seeing the wheels turning in their heads. He gratefully accepted a cup of steaming coffee from Cynthia and took a mouthful before continuing. "M'mm that is what I needed." She passed cups to the others and set the pot on the table along with a creamer and sugar dish.

"You all know that we are in for some rough times ahead," Alyn continued. "If things don't improve before long, we may find ourselves having to cut out some teachers and cut down on salaries of those left who will then have a heavier workload."

"Oh! Such a pessimist," Miss Ella exclaimed. "Do you really think that the government is in this much of a mess? If so, I'd better get busy with my investments!" she exclaimed with a hand to her forehead.

"Yes, Miss Ella. It is plenty evident, and we all need to prepare without anymore delay. Now, I realize we should have been on top of this two months ago, but the delay was unavoidable so let's get our heads together and get down to business."

He took a sip of coffee and cleared his throat to say more but was interrupted again by Miss Ella. "Wait just a minute, Alyn. I don't see how building an infirmary would be such a big problem."

"Well, it is, Miss Ella and we'll have to . . ."

"Just let me finish, dear," she said, using the "dear" that she called everyone. "I'll just save us all a lot of headaches and midnight oil. I will furnish all the funds for this project, and it will be a donation completely! How about that? . . . So, you can just skip on down now to number two."

Alyn threw back his head laughing while the rest of the members clapped except for Kate, who reached over and gave the old lady a bear hug and kiss.

"Now, that's what I call getting business done," Bob said as he stood up clapping.

Kate remembered just how this lady brought in funds from so many sources while they were planning on building the school in the first place. "I move," she said, "in naming the infirmary 'The Ella Fullman Clinic'!"

"I second it," Cynthia said, and the rest affirmed the motion.

Kate hurriedly wrote all this down in her notebook before Alyn even had time to put it in the form of a motion. "I suppose this is all legal," he said under his breath, grinning.

The rest of the items were checked off one by one, put into motions, voted on, and passed in legal order. Then Kate was eager to make motions that Priscilla Lyles be installed as school secretary and her husband, Cole, be hired as janitor and handyman.

As the octagon Waterbury clock on the wall struck midnight, Kendell Mountain School had an assistant principal, Kate Harris; a new music teacher, Patricia Russell; a new school secretary, Priscilla Lyles; and a new janitor and handyman, Cole Lyles. Robert Russell still would be principal and chaplain.

Chapter Fourteen

OCTOBER 1929. IT HAD BEEN FIVE MONTHS SINCE THE carnival came to Tony Howard's farm in southern Mississippi, and Little Bear still hated this flat land! He had never known hate before. There had never been room in his life for the word or the feeling of hate. But now, he grieved for his cave and his newly found friends on Kendell Mountain. He longed for the waterfall, the cool fresh air, and for the three boys who had become the children he never had. For years he had longed for a wife and family.

Little Bear was sitting behind the barn in the morning harvest sun thinking. He'd lived a lonely life since his parents died when he was a middle-aged man. His father, Running Wolf, died first and his mother, Red Bud, not long after. Once he was completely alone, he began to venture closer to the big house down the mountain from his cave, to get a look at people. He had always avoided them before. He was skilled at hiding unobserved, watching every movement of those who lived nearby. There was a little golden-haired boy and girl and sometimes a tall, lanky dark-skinned boy, who ran through his woods, jumping rocks over streams, and hiding secret messages in the hole of a great oak tree. The boy and girl were the ones who had another house built after the original one burned and now they were man and wife.

Little Bear thought about the golden-haired boy and the dark boy and how they liked to fish and hunt. They came in his cave and found the bag of money, and he was glad when they took it so the men who put it there would not come back. The men came too close to discovering him. Now, recently, there were two little boys, *di ni tla wa* (twins) who came and then brought another boy back to see Chief. They were nice boys . . . but . . . his agreeing to go with them to town to see a "carnival," they called it, had placed the old Cherokee in grave danger. The carnival people had taken him away from his lovely land where the bear and cougar roam and where the eagles flew high above the valleys below. Would he ever get to go home again? And that girl they also took away, Adam's great-granddaughter . . . he had not seen her lately and wondered if she, too, were homesick for the mountain.

Just as Little Bear thought of Sassy, she rounded a corner of the barn and saw him sitting on an overturned barrel. "Hello, Chief," she said. "I been looking for you." She flopped down on the ground beside him. "Are you alright? I mean, are they treating you good?" She looked up into his old wrinkled face and detected sadness in his dark eyes.

"Treat Little Bear good. Have food. Sleep on hay in barn."

"When the weather gets cold, you will need a warmer place to sleep."

"Will find place when time come," is all the old man said. He always thought things out before he said anything, and it was a few minutes before he said more. "Treat you good?"

Sassy looked at the ground and frowned. "Some do."

"Not all?" he asked.

She looked around to see if anyone could hear her complain and seeing none, she said, "That man in charge, his name is Tony . . ."

Little Bear nodded his head up and down knowing who was in charge for Tony had been giving him orders about what to do around the barn. Then Sassy continued. "Well, he is mean and I hate him with all my guts, and I wish we were back at home."

"Mm huh," Little Bear grunted in agreement.

"Chief, I'm gonna have a baby . . . what you say? A papoose?" Sassy told him sorrowfully.

"How you know this, girl?"

"Miss Lola tolt me."

"Father tell me how get papoose."

"Well, my mother did not tell me!" She emphasized the word "not." "I'm just plumb dumb, Chief. Real dumb!" Sassy started to cry and turned aside to wipe away the tears so he would not see.

Little Bear did see the tears. "When papoose come, we go home."

She held her head up and gazed into the old man's face and saw hope there. "Oh, Chief, could we? Do you think we could find the way back home?" Now she smiled.

"We find way." He reached out and placed his big hand on her head. A great sense of relief swept over her. She took a deep breath of air, letting it out slowly. "When papoose come?" Little Bear asked.

"Miss Lola say in the winter when it's real cold, right before spring time. She tell me to come stay in her room with her and she will look affer me. She a nice woman, Miss Lola, and the little bitty woman with the high squeaky voice, she nice, too, and she say she help me when it time." Then Sassy's expression changed to concern and fear of the unknown. Miss Lola told her that it hurts to give birth, and she wanted her to be prepared for this. "But, you know, Chief, I'm still sorta skeered."

"Be okay. You see. We make plan when time come."

THE TEXAS TRIP WAS SHORT BUT SUCCESSFUL. IT LIFTED Sassy's spirits somewhat because of her singing, and to Little Bear's displeasure, many bottles of the "Miracle Cure" were sold. The overall extra funds made would be a great boost to the slim savings that had been put away to carry them through the winter months. There would have been plenty of time for another carnival booking, but Tony Howard was tired and wanted to get everything at the farm done before his people began to get itchy for their winter leaves to begin. Some of them took a leave to be at their homes with families during the holiday season of Thanksgiving and Christmas and then for the cold winter months of January and February. They were now doing repair work on the rides and equipment, safely storing away tents in the huge barn, and the people who were staying on through winter had been settling themselves into the two-story house and barn.

Before Tony bought the farm, it was used as a ranch for raising and boarding horses. The barn was his main attraction to the place, a well-constructed building for his show horses and equipment. There was plenty of room that performers could use to practice their acts, and several rooms upstairs for some of them to live. The ones who worked in the house, cooking and cleaning and a few of the women performers would take the upstairs rooms there in the house. The seller had been happy to sell since he was wanting to retire.

Tony was happy to be home for a change, the routine of carnival life was always grueling and the moving about was tiring to the bone. Now, he had the men busy making ready for winter and the women working in the house. "That Indian wasn't much good for anything," he thought, "except to bring in money during carnival season," so he'd just let him lallygag about and do as he pleased. The young French girl was a delight to his desires. She possessed great potential as a performer. He knew that Sophie and Lola would do a good job with her, but they did not know that he would do an excellent job of teaching her in another field. Yes, he'd done well to get the Indian and the girl. Belle did not need money. He could readily see that she would be content to be a performer and, as an apprentice, she'd be satisfied with just enough pay to buy a few trinkets for herself. He had learned how to handle his people over the past few years and felt quite satisfied with himself.

Now, Tony met Belle on the staircase just as he started up and she was halfway down. "My, but you look like you don't feel very good this morning, Belle. Did you not sleep well?"

"No, not very well."

"You aren't sick are you?"

"Been throwing up a little."

He put his hands out in a pushing fashion as though to ward off whatever she might have come down with. "Well, don't give it to me," he said.

"Don't think you could catch it."

"Oh," he said, thinking it was a monthly thing. "Alright then, I'll just go out and see how the men are coming along."

Belle breathed a sigh of relief and realized that he had been on his way up to her room. She was thankful that they had met on the steps since it saved her for a few days perhaps. He went on out the front door, and she made her way toward the kitchen where she knew that some of the women would be gathered. Evidently Tony had already eaten his breakfast alone as usual, and the men were being served on the enclosed back porch at a long table with benches.

If Tony had met up with Lola since Belle broke the news to her last night, Tony would have no doubt dragged Belle back up to her room and given her trouble. Lola was biding her time until things could be straightened out in her own mind. She wondered if she should tell Sophie about this.

WHEN SASSY WAS NOT PERFORMING, SHE REVERTED BACK TO her natural speech. No matter how hard Sophie tried, the speech lessons were only for performing. The singing was a snap for her, and she sang the words exactly as Sophie taught them to her. Sophie recognized that Belle LaMont had a God-given voice for singing. Some had it and some didn't, but those who did had no trouble just opening their mouths and letting the melodious sounds come out. She could and did, however, show her a lot about actions and how to breathe, holding her hand and placing it on the abdomen as she inhaled air. The chest should go out with the air intake without shoulders rising. "Squeeze the stomach in," she said. It was evident that Belle was eager to learn, but one day she asked an irrelevant question in the middle of a lesson.

"Miss Sophie, has Tony Howard ever done anything to you?"

"Why, Belle! I'm shocked that you would even ask such a question! What made you ask this?"

"Because Miss Lola, she say he breaks in all the women here and he won' let me 'lone. I'm sick of him and I want you to tell me how to make him stop 'cause he done made me gonna have a baby."

"He what!" the woman exclaimed and backed up to a chair because she felt that she would faint if she didn't sit.

"Yess'um, dat's what."

"Well, he's married to me! I'll just see about this!"

"Oh, pleeze, pleeze, Miss Sophie," she folded her hands in prayerful pleading. "Pleeze don' tell 'im! He may beat on me an' Miss Lola say he got a mean temper. She say I come stay wit her so he won' bother me no more."

"I'll see to that for sure!" Sophie exclaimed. She stood up and put her hands on her hips, swearing "I'll kill the son-of-a-gun!" Her eyes shot fire, the fists now curled in knots.

"But, Miss Sophie, you can't do dat," the girl pleaded. "He deserve it, I knows, but that get you in plenty o' trouble fer sure."

With a belligerent scowl, Sophie said begrudgingly, "I'll grant you one thing, Belle, he'll rue the day that he broke you in! I might just make him into a woman!"

This last statement completely confused the startled girl. She knitted her eyes together and in all sincerity asked, "Just how you do dat, Miss Sophie?"

"When I get a chance, you'll find out."

Chapter Fifteen

OCTOBER 20 STARTED OFF AS AN ORDINARY FALL MORNING in Union Gap, . . . slow . . . with merchants out early sweeping off their storefronts and setting some wares and produce outside, stopping to call out greetings to one another. Some were discussing, over a second or third cup of coffee, the current main news item—the slowing economy of the country. The school bell rang, calling children inside; Cooter Potter ambled down the road with his old homemade wagon rattling behind him. He called out to the children, who turned and threw up their hands to him. Then, someone stopped and told Cooter where he might find some nice junk for his collection . . . always the same . . . but no one minded, because that's the way it has always been here in the Gap.

The morning train chugged past the station with a shrill whistle blowing, the engineer waving out his window to Billy O'Shields, stationmaster, who was standing out on the platform, his pocket watch in hand. "Yep, right on time," he told himself, shaking his head at the same time, and making an "okay" sign to the engineer.

Everyone seemed content with their lives here for everyone knew their neighbors and even those who lived up on Kendell Mountain. The slow economy did not touch many in this remote town for they had no need for an excess of money.

This day began the same as usual, but the devastating news on the outside of the area was announced when the afternoon train came chugging through, tossing off a supply of the daily *Atlanta Journal* newspapers. Standing and stretching, Billy shuffled out on the platform to retrieve them. Stooping, he took a paper from the bundle and read the headline in large bold letters that jumped starkly out to him . . . "NEW YORK STOCK MARKET FAILS!" The article went on to say that many people were immediately ruined, and some had jumped out of buildings to their deaths.

"Son-of-a-gun!" Billy exclaimed adjusting his glasses and spitting a stream of tobacco out over the platform to the ground. He wondered if this news would affect anyone there in Union Gap. "Maybe Doc and Kate Harris might have some stock in something or other, or Alyn and Cynthia Russell, and maybe that old Miz Fullman, I reckon." At any rate, he'd go spread the news before Cooter picked up the papers to deliver them.

Outside the Gap, falling prices and unemployment had affected everyone since the First World War was over. Joblessness was the principal problem right now. No doubt Billy would find many hobos riding in boxcars the same way he'd found the Lyles family not too long ago. They were among the lucky ones because they had found a home up on the mountain.

The town now buzzed with the news. People could be seen standing around talking, and the continuous checker game outside the general store even came to a halt for a few minutes, as though it were a silent prayer or in respect for those who had jumped to their deaths.

Alyn told Doc that the Butterfields had settled their affairs in Boston before their deaths, and he and Cynthia had been living off those relatives' investments. He was glad that he'd sold their house up there when he did, but now without those stocks, he would be penniless. "But, you know, we can always live off the land. I'm sure the apples this year won't bring very much in price but we'll manage."

Doc said that the only stock he and Kate owned was in the railroad, and he did not know just yet how the stock failure in today's paper would affect this. The country could not survive without railroads. He was sure Joan would be wiring Kate this very day to check on her security. Kate's sister and her husband, Bryan, depended solely on the railroad for their living, and up until today it had given them a good one.

"One thing for sure, Doc, Kendell Mountain School will not be affected for a good long while. But still, I'm glad we got into some programs to make it self-sufficient instead of depending so much on donations." Alyn said this after the tenuous shadows of reality began to sink in. For now, the school would be secure. The boarding students had paid for this year in advance, but come next year there would, without a doubt, be dropouts.

Chapter Sixteen

CORA BETH STOOD IN THE HALLWAY KNOCKING GENTLY ON the office door. When Alyn answered "Come in," she turned the knob and just cracked the door open wide enough to poke her head inside. "Misser Alyn, Will in de kitchen 'n he say he need t' talk wif you."

"Tell him to come on in here, Cora Beth."

"Yassuh, an' Miss Cynthee, she say tell you she 'bout ready fo' church and ax you t' hurry up."

"Okay. Tell 'er I'll be there as soon as I see what it is that Will wants."

Will came down the hallway in long strides, hat in hand and a concerned look about him. "Come on in, Will. What's the trouble?" Something evidently was wrong or he would not come in to see him knowing that he and Cynthia were about to leave for church. Just then Doc's car passed, the horn honking a signal for the occupants of the house to get a move on. Alyn had just gone in to look over a few things while waiting for his wife to put the finishing touches on her hair and pin her hat on.

"Well, Misser Alyn, I 'specks you might want t' warn Reverend Bob and his wife t' stay away from dee old Turner place 'cause it be hainted! Me an' Sam saw it wif our own eyes las' night."

"You saw what, Will?" Alyn asked, leaning back in the swivel chair and looking up at Will who stood in front of the desk nervously curling the brim of his hat with both hands.

"We seen lights inside dat house is whut. Dey moved all 'round, too, an' our dogs, dey barked lak sumpin crazy."

"What were you and Sam doing there in the first place?"

"We wuz possum hunt'n and dee dogs, dey run a big 'un true dee Turner yard. Dem dogs jes' let dat ole possum go on off true dee bushes an' dey jes' stopped in dey tracks and commenced t' barkin'.

88

Dogs, dey knows when a place be hainted. Dere hairs bristled straight up, too. Den dey quit barkin' and commenced t' whining, and Sam say dat ole Misser Tanner's ghost stay dere a-waitin' fer Misser Lonzo t' come back."

Alyn had a slight smile. He was amused with Will's tale, and it quickly reminded him of Luther (Sam's son, whom he grew up with) and how he believed so strongly in ghost tales. "Now, Will, there's not any truth in ghosts at all. Things like this are just made up in some-body's head. Sam has always been full of bosh like that and he even had Luther scared of his own shadow with all his tales."

"But, we seen dem lights, Misser Alyn. We sho 'nuff did." Will's eyes grew large as he spoke.

"There's a logical explanation somehow. Well, I'll talk to Reverend Bob. You just keep it quiet and tell Sam I said not to be scaring the women and children. We'll go over and investigate." Alyn heard Cynthia calling to him and stood up, dismissing Will, and they walked down the hallway together. At the kitchen door, Alyn put a hand on Will's shoulder, saying, "Things like this always have an explanation, so don't jump to conclusions before we take a look."

Will stopped and looked Alyn in the face. "I won' go 'round dat place so I hopes dat 'we' you done said don't include me none." Alyn just smiled and pushed the kitchen door open when he heard Cynthia talking with Cora Beth about the basket of food she had prepared for them to take to the church social. Cora Beth, Selma, and Ophelia always took turns preparing the Sunday dinners each week while the others went to church. Sometimes, they had company, and sometimes Alyn and Cynthia either went visiting or spent a quiet afternoon to themselves.

During the summer months the old one-room school building was used, but when school was open, church was held there in the chapel so there would be sufficient room for the student body. Today was parent visitation day, meaning the chapel would be packed with visiting parents from other towns, and the locals would supply their lunch baskets with extra amounts for the visitors. Reverend Russell would have a special message prepared, and Bo Dutton would be leading during the singing after the noon dinner meal. Bo was a big man with a booming bass voice. He could raise the rafters and make windowpanes rattle, and today he would surely show off for the visitors. Students would get to demonstrate their talents also at this time, with some playing instruments and some singing solos or duets or in quartets.

Miss Lettie Cromwell played the piano for the church services. Some had whispered that she had eyes for Bo Dutton, who had never married either. After his father's sawmill closed down, he just looked after his old dad and their small farm. Today, Miss Lettie would be dressed in her flossy Sunday-go-to-meeting finery and wide-brimmed hat with colored flowers to match the outfit, and she would play all over the piano, as she usually did, without any need for printed music. Bo Dutton had made comments before about her talent, and it was evident that he admired her, if for nothing more than her musical ability. They would make a good couple.

Out front, before the service started, Dan saw Becky Stephens talking with a group of girls. When she glanced toward him, he beckoned to her with a crooked finger. Startled to even be noticed, she pointed a finger to her chest and mouthed the word "Me?" Dan answered with a nod of his head that brought Becky to him as though he was pulling her by a rope. She adjusted her glasses and threw back her long blonde hair in a habit that he hated. When she smiled sweetly at him her buck teeth shined like a little rabbit's.

"What you want, Dan?" she asked when she reached his side.

"I'm not Dan, I'm Matt."

"Oh? Well, it's hard to tell. Then what do you want, Matt?" It wouldn't matter to her just which of the twins it was, she felt honored to be noticed by one of the most popular two in her class.

"I just wanted to tell you that I think you are pretty and that I like you. Will you be my sweetheart?"

"What! Me? Are you kidding?"

"No. Of course I'm not kidding. I've liked you for a long time. Haven't you noticed?"

"Not really but, sure, then . . . I'd be honored." Becky fluttered her eyes, sucking in her breath. "Okay, it's a deal. Bye for now, M-a-t-t," she drawled out his name and dashed back to her friends all a-flutter, leaving Dan standing there with his hand over his mouth hardly able to contain his laughter. Then Dan turned his back just in time to see Matt coming toward him and hoped he would not call out his name.

"Have you heard the news?" Matt excitedly exclaimed. "Guess what?"

"What news?" Dan inquired.

"About Sam and Will seeing ghosts in the old Turner house!"

"Aw heck, there ain't no such thang as ghosts."

"Yes there is! They said they saw 'em with their own eyes."

"Who told you?"

"Never mind. It's true."

"I hope Aunt Tiss won't be upset by this tale."

"They said it's true and there's lights floating around inside the house."

"We'll have to go over there and see about this. Have you seen Brad?"

"Yeah, I told him about it. He's gone on inside with his folks and there's Mama on the steps waving to us, so come on."

Then Dan decided he'd better warn Matt about Becky. "I heard some more news, too! Guess what?"

"Oh, just say it. What?" he asked Dan as they started up the steps.

"I heard that Becky Stephens is crazy about you and wants to be your sweetheart!"

Dan laughed and ran up two steps ahead of Matt who just stopped where he was with his mouth open.

"Come on up, Matt. Don't just stand there," Kate fretted. "I declare. You know how your father hates tardiness, and everyone will see us come in late."

Dan held the door open for them and made a mooning lovesick expression, fluttering his eyes at Matt as his brother came in punching at him. Now inside the foyer, Kate whispered, "Boys! Stop that. We are in church."

They saw David sitting on the outside of a pew next to the left aisle about halfway down and went to sit with him. He stood as they filed past, and the other occupants moved over to make room as Kate smiled a "thank you." Miss Lettie was playing the piano, and the service had not yet begun. Dan saw Becky sitting with her family several rows ahead of them. She turned to watch them as they came in and were seated. She smiled at the Harris twins, not knowing at which one to smile. After they were seated, Dan punched Matt and whispered, "See? I told you she is sweet on you." Matt retorted with an elbow in his ribs.

The chapel was full of students and their parents who had traveled from surrounding towns, many from the Atlanta area as well as the regular locals. It was a beautiful fall day for a church gathering, not too cool, just comfortable. There was no need even for fans that during the summer months could always be found along each pew, and not a dark cloud marred the sky. After the service, the meal would be spread outside on long tables under the trees without the worry of fanning away flies and bees. It was a lovely time of year in the mountains.

Trees redolent with bright oranges and golds still clutched their leaves until the late November wind would soon blow its harsh breath and the rains would come scattering them asunder.

After the opening prayer, the assistant principal, Kate Harris, was called upon to welcome the guests. She did not know that the principal, Reverend Bob Russell, would call on her, and she had not the faintest idea what to say. But never one to falter over words, she made her way to the platform trying to form in her mind just what would be appropriate. When David stood to let his wife pass from the pew, he admired her choice of attire this morning and the jaunty hat that framed her pretty face. He had no doubts that his wife would give a nice welcome to the visitors. Up on the platform, Kate whispered to Bob asking if she might introduce the faculty also. He nodded an affirmation.

As she called their names, each teacher stood and gave the subject that they taught. Then Kate gave her welcome as though she had been memorizing a speech for several weeks, and with her light air and lovely smile, everyone immediately liked the school board's choice of an assistant principal. The thought came into her mind suddenly that it would be nice if Bob would lift the spirits of the parents by telling how the students could attend another year without having to worry about finding the now hard-to-come-by funds. Maybe Bob had already planned on speaking of this, but if not, she would certainly get back at him for putting her on the spot and now it would be his turn.

It seemed not to bother him, for he stood up and explained what the school board had come up with during the October meeting and how it would be put into practice after the students returned from their Christmas holidays. Some parents already may have decided they were unable to let their children return before he spoke. Now their minds would be set at ease.

Several hymns were sung and no collection taken, which, of course, was very different for the usual Baptist church. Reverend Russell made a few announcements and also explained about the afternoon. After the meal, there would be a time of games or walking around the grounds before the singing program, and last, the parents would be welcome to inspect the building and classrooms and talk with each teacher about their children's progress. One class had made a book on the history of Kendell Mountain School's founding, and this book could be found in the foyer of the classroom building.

Preacher Bob lifted his chin heavenward, spreading his arms tenderly. "Our Heavenly Father," he prayed, his deep resonant voice captivating the audience. "We are your children, humble and grateful for this another day in your house; we thank you for your mercy and your love that covers us as an eagle's wings over her young. We are a rebellious, sinful lot, stained and spotted. We do not deserve your redeeming love, but because of your great mercy, we come to the throne of grace with the assurance that you are faithful to forgive if we but only ask. Look down upon us now and give your humble servant the message that you would have the people hear. Bless these dear children who are here to learn not only knowledge that would help them throughout their lives, but uppermost, the knowledge that you love them, Lord, and that you are forgiving. Take these hands as they are held up to you, and lead us all the way home. It is in your precious and wonderful name we pray. Amen."

During a general Sunday service, an offering would be taken at this point, but since there would be none today and for the sake of the afternoon program to come, there would be no more audience singing, only a special duet by Mrs. Patricia Russell and one of the male senior students. They came to the platform while Miss Lettie played the introduction to their song. Heads turned, eyes following the expectant mother down to the front. Some might have whispered that she should keep in the background and not flaunt herself in front of the children, but after the song was over, there was not a dry eye in the auditorium. The young man's part was merely the background and harmony. The song about a heavenly home set the stage for Reverend Russell's sermon. The sermon was shorter than usual, pleasing the students' growling stomachs and the desire of the younger children to run around outside.

A general stirring of the people followed as ladies reached for their handbags; others replaced songbooks and woke up small children who had their heads in parent's laps. Reverend Russell made another announcement or two and then asked old man Clark to have the closing prayer while he slipped to the door to shake hands as people passed by.

Tables outside were being loaded with food by ladies who had been asked in advance to take care of this job. The local people had furnished the dishes of food, and some were making trips to their wagons to retrieve them. Visiting out-of-town parents stood around looking helpless until they were rescued by teachers, who made them feel at ease and welcome. Before this afternoon would be over, their minds would be eased and they would feel like these people were all dear, old friends.

Students grouped with their particular friends to sit cross-legged on the grass, precariously balancing their plates and drinks while laughing and enjoying the beautiful day. Dan, Matt, and Brad sat with three other boys as they eyed a group of girls, and the girls looked at them, smiling. Becky Stephens's back was to the boys so she had to turn her head to look back at them. Each time she did, she inclined her head and smiled demurely, fluttering her eyes.

"Hey, guys, I heard that Becky Stephens is sweet on ole Matt," Dan snickered and took a bite of a chicken leg.

Matt exploded! He gave his brother a shove, spilling food and drink on his clothes. "She is not! And don't you say that she is!" He jumped up with curled fists, daring Dan to fight.

"Hey!" Brad said as he tugged at Matt's arm. "Take it easy now. Don't spoil everything. Just sit down. You'll have Reverend Russell on to you in a minute and your dad, too."

Dan did not take the dare but brushed off his clothes, gave Matt a dirty look, and trudged off to get another plate of food. His brother would really be mad if he'd known that he had started the whole thing. The girl had noticed the ruckus and figured the twins were fighting over her, which pleased her greatly.

While Dan was at the food table, the other boys decided to get up a ball game over at the field where the school held its games. "We'll have to hurry up before the afternoon singing begins," someone said. Then another answered that they'd have plenty of time, so off they went to induct enough players to make up two teams.

In the meantime, the group of girls nearby decided that they would walk down the pathway beside the creek for a nice stroll. Other girls joined them as they skipped along holding onto their hats or letting them flop to the back, secured by ribbons. They talked and giggled over everything that was said, told wild tales that could not possibly be true, exchanged dreams and desires, but most of all, talked about boys.

"I'll tell a secret if you won't tell Matt Harris that I told," Becky Stephens said, twirling around so that the girls behind her could also hear. She wanted to make certain that everyone could hear what she had to say. The girls chorused that they would not breathe a word of it to anyone, especially Matt. "W-e-l-l," she drawled out the word, to make certain that she had everyone's undivided attention. When they all assured her that they were listening and to go on and tell them what it was, she said, "Matt Harris has asked me to be his sweetheart!"

The girls, all shocked and squealing with delight, hugged Becky as they all jumped up and down. Becky felt like a queen. She was the first to have a sweetheart since school had started and the least to be expected to have one. "Becky! How does it feel to have a sweetheart?" Jenny Johns asked excitedly.

"Oh," Becky said, drawing in a deep breath, "Oh, . . . well, I'll tell you." Then she looked around and saw a big rock beside the creek and jumped up on it. She put one hand over her heart and the other up against the back of her hair. "I'll tell you how I feel. It is simply wonderful and I just absolutely feel like a queen." The girls all answered with "Ohs." Just then Becky's slipper slid and down she went into the rushing creek with a loud scream as all the other girls screamed also. "Help! Help me! I can't swim," Becky yelled, her arms flailing at the water, and then she began to be carried on down the creek by the rushing water. Three of the girls took off running back the way they had come over to the ball field, screaming breathlessly as they approached that Becky Stephens was being drowned in the creek. The pitcher dropped his ball and the batter slung the bat as they all took off to the creek running as fast as their legs would go. They ran to where Becky's friends were pointing and screaming, but Becky had already been washed around a bend in the creek. The boys raced along the path until they caught sight of the limp girl floating now in a calm pool past where the rapids had carried her.

THE HARRIS TWINS WERE BOTH FIRST INTO THE CREEK AND carried Becky to the bank where they laid her. Matt immediately pounced across her legs after Dan turned her on her stomach, and Matt started pumping on her rib cage. Water squirted from Becky's mouth as Matt kept pumping. Just as a crowd of parents came running down the path after they had been summoned by two girls, Becky groaned and fluttered her eyes.

"Whew!" Dan said. "I thought she was a gonner for sure."

"Yeah, me too," Matt said.

"How romantic," a girl whispered to another. "Oh, I could just die."

"Well, she nearly did," another whispered back to her.

"But she was in the arms of her lover."

"Which one? It could have been the one wiping her mouth with his handkerchief or the one pumping."

"I don't think she cares, she may love them both."

The Harris boys were congratulated by everyone and hailed as heroes by Becky's parents. Becky then could not make up her mind just which twin she was in love with. "What difference does it make?" she said to a friend. "They are just alike."

Dan could not put an end to what he had started!

Chapter Seventeen

THE SATURDAY BEFORE THANKSGIVING DAWNED COLD AND crisp with a northeast wind blowing leaves in swirls. The weather did not deter Alyn from crawling out of a warm bed to go hunting with Will and Sam. The Harris twins had begged to go along when they heard the men talking about the hunting excursion the afternoon before. Alyn told Will that one of the best things he remembered about growing up was going hunting with Adam and Luther and since Doc never hunted, he would like to take the boys along. "Be okay wif me iffen dey can be still an' quiet, lessen dey run everthang off 'fore we can shoot, an' we sho needs some turkeys fo' Thanksgivin'," Will said. So it was agreed upon that Alyn would go up and get the boys and be ready before first light.

The boys were all excited even though Doc and Kate were adamant that they were not to take a rifle. They were just to go along with the men, but they each could carry a lantern. They stuffed biscuits with sausage in their pockets and were ready and waiting the moment they heard the knock on the door.

"You mind Alyn, now boys," Kate called from the door as they ran out. "And don't stray off by yourselves. Stay together."

"Yes 'um," they called simultaneously, putting on caps and jackets as they dashed out the door and hopped in the back of Alyn's truck. They'd go back down to Knollwood and go out into the woods with Will and Sam.

"You ever kilt a turkey?" Sam asked as they walked along up toward the cave area.

"Nope. Never have," Alyn answered, "But Adam and I have got plenty of coons and squirrels and possums."

"Turkeys has got to be called up," Sam told him and showed him his turkey caller. "I'll jes' call 'em up an you shoot 'em." Then he turned to the boys and said, "Dis hea caller is older'n yore Uncle Alyn. I had it a long, long time. It's thu small bone of a turkey's wing. You jus suck air real quick-lak tru dis bone an' it makes little turkey-like yelps."

Will said that when you made the turkey call you put the bone back in your pocket and don't do it again because a gobbler could hear it a way off and he'd come creeping up before long even if he were a mile away. If you gave another call, he'd get wise and go the other way. "We'll make a blind with bushes and sticks and get behind it," he said, "An' 'fore long, iffen we don' bad a eye, he'll come right to dis spot affer he gobbles twice."

"And then we'll have turkey for Thanksgiving dinner," Dan laughed. "But you know, I think I might not like being still and quiet so long."

"Well, we half to Dan, so button your lip," his brother told him and received a shove for it.

"Now, boys, you don't want to have to turn around and go back home, do you?" Alyn asked as a warning. Neither of the boys answered, but shortly Dan asked just where they were going.

"On up tuther side of thu cave."

"But how do you know that turkeys are up there?" was the next question.

"Aw-w-w-w, I ain' nebber seen thu like. We might get inna flock er maybe twenty er twenty-five. But turkeys, dey don' gobble much in thu fall o' th' year so yo jes' haffa lissen real good."

Will broke in with, "Sometimes dey gets tuh squabblin', you know, like a young tom an' a old one and dey sho does put up a racket. You boys gotta set still jes' wher' we tells ya and don' move none 'til you hear us shoot er you might get shot, too. An' dat gobbler, he a smart ole cuss and can hear a pin drop an iffen he do, he be long gone fer sho."

"I suppose that's where the old saying 'He can run like a turkey' came from," Alyn laughed.

"I found a place dat had been scratched plum bare where acorns had fell offen a tree. Looked lak chicken scratchin's but turkeys done it." Sam said this and then stopped to catch his wind from the climb, the group stopping below him. "Be light 'foe long and dey be a-comin' down from roostin' in trees."

Then Will told Sam not to shoot at a hen turkey. "Ain't I de one what tolt you not to shoot 'em in thu firs' place? We 'ud be a-wiping out all turkeys iffen we shoot thu mamas."

"I think I'd rather go with you when you take the dogs, and they get to running and barking like mad. It will be more exciting," Dan said feeling bored already. "My father said he heard an ole bear the other night out back of our house. Now, that's the kind of hunting I'd like to do."

"We'll have to go after him, Dan," Alyn told him, "because Adam told me that the hogs have been real nervous lately, and he thought they were frightened by a bear."

"Alright! Let's do it then."

"We'll see about it."

As soon as the first light slanted through the dense forest, they reached the spot that the men had been talking about. Sam took his turkey caller out of his pocket and pressed it to his lips, making the sucking sound. The air came out with a sound like a hen turkey, then he slid it back into his pocket and began to pile up brush for a blind. "Get back dare, boys, and don' make no sound," Sam told them. Dan stretched out on the ground and went to sleep but Matt was anxious to see the gobbler come walking up. He crawled up beside Alyn and crouched down.

Alyn propped his rifle through the sticks of the blind and let Matt look down the barrel. It was not very long before a big turkey appeared. He stood there looking around and gobbled twice, then Alyn punched Matt in the side and whispered softly in his ear to get the gobbler in the center of the sight and pull the trigger. He did and got his game on the first shot. If he had missed, there would not have been a second chance. Matt immediately jumped up to run and get the gobbler, and Will went with him because he could see that this was a heavy one. Matt's squeals of delight made Dan sit up with a start.

"What's going on?" he asked rubbing his eyes.

"Your brother got a turkey," Alyn said. "Blow that caller again, Sam!

"Dat all fer dis spot. We haffa move on."

On that excursion the hunters bagged three turkeys weighing at least twenty or twenty-five pounds each.

ALYN ENJOYED THIS OUTING WITH THE BOYS. HE WAS thinking about it while going to sleep that night, deciding that this is the way it would be with his own son. They would do things together that fathers and their sons do. He would take him on trips to interesting places and teach him how to live a good life. He hoped that his son would love the mountain as much as the twins and stay there to live when he became a man. But, these days, he was still thinking, children wanted to go away on their own and make a life for themselves in the cities. Would anyone ever get to do this again? The depression had put people's dreams on hold. Then another thought came into Alyn's mind—the baby may be a girl. "Well, fathers can be just as close to a sweet little girl; they just did not go hunting and do things that men like to do. And there would still be other children that we will be blessed with," he thought. When Cynthia jumped in her sleep, Alyn turned over and placed his hand on her abdomen, feeling the baby move.

Then, he thought about the promise that he had made to Dan. He would take him bear hunting, and they would investigate the goings-on at the Turner house.

Chapter Eighteen

ON THE SATURDAY AFTER THANKSGIVING, THERE WAS A gathering at the community house in Union Gap. Ella Fullman planned and put together, with some of the ladies' help, a box supper and dance. Miss Ella always enjoyed delegating the decorating and planning every detail of things to be done beforehand. She decided that the money collected for the bids on the box dinners was to be given to the person holding the lucky ticket. Among the young unmarried couples, the boxes were bid for, and the winner shared the meal with the girl who had prepared it. Then, of course, they spent the evening dancing together. Someone must get the tickets ready, and Ella cornered Priscilla Lyles for this. The local musicians had been practicing for the affair and looking forward to a grand time. "This time the men are to leave the corn liquor at home." She was passing this word around, remembering the ruckus which the spiked punch had caused at the last affair they'd had. "And I hope no one comes riding through the double doors like Alonzo Turner did that time when Alyn and I were children," Cynthia commented to Kate. "Oh, no! And that same time my mother came and David got her drunk on spiked punch! The very idea. He thought it was funny. I could have wrung his neck for that." They both could not help but laugh. Cynthia did not attend that affair because her mother was confined to her bed; it was right after the hanging.

"Well, I'm sure the sheriff will be there as usual, and he will give all the punch a taste test, I'd bet you on that."

"After he does his tasting, someone will come along with one spiked bowl somewhere in the building. I'd bet you on that, too!"

As usual, everyone worked all day decorating the community house with colored leaves for the festive occasion and adorning tables with pine cones and whatever else could be found to make them pretty. There was always an abundance of corn shocks in corners and a tub of apples from Knollwood for bobbing.

About an hour before time, the musicians arrived to set up their corner and do some practicing. As the ladies worked, it sounded like the party had already begun. Wagons arrived early to assure the drivers of choice hitching places and to enable children to gather and "run wild" as mothers warned them not to do. They splashed in the creek, heedless to previous warnings, the weather now too cool for this. They chased one another around the building, dashing in and swiping a cookie or a piece of pie and back out again to eat the coveted prize. It was the perfect time of evening to have a game of hide-and-seek.

The local Knollwood School children naturally would be along with their parents, but the boarding children never got to attend the local affairs. The school made certain that these students had enough entertainment among themselves.

At a box supper, bidding for the boxes would be first, then the meal, and last, the dancing. So promptly at seven o'clock Mayor Marvin Cates entered the building with his wife, a short, stocky lady, and began shaking hands. (Elections would be held this month.) Cynthia and Alyn had arrived just before the mayor, and after he placed their offering on the table already laden with all sorts of food, he turned to the hand held out to him. The mayor placed one hand on Alyn's shoulder, shook with the other hand, smiled, and said to him, "Well, Alyn, have you climbed up any silos lately?"

Alyn shook the hand of the mayor, who was not one of his favorite acquaintances. "No, Mayor, not recently."

When they were young, Marvin and his brother were rascals who tried to overrun any boy they could, and they tried to do this to Alyn whenever he came to town with Aunt Joyce.

"And have you knocked over any fishing rods in the general store lately and blamed it on anyone else?" Alyn added, smiling all the time he made this remark.

"Now, Alyn, you don't still hold that against me, I hope, particularly now at election time!"

"I suppose not, since there isn't anyone running against you."

The mayor caught the slur and turned to shake someone else's hand instead of making another remark.

Reverend Russell and his wife, Tissy, entered, followed by Carlotta and Smiley Phillips.

"Hello, Smiley and Carlotta," Alyn said to the couple after he had spoken to his Uncle Bob and Tissy. "Where's the pretty little daughter?"

"Hi, Alyn," Smiley said as Carlotta turned to take her bowl of something-smelling-good over to the food table. "Emily saw her friend, the little Lyles girl, outside so that's the last we'll see of her for awhile. How's things going? Your wife faring well?"

"Yes, she is. She finally got past her sickness and is putting on weight now."

"That's good. I noticed the Reverend's wife is, too. Say, what's this I hear about her folks' old house having a spook residing there?" Smiley grinned when he asked this question.

"Oh, those tales get around. When somebody comes up with a tale, it gets added to and goes on until it makes the rounds and then finally dies down. You know how it is. Two of the men up at Knollwood seem to have gotten that one started. When I was a kid even I heard spooky tales, and it scared the wits out of us kids. We couldn't quit talking about whatever it was at school."

"I guess people always have to have something to talk about, like it is entertainment or something."

"Yeah, something like that. Oh, excuse me, Smiley, I see David Harris motioning to me." Alyn walked over to where David was standing, and Smiley turned to talk with a group of men nearby.

"I see you've already hit the punch," Alyn grinned.

David gulped down the mouthful he had taken and grimaced. "It's sure flat. When you discover the good bowl, lead me to it."

"It must be pretty close to where all those men are standing," Alyn pointed. "Where's Kate?"

"She let the boys and me out and went over to the boardinghouse to pick up Miss Eva and our visitor. You've no doubt heard about our good luck."

"Don't believe I have. What good luck?"

"Of course, that was meant to be a slur, it's really our bad luck." He took another mouthful to finish off the cup of distasteful punch and kept Alyn in wonder for another few seconds. "Kate's sister, Joan. She came in on the afternoon train for what I hope will only be a few days or possibly the weekend."

"Well, what'er ya know! Wonder what brings her to our boring town? From all I've heard about her, she's like her mother and prefers hoity-toity events."

"All I know right now is that Kate said she seems rather upset about something but hasn't come out with it yet. When she lowers the boom, I'm sure she will say a mouthful."

"I haven't seen her since I was a kid, but back then I could readily see that she and Kate were nothing at all alike. I heard Uncle Anson tell Aunt Joyce that she was just like her mother, Candice, in ways and, from what I could gather, that was not a compliment by any means. By the way, is her mother still living in the house that her parents left her?"

"Oh, no. She sold that a long time ago and made a killing on it. Then she built an apartment building and rents to rich people from up north who come down to winter there. She has one of the apartments for herself."

"Well, she must have gotten some of the cobwebs out of her brain for once. I believe Kate said something to Cynthee that awhile back you folks made a trip down there to visit her."

"We've made several trips to visit back before you returned to Kendell Mountain—short trips, mind you. The boys enjoyed themselves, going to the beach and just seeing Florida in general. Candice made our stays rather sour by still going on about 'how Anson did me by leaving me and marrying that mountain woman, and look what he got for it and I didn't get one bit of insurance!'"

"But," Alyn broke in, "it was the other way around. She left him. Didn't want him in the first place."

David nodded his head up and down in affirmation as he pointed his empty cup toward the door. "Here comes Kate and Joan now." Both men turned to watch them walk in, as did every other man in the place, and the ladies at the food table all stopped what they were doing to get a look at the attractive woman with Kate.

"As I live and breathe," Ella Fullman told the woman next to her. "That woman hasn't aged one bit in years! What's she doing here? That is Candice Kelly, isn't it," she asked Cynthia who was taking a cloth off of a plate of food she had placed on the table.

Cynthia turned to see Kate and her sister coming toward her. "No, of course not. It's Candice's other daughter, but she does look just like her. Acts like her, too, so I've heard." Then Cynthia left to meet them and smiled a greeting to the visitor.

"Cynthia, I don't know if you've met my sister, Joanie." She placed an arm around Joan's shoulder as her sister corrected her statement by saying, "Joan."

"Hello, Joan, it is a pleasure to meet you since you are Kate's sister, and we love her so dearly."

"Thank you," Joan said, "But we aren't anything alike in looks or ways. I don't see how she has buried herself here for years. As for myself, I prefer the city."

The smile left Cynthia's face. She made a quick observation of the woman and saw a trim, well-dressed lady who would be even more attractive if she'd possessed a soft, sweet countenance like Kate. "Oh, we make do around here, and if we become too bored, we hop on the train and head for Atlanta. Generally, there's too much to do here to even think of being bored. I do hope you will enjoy your stay. How long are you planning on being here?"

"I don't know, yet, maybe a few days, maybe longer. I have a little problem to discuss with Kate and David."

"If there is anything that Alyn and I could do, you only have to ask, after all, you are Alyn's adoptive sister, like Kate." Cynthia looked Joan squarely in the face and saw astonishment there when this revelation dawned on the woman staring at her. Then Cynthia added, "I hope your mother isn't ill."

"No, she's fine as long as she can boss everyone around." Then Joan turned her head looking all about at the people staring at her and changed the subject. "Looks like quite a crowd gathering here tonight." She turned and asked Kate, "Where are your boys?"

"Outside with the other children. They'll all dash in for plates of food and take them back outside to eat.

"Well," Cynthia said, "It looks like Reverend Bob is about to say the blessing."

Bob had stepped up on the platform, held up his hands for silence, and then began the prayer. As usual at every gathering, the sheriff took this opportunity to glance around and search each man for bulges from their pockets or jackets. He hoped that there would be no guns or any loaded fists or hidden moonshine. This was not as prevalent these days as it had been in the past, but a sheriff could not be too careful. There were a few individuals who still were not of the highest honor. This sheriff, Junior Eason, elected during the last election, proved to have been a wise selection of the three men who were running. Junior, nephew of a previous sheriff, Todd Eason, grew up tagging along with his uncle and learning the job at a very early age, so he felt as though he had been cut out for this position.

After the prayer, people began finding seats to see who would bid for the boxes that had been placed on the end of the food table. After the contents of the boxes were eaten, the participants, if they still had room, could go to the table and replenish their plates. Reverend Carder of the Presbyterian church was in charge of the bidding. There was teasing and catcalls to the young men who stepped up to claim the boxes they had bid for and won and take the young lady by the hand. They already knew who had prepared each box. They found places off by themselves to eat, or they went outside to enjoy the peace of being alone, if they could find a quiet place without any children around. Some of the men found merriment in keeping the bidding going, raising the price of the box that some fellow was after, until some had to count their coins to see if they would be able to bid again.

With this out of the way, children came running in to fill their plates and take them to the place they had chosen at picnic tables outside. Becky Stephens's mother loudly told her daughter to stay away from the creek as she hurried out to join her friends and hope-fully get to sit with the Harris twins.

After the meal was finished and leftover food replaced in baskets, the musicians returned to their corner to start the dancing. "Uncle" Abner Purdy, still possessing the booming voice he'd always had, started off the first song as chairs were pushed back against the wall and dancers came out to the middle. David remembered the dance he'd had with Candice Kelly years ago and the spiked punch he kept offering her when the dance was finished. "Wonder if this would work with her daughter, Joan," he thought to himself, smiling. He decided he'd best dance with his wife first just as he saw Smiley Phillips walking toward Joan and then leading her out on the floor. Joan did not look too pleased but allowed herself to be led.

As David and Kate danced among their friends, David asked each man to break in on Smiley and Joan's dance, suggesting that they needed to keep her dancing to make her feel very welcome at their party. Making Joan feel welcome was not David's intent. So, the plan was passed around, and every few minutes, Joan found herself with another partner until her feet began to ache in her dainty pumps, which were not made for dancing. Several feeble attempts were made to "sit this one out," but those fell on deaf ears.

Now, Joan was dancing with David, and the music was louder and faster. "For heaven's sake, David, I have to sit this one out! What's wrong with all these men, anyway? They act like they've never danced with any other woman but their wives before."

"Ah, now, Joanie, they're only being nice and friendly and after all, it's a great compliment to have them all wanting to dance with you. They think you're a beautiful woman." He swung her around, pushed her out, and pulled her back.

She reached up to push a lock of hair back that had fallen out of place. "Slow down, David! This is not funny!"

"How can I slow down when the music is so fast?" he grinned capriciously with satisfaction.

"I insist that we stop this now!" she exclaimed as she jerked her hand away from his shoulder. He held on to the other one and stopped dead still.

"I tell you what, then. If you're so tired, let's go over for a cup of punch and have a rest."

"I think it's about time." Joan took a dainty embroidered handkerchief from a tiny purse that dangled from her belt and dabbed at her forehead as she was led to the punch bowl. Her bobbed hairstyle and flapper dress were causing many whispers behind cupped hands. All eyes watched her every move.

"There's too many people at this bowl, let's go to this other one over in the corner."

The men gathered at this punch bowl stepped aside as the couple approached and watched Joan take her first sip from the cup offered her. "Mmm, this is very delicious," she said demurely.

"Yes," David agreed wholeheartedly, "and I recall that your mother liked this punch, also. She came up here one time when we had this harvest affair and was the hit of the party." Turning toward the men standing there, David said, "I'm sure you gentlemen all remember when Candice Kelly was here?" The men all smiled sheepishly and agreed that they remembered Joan's mother.

Joan quickly drained her cup and held it out for more. She drank that one slower, but as Kate surveyed the area for her sister and spied her laughing with the men and holding her cup out for the third round, she dashed across the room toward the group. Her scowl gave evidence that she was unhappy, and the men scattered except for David.

Kate reached out, intercepting the cup that was held out for Joan. "Oh, no you don't, David Harris! You should be ashamed of yourself. And what do you suppose people would think of the Christian school's assistant principal if they knew that her husband had given her sister spiked punch? You should know by all the men gathered around that this bowl was surely spiked with moonshine!" Taking Joan by the hand, she headed for the chairs that were pushed against the wall, and they sat down. Joan, happy to find a cardboard fan on the chair next to her, kept it flapping, commenting all the while that it certainly was hot for this time of year and what did she mean by saying the punch was spiked?

"JOAN, THAT PUNCH YOU DRANK HAS LIQUOR IN IT, AND IF you'd had that third cup, you would be lying out on the floor!"

"For crying out loud! Then, why did David let me drink it?"

"He must have thought it would relax you and help you to have a good time," Kate told her sister, but to herself she was thinking, "just wait 'til we get home!"

Chapter Nineteen

ON THE WAY UP TO THE NORTH RIDGE, IT TOOK ONLY A VERY few minutes for the twins to fall asleep on the backseat. At an interval in conversation from the front seat, Joan felt compelled to tell Kate and David the reason for her visit to Kendell Mountain.

"I did enjoy the get-together tonight, but that won't help my despondency for long I'm afraid."

This interested David from a medical standpoint. "Despondency? You didn't seem so despondent to me this evening."

"Joanie, why should you feel like this? Has something happened that we don't know about?"

"Yes, I'm afraid so."

A wheel hit a rock that made the car swerve as it bounced along over the rough road that now had become steeper. David shifted into high gear. They were waiting for Joan to continue.

"It's Bryan, as you may suspect. He's gone off with a woman." Her chin quivered, and it was all she could do to keep from crying. "I've discovered that he's been having an affair with her for the past two years. Can you believe that!"

"Oh, my, I'm so sorry, Sis," Kate said almost in a whisper as she placed an arm around Joan's shoulder and drew her close. Joan was fumbling in her purse for a handkerchief and, when she found it, dabbed at teary eyes.

David looked over toward Joan and asked if she had confronted Bryan.

"Yes, I did when he took out a suitcase and started packing. This was the first that I knew something was going on. The very idea of him doing such a thing to me, and our girls, even though they are grown-up, were devastated when they learned that their daddy had left without so much as a good-bye. I don't know how he expects to live when he didn't work and depended on our railroad income completely. Evidently, the woman has money. Well, she'll have to keep him up because I will not!" Her voice sounded spiteful. "I know I am better off without him but just knowing that after all these years he would leave me . . . just simply take off with another woman." At this point, the tears rolled down her face like rivers, and she had to blow her nose.

"Have you told Mother?" Kate asked.

"No. She would only say it was just like Daddy did and that isn't so. You know that, Kate. I thought I'd come up here until my feelings ease up somewhat, or does it ever ease up?" When she asked this question, she immediately was sorry, especially in the presence of David, as she thought of Paul leaving Kate. Her words died in silence.

"You can make your own life, Joan. The world hasn't come to an end, and there will be other things open up for you, you'll see. We'll talk more and you know you are welcome to stay with us until you decide what you want to do." Then David agreed with his wife, feeling sorry that he'd told Alyn he hoped she wouldn't stay long.

NOVEMBER PASSED SWIFTLY, AND DECEMBER FLEW IN ON ICY wings, chilling everything within its frosty grasp. Some days Joan went to school with Kate and the boys and accepted menial jobs in the office with Priscilla. Kate wished that her sister had studied to be a teacher, for classes taught by Cynthia had to be split up and crowded into another class since Cynthia had to give up teaching. Now very heavy with child, it had become a laborious task to climb the school's front steps and to hold out to do a full day's work. Alyn, as well as Dr. Harris, insisted that the time had come for her to stay at home.

The same was true with Tissy Russell. Even at Ella Fullman's advanced age, she was called back to fill in for Tissy as the music teacher. If the two ladies could return to teaching at a later date, then so be it. Joan was not a teacher, and she just may get up one morning and announce that she would return to Atlanta.

On a dismal Saturday around mid-morning, the twins decided that they would take their Aunt Joan and show her around. One boy told the other that Aunt Joan did not seem to be the outdoors type and may not want to go traipsing through their woods. The other twin suggested that they show her through the cave. It was so awesome that they just might start charging admission for folks to explore it! "But ole Chief Little Bear would not like for us to do that," the other one replied. "It's his house, and he just might show up again some day." Well, this time they would show Aunt Joan, surely he wouldn't mind that. So after breakfast, the three put on their heavy coats and caps and, each bearing a lantern, started out. Joan, reluctant to go, felt that she should spend some time with her nephews and relented. True to their feeling, Joan was completely amazed and enthralled with the cave. The boys gave her the history of their friend, Little Bear, as they went along through the cave, and they told her about the kidnapping of the Indian and Sassy.

"That is simply unbelievable! They couldn't just completely disappear from off the face of the earth!" Joan exclaimed. "What's the matter with the sheriff here? Can't someone do something? How could they just forget about it and sweep it under a rug like it never happened?"

"We don't know, but no one has found out anything at all."

"If your granddad was still alive, he wouldn't let this rest until they were found."

"I know," Matt said. "He could get anything done."

They let the subject die as they approached the cave entrance. Before they'd gone very far, Joan became frightened. She said it was hard for her to breathe in that place and was afraid that they would become lost and no one would ever find them. "Let's get out of here, boys, now. I-I-I've always had a problem with claustrophobia. Please forgive me. I wanted to please you by coming here, but let's go now." She turned to go back the way they'd come and commented when they emerged that the weather looked stormy. Maybe they should return home now.

"Aw, not now, Aunt Joan," Matt said. "Just a little while longer."

Dan, the adventurous one, said, "I know what, Matt, let's go over to the old Turner place and have a look around."

Both Dan and Matt had been wanting to go there, but their parents said "no." But now since Aunt Joan did not know about the lights over there, they wouldn't tell her and just go ahead.

"What is the old Turner place?" Joan asked.

"Oh, it's just an old house, and we thought it would be a good place to camp out sometime."

"Yeah, we thought we'd check it out in the daytime first. Several of the guys at the school and us thought it would be fun to have a camp-out. It's on up further from here on Possum Ridge, but it wouldn't take us long to get there from here."

"Come on, Aunt Joan, be a sport and come with us."

"Alright, this time I will go on with you, but you boys are just going to simply wear me out with all this climbing up the mountain and walking. I may have to stop and rest along the way. My daughter's little boy would love all this. He's a real outdoorsman."

"Why didn't you bring him with you to visit us?" Matt asked as he grabbed hold of a low branch in passing and stripped off a few leaves.

"His mother wouldn't hear of it. Maybe another time she will let him come. He needs to get away from her for awhile."

"Oh, oh! Look at that! Did you see that, Aunt Joan!"

"Yes, yes! A doe and her baby! How magnificent they are!"

"We frightened them from that cluster of bushes. I'll bet they were bedded down there."

The deer were gone out of sight as quickly as they saw them and at the same time thunder rumbled across the mountain.

Joan stopped with a flash of fear through her chest and she seemed to shiver. "Boys, we must go back now before we are caught in a storm. Your mother won't even know where we are."

They had been climbing constantly while talking and had put a good deal of distance between the spot where they now stood and the cave. "But we are closer now to the Turner place than going back down the mountain," Dan said, "and besides if it starts to rain, we can take shelter there until it passes."

Then Matt added, "Yes, just down this slope and up the next one and to the top is Possum Ridge. There's a little rough road that runs over the ridge and around the mountain. It's a long way that'a way down to town."

And Dan took up the explanation with, "We'll be there in ten minutes."

"Maybe by the way the crow flies, but not by the way I walk," Joan puffed, trying to catch a second wind. "I really think we should be heading back the other direction for home."

Dan put an arm around his aunt's shoulder and patted her. "You are really a good sport, Aunt Joan, and I'm glad you came to visit us. I knew when I saw your bobbed hair that you were the adventurous type. I really like you."

"Thank you, Dan. That's very sweet of you." She stopped long enough to flash a smile of pleasure at the boy. "Let's get on with it and find that house so I can rest. It certainly must be a special place for you to want to go there now."

"No, there isn't anything special about it at all. In fact, it's kinda tumbledown, but it might be neat for the guys to have a camp-out there."

True to Dan's words, the old house came into sight in about ten minutes or so. It sat up on a knoll, forlorn and desolate with broken-down wooden steps leading up to a porch. The house had evidently been built by someone who knew nothing about construction. Several rooms had been haphazardly added at some later date, no doubt in order to make room for the Turner's growing family.

"Do you mean that someone actually lived here?" Joan asked amazed at how simply these mountain people lived.

"Oh, sure, like we said, it was the Turners. You know, Aunt Tissy Russell was one of the people who lived here."

"Yeah, and she seemed to turn out alright, but the rest of them didn't."

As they went up the steps, Joan suggested that they should check with Tissy first before the group of boys made any plans. Up on the porch, Matt had his hand on the broken doorknob about to turn it when a noise from inside stopped them in their steps. Remembering what Sam had told Alyn about the place being haunted, the boys looked at one another, both feeling chills down their spines.

"Well, boys, it sounds like someone still lives here," Joan said. "That sounded like hammering to me. Go ahead, Matt, knock on the door."

Dan stepped up next to his brother and grabbed his hand. "No, don't knock, Matt," he said in a whisper. "Let's go around and look in some windows first and see if anyone is in there."

"Just don't leave me here by myself!" Joan demanded. "I'll go with you." And she turned to follow the boys off the porch and around to the back of the house. They had taken off just as soon as Matt had made the suggestion, leaving Joan to catch up with them. Just as Joan rounded the corner of the house, a dusty curtain hanging by threads was pushed aside by an unseen hand with a flicker of a person peering out. The curtain fell back into place.

Joan found Dan bending over with Matt standing on his back looking in a window. "Get off, Matt, quick. I can't take it." Instead of waiting for his brother to jump, Dan fell to one side and down Matt went also.

"Guys, if someone is inside, you have already frightened them away with all your racket!" Joan reprimanded with hands on her hips.

"Let's get away from here; we are the ones who are trespassing."

"No, if someone is in there, it certainly won't be Aunt Tissy." The twins had always called her "Aunt" and Reverend Russell was "Uncle Bob."

"Try the doorknob, then. The door just may be unlocked."

Matt tried the door and it opened, slightly squeaking when he pushed on it and motioned for his aunt and brother to follow. "Shh. Let's tiptoe."

Joan did not care for the idea at all. "But," she protested, "what if we bump into someone in there?"

"Leave the door open and we'll scadoodle outta here!"

The room they entered was a kitchen. A dusty old worktable sat underneath the window, a small table in the middle of the floor, and an old iron stove against the far wall. There were scattered items on the floor where they had been pulled from underneath an open cabinet, obviously when someone had been looking for something. A crudely made pie safe sat next to the worktable. Spider webs dangled from the corners and one across a doorway that led to the next room. The sound of hammering had ceased and only the sound of Joan nervously blowing out her breath was heard. With a finger on his lips, Dan motioned that they follow him into the next room, a bedroom. An old iron bed pushed up against a wall held a mattress that had mouse holes in it and cotton poking through. A dresser with empty drawers hanging out was the only other piece of furniture in the room. Joan grimaced with disgust, feeling thankful that she had never had to live in such a crude environment, as she turned sideways to go through the door in order not to touch it. She had worn flat shoes but now wished that she had on the one pair of slacks she had packed for her trip. None of the women on Kendell Mountain ever wore slacks, and if she had been seen in them, it would have caused her to be even more of an oddity than just her short hair.

"Come on, boys, let's go now."

"Shh, Aunt Joan. Whisper. I have a feeling we are being watched."

"Who by, a ghost?"

"There's no such thing as ghosts. It's somebody real."

This room had no outlet, and in order to go further, one would have to return to the kitchen and take a small hallway from another door or go out the back. As Dan turned to go out the door they had come in, a noise was heard as though someone had dropped something. The trio all looked at one another, each feeling a grip of fear, and now anxious to get out of the house. Before they reached the door, however, a man with a mean scowl and a gruff countenance entered and blocked the doorway. He put one hand up and held the door facing; the rest of his body filled the doorway. Then he grinned a toothless grin, looking at first one and then the other twin, but as his eyes fell on Joan, he smiled halfheartedly and said, "Well, if you ain't a pretty li'l lady. I jes' might take a fancy tu you." He took two steps and reached out to touch her hair. Joan slapped his dirty hand away as they gazed into each other's eyes, challenging one another.

"Keep your filthy hands off me, you monster!" Joan demanded.

Dan and Matt stood there with wheels turning in their heads. They tried to decide just what to do and glanced at one another. They had always felt so close that one could nearly judge what the other was thinking in any given situation.

"Ain't choo thu brave one," the man smirked, "but then, I like a feisty li'l fireball." He motioned with his hands for her to come on. "Let's just see what choo can do now. Step back boys, ya'll er jes' runts and can't do nuthin' to hep 'er noways."

Joan took the few steps necessary to face him, and when she got close enough, she spit in his face and then kicked his ankles. He caught her by the hair and gave her a hard slap and then a fist on her cheek that left it stinging and throbbing. Then the two boys jumped in kicking, pulling his hair, and biting. The force of the three of them pushing on the man knocked him to the floor with all three on top of his back. Dan sat across his shoulders, grabbed his long hair, and pulled his face up and down, knocking it hard against the floor. Joan got up, kicked his legs apart and gave him a swift, hard kick in the crotch just as his head hit the floor again. Both blows made him see stars and then total blackness.

"Come on, both of you, run. Now! Let's get out of here!" Joan had already gone through the door and headed to the kitchen when the boys caught up with her. They sailed out the back door and through the woods. Dan caught Joan by the hand and dragged her along, her other hand flailing through the air. A loud clasp of thunder shook the earth, then rain started in a sudden downpour.

Chapter Twenty

"I WONDER WHO IN THE WORLD THAT MAN COULD BE?" Kate asked David the next morning as they were getting ready for church.

"Beats the life out of me, but those boys should have known better than to go way up there and take Joan along. Sakes alive! He could have killed them."

"They said they heard banging like someone using a hammer." Kate was brushing her hair and staring in a dressing table mirror. She watched David's expression as she brushed.

He was putting on a tie and undoing the knot for the second time. "I hate these blasted things. Never could understand why men must wear them to church. I feel like I have a noose around my neck." He did not comment further about his wife's last statement but said that they would have a talk with Bob and Tissy this morning about the incident.

"Do you think that they may have told someone he could use the old house." Kate would not let the subject die.

"They could have, of course, but it isn't probable. I'd guess that they don't know a thing about anyone being on the place." David stepped over to glance above Kate's head at himself in the mirror. "There, that's done. I'll go and check to see if the boys are ready . . . what about Joan?"

Kate stood and looked around for her purse and Bible. "She said she is completely whipped and has taken a cold from being out in that weather, so I suppose that means she will sleep in this morning."

"From the story I heard, the man may be needing some medical services himself. Guess he learned not to mess with your sister!" David gave Kate a peck on the cheek and a pat on the backside as he went out the door. "All she needs is a big dose of castor oil," he grinned and closed the door.

116

During the night, the weather had turned colder and little icicles that dangled from tree limbs tingled softly in the breeze, turning the woods into a fairyland. Only a few church members braved the cold that morning to attend church; they were the ones who lived close by as well as the school's students and teachers. Bob's sermon was short and to the point, and even his wife stayed in their quarters, which adjoined the chapel on the opposite side of the school. As the people were leaving, Reverend Bob shook hands in the foyer instead of standing with the door open to the wind. As David and Kate came by, they were about to ask to speak further with him (to inform him about yesterday's incident), when he asked if the doctor would take a look at Tissy; she was not feeling well this morning.

"Certainly," David said and went to the car to get his medical bag. Kate told the boys to go and visit with the Lyles boy, and they would pick them up on the way home. Delighted, the twins ran off to see if they could catch up with the Lyles before they left in their wagon. As they bounced down the front steps they saw their father talking with Cole Lyles who was unhitching their mule. "Hey, wait for us," they both yelled, picking up speed. They could hardly wait to tell their friend, Brad Lyles, about what happened to them the day before.

Kate and Bob had gone on in the Russell's apartment and found that Tissy was in bed, awake, and reading a book. "Oh, Bob! Should you bring guests in the bedroom?" She hugged the covers up higher. Her embarrassment was obviously at her protruding stomach looking like a mountain beneath the covers.

"Just stay right there, Love. David is coming in just a few minutes. He thought it best to have a look at you." Bob stooped to kiss his wife on the forehead and wiped her hair back from her face.

"Well, excuse me, Kate. I must look a fright. Please have a seat."

"So, you haven't been feeling well? Just how long has this been going on?" Kate asked, knowing that David would ask her the same question shortly.

"For a couple of days, I suppose, and I've just been lazing around." She ventured a smile even though she did not feel up to being jovial. "Is it suppose to be this way, Kate? You should remember."

"It's very easy to forget, but I do remember that I thought it would never get over. You have to remember that carrying twins was much more difficult, and I felt terrible a lot earlier than you have. I had to take to my bed for the last two months."

"I'd hate to know that I had to get any heavier. That must have been very hard for you, and I remember you worked in the office probably longer than you should have," Tissy answered, and Kate noticed that she winced and rubbed her stomach.

"Are you having pains, Tiss, or just uncomfortable?" Bob asked, but before she could answer, David came through the door carrying his black medical bag.

"Okay, little mother, let's have a look at you. Now just how are you feeling?" David asked as he opened the bag and took out his stethoscope, plugging it into his ears. Tissy told him the same thing she had told Kate. Her stomach hurt every now and then and has been griping since the day before. David turned to Bob and asked that he go to the infirmary and fetch a wheelchair. "We should take you into the infirmary and do an examination. And if this baby has decided to make its appearance early, you will need to be in the hospital over in Clayton. The infant will be small and will need a lot of care."

IMMEDIATELY, TEARS BEGAN TO ROLL DOWN TISSY'S FACE. "Oh, we can't lose this child. We just can't."

David sat down on the edge of the bed and took hold of the frightened young woman's hand. "Don't do any worrying now. That won't help you one bit, and the baby may not be on the way. We'll see." He asked her to pull the covers down and her gown up so he could have a listen to the heartbeat. Then smiling, David patted her on the shoulder and assured her that the heartbeat was nice and strong. "It will be fine even if it does come early, Tiss. Don't you worry now."

After Tissy was wheeled into the infirmary and assisted up on an examination table, David told Bob to go out and do some praying while Kate assisted him with the examination. He was glad to go. It made him think of years ago when he had filled in for the doctor while David was away tending to a sick person. Bob only had a year of medical school when he felt called to go to seminary. And then, his first wife had died giving birth; the baby died with her. Now, Tiss was in trouble, and he certainly could not take losing her, too. Yes, he'd go out to pray, but first, he'd alert others to do the same.

The doctor quickly rolled up his sleeves and washed his hands. It took him only moments to discover that the cord was wrapped around the baby's neck. "Kate, talk to Tissy. Keep her mind off what I'm doing," Bob whispered to his wife. "This baby must be turned around at once. I'm not going to take time to sedate her." He started to work immediately, while Tissy, with tears running down her face, held tightly to Kate's arm. With the other arm, Kate reached for a nearby towel, drying the frightened woman's tears away. She spoke soft, soothing words in her ear, assuring her that it would be over in just a few minutes and that Bob was praying for her. Kate wiped her friend's hair that had become wet from perspiration. "What's going on, Kate? Am I losing the baby?" Tissy was plainly afraid.

"No, Tiss. You aren't losing it. David is merely getting it in a position to have more room. Try to relax; don't tense up and it will be easier." Kate had assisted her husband many times with births. He commented once that she could do it by herself if need be.

All the pulling and pushing made Tissy wince with pain. She was determined not to cry out. This baby had to be alright! She knew David would do whatever he could. And he did. Before long, he raised up and reached for a towel to wipe his own face of perspiration. The towel could not erase the relieved smile across his face. "My dear, Mrs. Russell," he said in a light, teasing tone, "Your child is fine and so are you. She just needed to turn around and got sorta lost in the process and gave me quite a scare."

"She!" Tissy exclaimed. "Oh, my! Are you sure, David?"

"Yes, Ma'am. Without a doubt. But, just don't be mopping any floors or digging any ditches. You'll have plenty to do later so just take it easy for now and let others do for you."

"Oh, Kate! Please call Bob in here. We are really and truly going to have a baby!"

Kate smiled and blew her breath out in a sigh of relief as she left the room. David gave Tissy a strange look and said, "But, I thought you knew that you are going to have a baby."

"Of course, who wouldn't with all this weight stuck out front, but it just didn't seem real until you said it is actually a girl. A real little girl." She struggled to get up. "Oh, I am so clumsy. Please help me up from here. I have to go and tell the world that our little Bess will be here before long. She will actually be in my arms!"

"So she now has a name? What will the full name be?" David inquired.

"Bessie Leigh Russell. We'll call her Bess."

Chapter Twenty—one

DOWN IN THE ATLANTA PENITENTIARY, TISSY RUSSELL'S father, Alonzo Turner, sat in the visitor-receiving room behind a glass, with his visitor sitting on the other side, speaking through a small cut-out circle fortified by metal mesh.

"I tell you, it ain't there, Alonzo. Are ya sure ya put it where ya said?" He leaned forward in his chair speaking in low tones through the hole in the glass, looking nervously around to see if a guard was listening.

"Yer durn-tooting I put it there, Biggs! It's gotta be there, and ya jes' did not pay attention when I was trying to splain how to get at it. Now I'm a-gonna tell ya again and I won' cha to listen good."

"Well, that woman up there in thu house nearly kilt me, and . . ."

Alonzo cut him off in mid-sentence. "What? A woman, you say? Whut was she doin' in my house? Who was she? Could it have been my daughter?" Completely baffled about what woman it could have been other than Tissy, Alonzo asked another question before waiting for any answers. "Wha'd she look like? Describe her to me."

"I didn't pay much attention to 'er looks. She was a trim little lady and had short hair."

"Haw! A woman with short hair?" Then Alonzo gave a hearty laugh that made his ample belly shake.

"That there's true. She did. She had short hair and there wuz two younguns with 'er. They wuz twins. Jes' alike. They gimme a beating, too. No sirree! I don't wanna tangle with that trio again."

"Well, if you want half o'that money, you'll go back up there and get that stash I hid in thu house and on thu double before those boys go back and find it with their nosing around. Okay. Listen an' I'll tell you agin. We only got about three more minutes so get it right now. You pull up two planks of floorboard in thu kitchen in thu southwest corner and it will be right there, plain and simple. Ya got it straight this time?"

"Yea, I got it, Lonzo, butcha tolt me in thu bedroom next to thu kitchen."

"I didn't do no sech-a-thang. Here comes thu guard. Do what I said with it, cha hear me, Biggs?"

"I hear ya."

"Time's up, Turner," the guard said. Alonzo stood to be taken back to his cell. He turned his head to watch his former cell mate go out the door, wishing it were him going out to freedom. Ahh! To breathe fresh air again. But this was only wishful thinking. With two life sentences, there would be no chance for a parole.

Chapter Twenty–two

DECEMBER. A DELIGHTFUL MONTH! A MONTH OF CELEBRATING, a month of joy, a time when people put aside any petty differences to extend a hand where it might be needed. A cold chill may fill the air, but inside there is warmth of the hearth and the heart. Wonderful aromas waft through gaily decorated rooms; excited starry-eyed children anxiously await the arrival of Christmas morning.

Christmas of 1929 would be no different on Kendell Mountain. Before the depression the children usually received homemade toys and homemade clothes. If they were lucky, there may be an orange and some nuts in a stocking hung beside the chimney. And for as long as anyone could remember, there had always been a gala celebration at the church on Christmas Eve. Someone would have brought in from the woods the nicest tree that could be found and others decorated it before the pageant that night. Then there would be the usual singing of carols, the giving out of a present to each child from Santa, the pageant put on by the children, and then the supper. School closed down a week ago for two weeks, and boarding students left then to spend the season at home.

On Christmas Eve morning, there came a knock on the door of Reverend and Mrs. Russell's apartment door. Tissy Russell laid down her knitting and with difficulty, lifted her heavy body from the chair.

"A visitor so early in the morning," she grumbled out loud, wishing her husband had been there to answer the knock. She was finishing up the last of the scarves and needed to get them all wrapped. Being a new knitter, this had been a tremendous undertaking. One of the ladies in the church had graciously taught her how to do the basic stitch with fringe at each end. Tissy was proud of her accomplishment, admiring each finished product as she folded and placed them in a drawer. Now it was time to take them out and begin wrapping.

She smoothed her dress, at the same time tucking her hair in place, and waddled on swollen feet to the door.

There on her steps stood a man and woman that she had never seen before, the man holding a hat between each hand. He had gruff features, a large frame, like a railroad workman or a lumberjack perhaps, and a full beard with dark eyes beneath bushy brows. The woman, evidently his missus, had a small frame and the face of a dependable mule. She wore a dark coat with her dress hanging below it and a scarf over her head. She stood on the step below him, holding her coat together against the cold wind that was blowing.

"Good morning, missus," the man smiled, showing a blank place where a tooth was missing. "We don't mean tu trouble you so early but we wuz tolt that per'aps you might find it in yore heart tu let us have thu use of thu old Turner place up on Possum Ridge."

Tissy did not intend to invite the couple in. She wished again that Bob would return at once and was at a loss for words. She sized them up, thinking that maybe they were in the same fix that the Lyles family had been when Cynthia allowed them to use her parents' old house. She cleared her throat to give herself another few seconds to think of something to say. "My husband is in the other building. I would have to consult with him. Who did you say told you about the house?"

The man turned to his wife, and Tissy thought that he was expecting her to answer the question. But he returned his eyes to her and answered, "Well, it was that railroad station man I think."

"Oh, Billy O'Shields. That figures." Then Tissy figured that they, too, like the Lyles, came in on a freight train, but she wondered why he seemed unsure about who told them. "Do you have any other family that would be staying with you?"

"No. Not nobody but us."

"Well, the place is very dirty and it doesn't have much furniture in it."

"That wouldn't make any matter, Ma'am. We'd even be willing tu sleep on thu floor, if need be."

At this point, Tissy felt a pang at her heart for the couple and decided that Bob would be very upset if she turned away someone in need. "I tell you what. Just go over there to the church door." She pointed in the direction of the church on the other side of their apartment, which was a part of the school building. "You just go on . . . the door is open and have a seat in one of the pews, and I'll find Reverend Russell. He'll be in there in a few minutes."

"Yes, Ma'am, we'll be pleasured to do that." The man who had not given his name, bowed his head with his hat over his heart as he and his wife turned to go back down the steps. Tissy closed the door behind her and retreated to find her husband. They met just as she opened the door that led into a hallway behind the church auditorium.

"Hi, Sweetheart, are you feeling alright." He kissed her lightly on the forehead.

"Yes, I'm alright but we had baffling visitors just now."

"Oh, really. Who? Have they already left?"

"They didn't give their names. I was taken by surprise and did not even ask who they were, but they are waiting for you in the church. They were asking for the use of my family's old house and seemed to be homeless. They said that Billy O'Shields told them about it."

Bob ran a hand across his mouth and rubbed his chin in a thinking manner and replied, "Evidently they got out of a boxcar."

"I had the same thought, but they didn't offer any information about where they came from so I didn't ask."

"Okay, Love, you just go on back in and I'll talk with them. If I decide that they are alright would you care if I tell them they can use the house?"

"Of course I wouldn't care. Whatever you decide will be okay with me but do ask them a few questions first. We don't want some oddballs hiding out on our mountain."

Bob smiled and disappeared through the sanctuary door. It was his job to help people in need whether it was their bodies or their souls, and he knew the right questions to ask. But he hoped that he would not be lied to. That would be a problem between the couple and their Maker; his job was only to provide.

In a little while, Bob came back to the apartment telling Tissy that he had agreed to let the couple use the house with a few stipulations. There was to be no drinking or moonshining, they were to keep the place in good condition, no trash was to be thrown about the yard, and the Russells would be allowed to inspect the place at any given time. If they needed food, they could come to the school and receive it twice a day in exchange for their help with the livestock and chickens.

"That seems to be very feasible," Tissy agreed. "Did you ask their name?"

"He told me that his name is Grover Biggs and his wife is Jasmine. I do hope that we will not be sorry about taking them under our wings."

"Did you ask God for help with the decision?" Tissy asked calmly.

"Of course, on the way in to meet them, but there wasn't much time to listen for an answer."

"I believe if it had not been the right thing to do, something would've happened to prevent your decision." She placed her arms around him as well as she could with her girth in the way. "It'll all work out, I'm sure. Just keep praying about it."

As the Biggs couple left the building, they looked at each other smiling and then broke into laughter before they left the school yard. "Guess that wuz plenty slick, huh?" Grover said to his wife, and they slapped each other's hand in success.

THAT SAME NIGHT, THE SCHOOL YARD WAS FILLED WITH tethered horses and mules, the wagons already empty of the people, and the tables held the food that had been brought for the pageant and festivities. The dining hall had been decorated with pine boughs, cones, and candles. Each table was spread with sparkling white cloths with a decoration in the center, and a tall cedar tree, draped with handmade items and paper chains, graced the side of the platform. On the platform was a nativity scene where the characters in the play would perform. Miss Lettie was already at the piano playing carols. There was a warm glow felt in the room from the stove Cole Lyles had stoked earlier, but mainly the warm glow came from the Christmas atmosphere. Children were hyper from the excitement of knowing that Santa would come in and give each of them a gift of some kind, always something small. But no matter how small, they would feel blessed and happy. "Who would play Santa Claus this year?" the grown-ups wondered and asked one another. From the crowd in the dining hall, no one seemed to be missing who could be out somewhere putting on the old, worn suit that had been passed around for years.

As Bob and Tissy were coming down the hallway from their apartment, they met the Biggs couple face-to-face.

Bob greeted them first and then Tissy spoke. "Did you find everything in order up on Possum Ridge?" she asked.

"Oh, Yes'um. But we was a-thinkin' about how thu Reverend tolt us that we could come and get a plate of food and thought we'd jes' come on down tonight and ask you if we could have a bite."

Then his wife added, "We didn't know that there was a 'to-do' a-going on and didn't mean to jes' barge in."

"All are welcome. Just come on in with us. There will be food a-plenty and some left over. Did you think about what I said about helping out with the livestock and barnyard fowl?" Bob reminded them in the form of a question.

"We did, and we'll be glad tu come back down here tomorrow."

"It will be Christmas, you know," Tissy emphasized the "will."

Mrs. Biggs told them they did not have anywhere to go anyway so they'd be glad to spend Christmas morning with the chickens, pigs, and cows.

When the group entered the dining hall, all eyes turned to greet the pastor and his wife and the couple with them. When one of the twins saw Grover Biggs, he pointed a finger and said loudly, "That's the man that attacked us and beat up Aunt Joan!" The room became still and quiet and one could actually hear people's breath being sucked in with astonishment. Joan turned from someone she was talking with and exclaimed out loud, "It is him, and he nearly killed me!"

Bob held up both hands for silence and said "Wait!" Biggs and his wife turned to go out the door. "Let's talk about this right now. Joan and the Harrises, come with us and you too, Mr. and Mrs. Biggs. Follow me to my study." He beckoned with a finger to Alyn. "You'd better come along, too, Alyn."

"You'd better believe I'll come and give that man a piece of my mind!" Joan retorted. She pranced, with clinched fists, behind the group.

No one knew just what to do so they stood around in little groups talking. Some had not heard about the incident at all. Miss Lettie started playing carols again but this time very loudly. Bo Dutton walked over to her, and they both started singing, hoping others would join in. However, it seemed they'd rather talk.

In the office, Reverend Bob seated his wife in his chair behind the desk and motioned for the others to take chairs. There weren't enough chairs so Alyn and Grover Biggs stood.

"Mr. Biggs, why did you not tell us about the incident up at the house when you asked us for permission to stay there?" Bob questioned.

"Yes, and what was all that hammering you were doing and why did you attack a woman and children!" Joan exclaimed with fire shooting from her dark eyes.

"Now, Joan, just let Bob speak, please. Let's wait a minute and keep cool," David Harris spoke in his calm manner. Joan crossed her arms in a huff.

"I'm real sorry, Miss, if I hurt you and them boys," Grover Biggs began in a meek voice. "You folks jes' came in and startled me and I didn't know what was a-happening."

"If I remember correctly, you came into the room where we were, stood in the doorway, and threatened us," Joan shot back quickly.

"I don't remember zactly how it happened, but when them boys jumped on me I thought it was a couple of wildcats, and Preacher, I was tolt down in town that we might could use the house so we went on up there close tu dark time thu day before. I seen this loose board and a hammer and some nails close by so I was just a-hammering away when this here lady and them kids came in." This version seemed feasible.

"Where was your wife when all this was going on?" Alyn spoke up.

Jasmine Biggs answered the question herself in a tiny little voice like an elf. "I, uh, I was out back in thu outhouse. I fount a interesting magazine in there and s'pose I jes' stayed a long time." Bob could not help but smile at this and so did Alyn, he noticed.

Bob cleared his throat, thinking just what he should say. It seemed like a courtroom; he was the judge and the others were the jury. "Mr. Biggs, I feel certain that you could see your intruders were innocent children and a lady who would do you no harm. You did not have to attack them or even fear for your safety. They held no gun on you. If our friend here," he pointed to Joan, "and the boys' parents, Dr. and Mrs. Harris, will accept an apology from you, then we will not involve the sheriff."

The last thing Grover Biggs wanted was to have the sheriff involved! His parole would be revoked and he'd land up back in the pen! "Oh, Ma'am, I'm sure sorry as I can be and I hope I didn't hurt cha too much and them boys, neither, an' you sure nearly ruint me." He looked first at Joan and then Doc and Kate. "I ain't a mean man and I ain't never laid a hand on my wife, here, neither, have I, Hon?" Jasmine shook her head in answer. "We'll be ever so obliged fer thu use of that house and I won't cause no more trouble."

Bob looked toward Joan and then to Doc and Kate. "What do you say, folks? Is the apology accepted?"

"I suppose so," Joan said grudgingly, and Doc said that if he ever came around his boys again Grover Biggs would have to answer to him.

Bob was sitting on the corner of his desk. "Mr. and Mrs. Biggs," he hesitated, thinking just how to say what was on his mind. "I don't think even a courtroom judge should require that people go to church after he releases them from their crime, but since you have agreed to work for your food at our Christian school, it would be only fitting and proper that we ask you to attend services here regularly just as our teachers and other employees do." He paused and looked both of them straight in the face to get their reactions. Their faces were blank and could not be read. "It is your decision. You can accept this requirement or you can find another place to live and get your food."

Tissy tried the best she could to hide her smile. She was proud of Bob's wisdom and his quick decisions. She always knew that he would do the right thing in any given situation. Over the years, he had become very wise; she knew where that wisdom had come from.

Grover Biggs did not take more than one second to give his decision. "Oh, we'd be happy to attend, Your Honor, uh . . . I mean, Preacher, in fact I was jes' about to ast ya if we could come. Wouldn't that be nice, Hon?" he turned to his wife and asked.

Later, Alyn told the Biggs couple that they could spend the night in their barn; there was plenty of clean hay to sleep on. It would be impossible for them to make the climb up to Possum Ridge after dark. Adam would wake them when he went in to do the milking. Grover said that would be fine and they'd just go on back down to the school when they got up to do the chores and have some breakfast before they went on up to the house.

As Grover was waiting for sleep to overtake him, his mind was busy thinking about finding the money that Alonzo Turner had stashed under the floorboards, or so he said. Grover and Jasmine would have enough money to live on for the rest of their lives and Alonzo would never see them again, and besides, since Alonzo would never get out of jail, what good would the money be to him? He'd told Grover to give it to his daughter and the preacher. Ha! That would certainly be a joke! He studied on this long and hard after he heard Jasmine's snoring.

Grover, now forty years old, had escaped the everyday drudgery that was a pattern of life for his parents and their eight children. At twenty years of age and with no foreseen hope of a better life, he was bone tired of the hard work with absolutely nothing to show for it. On the day that he left, he was in the cotton field hoeing weeds from the rows that just seemed to get longer and longer with each step. There was never an end! He looked up into the scorching sun, shaking a fist in anger. Deep down inside him there had been this rebellious determination to escape, and this determination had grown faster than the weeds. Leaning on his hoe, he thought how life had to be easier in the cities and decided right then that this day would be as good as any to walk away and never look back. From this day forward, the cotton fields of Alabama would merely be a gruesome memory.

As late afternoon was darkening swiftly into twilight, Grover walked quickly in the opposite direction of the Biggs' run-down house where the family would be gathered now for their evening meal of cornbread and buttermilk. In the crossroads town seven miles away, he hopped a freight, feeling free as a young bird sailing on a springtime breeze.

Yessir! He'd paid his twenty years for his part in an armed robbery. It hadn't been his fault the old man lunged at his partner's gun and been shot to death. Now he could take Alonzo's money and be long gone again. He'd appease the preacher for a few days so as not to arouse any suspicions. After he thought on these things, he rolled over on his side and went to sleep.

For the rest of the cold winter months, December, January and February, the Biggs couple were true to their word and even found themselves enjoying what they were doing. Jasmine enjoyed sprucing up to go to church. Kate told her to look through the missionary clothes closet there in the school and see if there were any clothes that she and Grover could use for church. At first, Jasmine wanted nothing to do with any of the handouts, but when she was shown a nice-looking dress that Ella Fullman had donated, she could not refuse. Then she selected another, plus a hat and shoes and some things for her husband. Kate also offered them sheets, towels, and soap, with hope that these would be used!

When the couple was invited to attend extra functions, they began to feel as though they actually belonged among these kind, benevolent people. Grover did a lot of thinking about the money that he'd been searching for inside the Turner house. He had not been back to the Atlanta Penitentiary to visit with Alonzo since he had been told that the money was hidden under the kitchen floor. However, when the money wasn't found there, some of the floorboards had been taken up in every room where it was suspected that this or that would be a good hiding place, and the boards carefully nailed back in place when nothing was found. Maybe after all these years Alonzo had forgotten exactly under which room he'd hidden the money. All Grover received for his labor was muscular arms and a sore back.

With this on his mind, it was hard for him to concentrate on Reverend Russell's sermons each Sunday morning. But one Sunday in January, something the preacher said in the sermon struck Grover as interesting, and he listened intently. Everything said seemed to search him out individually. It caused him to squirm so that Jasmine cut her eyes toward him several times before she actually punched him in the side with her elbow and sent him a frown. Each point that the preacher made singled Grover out making him feel that a finger was being pointed straight to him. As a child, Grover's parents took him (and his siblings) to church. Grover was totally bored at that time, offering any excuse that could be concocted to stay at home. He'd rather take a cane pole and strike out for his favorite fishing hole than sit for an hour listening to a preacher prance from side to side, ranting and raving. He had not been to church since becoming an adult.

The Sunday that he felt singled out, he hung back to let others shake hands with Brother Bob at the door after service. When Jasmine had gone to talk with some lady, Grover timidly asked Bob if he could make an appointment to talk with him in his office one day soon.

"Why certainly, Grover. You aren't planning on leaving us are you?"

"No, Preacher. It ain't that. I'm jes' needing some advice, you see."

"Well, if I can help you in any way, you just come on in when you finish with your morning jobs and hunt me up. I'll be about the place here somewhere."

Grover mentioned nothing at all to his wife about talking with the preacher, so one day while she was busy with one of her jobs inside the school, he slipped away from what he had been doing and went to look for Bob. In the hallway he saw Dr. Harris coming toward him at a fast pace, swinging his medical bag along.

"Morning, Doc, got any sick younguns?" he asked.

"Hello, Grover. Nope. No sick younguns, but Mrs. Russell is in labor," Doc replied and hurried on by to the infirmary.

It was a week later when Bob remembered his promise to have a talk with Grover Biggs. The infant and mother were doing fine, but they would need someone to help out while Tissy was laid up. It was Tissy who thought of Jasmine Biggs. Bob told his wife that he'd go get Jasmine, and while she talked with her, he'd see what it was that Grover needed with him. Bob's next class was not for another hour yet. That would give him plenty of time to help the man sort out his problem.

Inside the office, Bob sat behind his desk pointing to the chair to his left. Grover sat down meekly, not having the faintest idea how to begin the conversation or just what to say. He waited for the reverend to ask, timidly holding the hat with both hands on his knees. "How's the wife and the little baby?" Grover asked for an opener.

"They are both just fine, just fine, and I'm really happy that the waiting is over. My wife has been quite uncomfortable for the last month or two." He waited for a few seconds, turned sideways in the chair to face Grover and asked what he could do to help him with his problem.

Grover cleared his throat, glanced down at his feet, and sat forward in the chair. "I don't know just what to say, Preacher, but I kinda think you was a-preaching just to me this past Sunday."

"Oh, and how's that, Grover?"

"Well, you said some things that just put me to thinking." He cleared his throat again only to give him some time before answering further. "I haven't been a churchgoer since I wuz a kid and went because my folks made me, and frankly, Preacher, ever since I been growed up I just been blamed sorry . . . a no-account, in other words. An' I been a-thinkin' on what all you said an' I want tu change my ways an' be a Christian. When me an' Jasmine come here we didn't have nuthin' like that in mind a-tall." He leaned an elbow on the edge of the desk now. Once he had said this, the words kept coming. "Now, I'm not proud of telling this here so I'd really 'preciate it iffen you'd not tell it to nobody, but it's like this, Preacher, I been a jail-bird for thu past twenty years. I got out just three months ago and me and Jasmine got married right off thu bat. We been knowing each other for years. She used tu come to visit her husband . . . he was in jail, too, but he upped and died and I went to see her when I got out." He glanced toward Reverend Russell to see his reactions to this story but could read nothing in his face.

"I see," was Brother Bob's answer. He made his desk chair rock, then leaned toward Grover and asked, "Would you care to tell me what you were in jail for?"

"It wadn't jus' jail, it was the Atlanta Federal Pen and I was in for armed robbery but I didn't know that my partner was gonna shoot thu man we held up. The man died so it went purty hard on me, too. I served my twenty years and behaved myself, too, thu whole blessit time. And, oh, I wanted to tell you about somethin' else . . . I got put in a cell with a 'lifer' by thu name of Alonzo Turner."

Bob sat up with a start and said "What!" He slapped a hand on his desk.

"Yessir and he's thu one that said I could use his house. But that ain't all."

"Do you mean there's more!"

"There shore is, but it's like I tolt cha, I ain't proud of none of it."

"That's alright, Grover, just continue." He was anxious to hear what else the man had to say.

"Well, Lonzo said that he had some money that would have belonged to Jim Abernathy for some 'shine he had a large order for. I guess you knowed who he was?"

Bob nodded, affirming that he knew and waved his hand for him to continue.

"Lonzo, that there's what I called him, he said that Jim is dead and since he, meaning his own self, . . ." and Bob nodded again wishing he'd just talk without all the side remarks. "Well, meaning that he certainly would not be released from the pen so he asted me if I'd come up pere and get thu money and give it tu his daughter. He said it was a whole lot of money and he never did count it all and I reckon it was 'cause he couldn't count that high. He had made the 'shine and delivered it several days before they got caught up with because Jim had not come back from wher he had been and thu man that ordered it was pressing him purty hard-like. Jim didn't even know yet that Lonzo had delivered the stuff and got paid fer it. Lonzo said he had hid the money until Jim got back, but they got caught up with and thu money was still wher he hid it. But here's thu catch, Preacher, the money ain't wher he tolt me I would find it, and I've done searched thu whole house over an ain't fount it yet." Biggs coughed, rubbed his beard, and continued. "Since Lonzo went ta all that there trouble . . . he orter be entitled tuit, don't cha think, Preacher?"

"So that's why you wanted to stay in the Turner house?"

"Yessir, I reckon it was thu reason, but since we didn't have nowheres to live, we thought it would be real nice to have a house, too."

"I'll tell you why you couldn't find the money, Grover. It's because it had already been found by me. I could tell that the boards had been pulled up. He cracked them when he took them out and did a very sloppy job of putting them back. It was very evident that they had been taken out and replaced so I took them up again and there was the money in a suitcase, just like he told you."

Grover's eyes grew large, and he felt his pulse beating hard. "What became of it?" he asked, running his fingers through his thick hair and sitting up straight in the chair.

"It was donated to the Kendell Mountain School," Bob said softly, looking straight into the startled eyes of Grover Biggs. "That was the best place for it to do the most good for a lot of people, not just one greedy person who did not deserve it.

In a way, Grover felt defeated. However, since he had the new feeling inside him that he really wanted to turn over a new leaf, he actually felt relieved. "Preacher, I hope you will believe me when I say that I'm really happy I did not find the money. I know from 'sperience that money does terrible things to a person. I never heard of a rich person that is totally happy, have you?"

"Oh, there may be a few but not very many. Most folks don't know how to handle money. They let it go to their head and become more greedy until it actually becomes their downfall in the long run."

Grover gazed down at his hands that were clasped together on his lap. "Since me and Jasmine have been here, we have come to see that people living here don't really need a lot of money." He looked Bob in the eye and asked, "Could we just go on livin' in that house and working at the school for ya'll?"

"Grover, we'd be happy if you'd do just that, but I wonder if you'd agree to do one more thing." The man expected him to give him another job to do around the hog pens or the barn, maybe some plowing up the fields to get ready for the spring planting. Bob had other plans for Grover. "I would like for you to sit in my Bible class every day with the students. It is only a one-hour class. I would not require you to take any tests or do any written work, however, like the kids must do. Would you do this?"

The man grinned and said he'd be glad to do that. Bob asked him not to tell anyone that he had been in jail because the parents would not like it, and the school board would not agree to his being there. Not that the board would want to hold him back from being involved with church, but because there would be many parents who would take their children out. Grover understood and said he did not want anyone else to know anyway because "he was tired of feeling lower than a egg-sucking dawg!"

Grover Biggs left the church office feeling that a great load had been lifted from his shoulders, and for the first time ever, he felt satisfied with his life. Before long, he knew that he would come down to the altar and make it known in public that he'd asked God to forgive him for all the sins he'd committed, and they had been many.

Chapter Twenty–three

ON A COLD WEDNESDAY EVENING IN THE MIDDLE OF February, Cynthia, sitting in her rocker in front of the fireplace watching flames lick around the logs, rocked slowly, her mind playing pictures of the past as though it were a movie reel. The red wool sweater she had on felt warm and snug. She was thinking how her granny, known to everyone as "Miss Maudie," but just plain "Granny" to her, would have loved the baby and have been forever crocheting little jackets, booties, and blankets. Her father, Hugh Tanner, would have whittled toys and he would have told his wife, Amy, to stop spoiling the child.

Cynthia was smiling when Alyn came into the room with a tray of coffee cups and some teacakes. "You look like the cat who just swallowed a mouse. Now what were you smiling to yourself about?"

"Hi, Sweetheart, I was only daydreaming. It's funny how it's so easy to do that in front of a fireplace." Alyn handed her a cup of the steaming coffee. He had already put milk in the coffee, knowing just how she liked it. "Thanks, I was just wishing for a cup of something hot to warm me up. I could easily get used to all of this being waited on." He placed the tray on an end table, took his cup, and pulled a chair beside his wife.

"Well, here we are, two old married folks already gone to seed and taken to our rockers," he teased.

"But the seed will be all sprouted out any day now, and I know you will be the most perfect daddy in all the world." She reached a hand out and pressed his arm. Her happiness and contentment showed in her expression. In a minute or two, she noticed that he gave a slight wince and rubbed the calf of his right leg. "What's the matter, Hon?"

"Just an ache. It's right where I got some shrapnel during the war. Guess you'll have to wheel me around in my old age."

"I'll rub it with liniment when we go to bed."

"Then I will even smell like an old man," he grinned.

Cynthia chuckled and rested her head against the back of the rocker. "Alyn, did you ever think of me before you came back here." She stopped rocking and turned her head to face him.

"Yes, of course I did. And I wondered if you dreamed the same daydreams I did. I've looked up at the stars and thought, 'Does she ever make a wish on the first evening star like we did as kids.'"

His saying that made her feel a warm satisfaction, but her guilt at giving up on his returning still remained. Looking into the fire, she said dreamily, "I spent countless lonely nights before I resigned myself to the fact that you would never come back. With my family gone I felt all alone in the world with no one to love me. You had no one either, but I didn't wait any longer; that's why I married." Then, almost in an inaudible whisper she said, "I'm so sorry I didn't wait awhile longer, Sweetheart."

Alyn's coffee cup had been replaced on the tray and now he was bent over with his elbows on his knees staring into the fire. Yes, she had been married before for only a short time. When they married, she still wore the traditional white wedding gown, and the wedding was in their church with bridesmaids and the whole works. He saw her in the flames now, his beautiful bride and soon-to-be mother of his child. Sitting back now and looking at her, he saw a tear slide slowly down her cheek. He stood and bent over to kiss the tear away. Holding her head with both hands, he turned it up and kissed the sweet soft lips. "It's all in the past, my darling. Please put it all behind us. We'll be together for the rest of our lives and God willing even in eternity." He took her arms and lifted her to her feet. His arms were around her as close as possible with her large fullness protruding between them. He kissed her forehead, then their lips met. When he opened his eyes, she looked up into his and whispered, "Oh, Alyn, I do love you so. More than you could ever know." The war did not succeed in hardening him; there was still the gentleness he'd always possessed and which she loved. He evoked in her feelings that she had never felt for her first husband.

"And we love you very much."

"We?"

"Certainly. Junior just gave me a swift kick. He wanted to let you know he loves you, too."

"And how do you know it is a he?"

"Simply because he kicked like a football player." They both laughed. He had succeeded in lifting her spirits. He yawned and said,

"Let's turn in; I haven't forgotten that you promised to rub my leg."

Cynthia retrieved the book she'd tried to read before her husband came into the room but found it uninteresting and had abandoned it. Passing into the bedroom, Cynthia observed herself in the dressing table mirror without any enthusiasm. The pretty face now looked full, her figure completely out of shape. Alyn had told her only today that she was even more beautiful than ever. Her dark brown eyes held a brilliant sparkle and the blonde hair a glow that gave off a halo effect. But Alyn's sweet words fell on deaf ears . . . she still felt ugly. She sat down on the dresser stool and taking up the brush, began stroking the long silky hair. He had asked her pleadingly not to cut it off when she mentioned that Joan's short hair looked so simple and easy to manage. Now, sitting on the edge of the bed, taking off his shoes and letting them plop to the floor, he gave an approving look and mentioned this again.

"Oh, I meant to tell you that someone is coming to live with us soon," he said casually in a matter-of-fact manner as though this were a cut-and-dried situation.

Cynthia laid the brush down and turned to face him. "Really? Is this anyone I know? Or, is it to be a surprise or something?"

He laughed as he stood to pull off his shirt and undershirt. She noticed his broad shoulders and arm muscles and the light hair on his chest that she loved to run her hands through. "No. You don't know him yet, but I know you will learn to love him."

"For crying out loud, Alyn, just come out and say it. Who is it? I may not want someone else living with us."

"But you will. He's small and helpless and he's only six weeks old."

"I don't think I can manage two babies! What in the world are you talking about?"

"I suppose I forgot to mention that he is a puppy," Alyn grinned happily like a little boy knowing he was getting a dog of his own.

"For heaven's sake! Why couldn't you say that to begin with?"

"I hoped you'd agree with my telling Bo Dutton we'd take him. He's one of a litter that would be a great-grand youngun sired by my old dog, Beans. Beans lived to be about twelve. He was only a year younger than me."

"I know. Poor old Beans. He was such a good dog. I loved him, too. Whatever made you name that dog Beans anyway?" She had started spreading cold cream on her face to clean it.

"He dearly loved green beans; in fact, he loved any kind of beans. He'd eat as many as I could hand him under the table. Aunt Joyce would usually catch me at it and tell me to stop and put the dog out."

"Well, I hope this puppy will grow up to look just like Beans. What will we call him?"

"I kinda liked the sound of Jasper. Several times I've said 'Come on, Jasper . . . Here, Jasper, come on boy,' and it sounded right. What do you think?"

"Sounds fine to me. Do you think Sam and Will's hunting dogs might hurt him?"

"They'll get used to him. We'll keep him in the house until he's older. Oh, and Matt and Dan are getting one of the pups, too."

Cynthia stretched, yawned, and got up to undress. "Puppies and children. They go together. I hope Brad doesn't get one or we'd have too many dogs around this place."

In the middle of the night, well before dawn, Cynthia was awakened with stomach cramps. She crawled quietly out of bed so as not to disturb Alyn. She walked to the bathroom and then to the living room where she knew the fire would be smoldering still in the grate as Alyn had banked it, a fire screen safely in front of it. She sat down and then wished she had brought along a blanket. Then, she felt that a cup of hot cocoa would be soothing. So she got up to get these items and as she stood, felt another stomach rumble and more aching. "This could possibly be the time," she thought to herself remembering the date. "It was due last week. I wonder if I should call Alyn. No, maybe I'm hurrying things." Then her mind replayed some things that Kate had told her to look for. "The pains are supposed to get closer together and Kate said there would be drops of blood and the water would break." So she decided to have the cup of cocoa at the kitchen table and read some of the book. "Oh, shoot, I took it into the bedroom. Well, I'll go sit in front of the fireplace and write down some names. This child must have a name when it arrives." She finished off the cocoa and struggled to raise herself from the chair. It was hard to feel comfortable anywhere. There was the aching again but still no hard pains. In the hallway, she took a couple of sheets to fold for padding in the chair and a throw to wrap around her. The mantel clock struck four times.

At six o'clock, Ophelia came in through the back door and saw a light shining from the open living room door and went on down the hallway to investigate. She found Cynthia curled up on the couch, lying on her side with knees drawn up in pain. "Oh, Miss Cynthee, dat baby be ready to come! Wher Misser Alyn?"

"Please go wake him. He'd better go get David and Kate before they leave out."

Ophelia rushed out the door to call Alyn just as Selma came in and heard them talking.

"Let Misser Alyn stay and I go and get Tad to go fer Doc Harris." She turned and hurried on her mission. Things were beginning to buzz as the first rays of light streamed down on Knollwood.

It was only a short time until Doc's Model A Ford was heard turning onto the gravel driveway, and Doc and Kate came on the back porch. Kate poked her head inside the kitchen where Selma had just set the coffeepot on the stove. "Selma, would you please ask Tad to go up and get the boys off for school. They'd sleep right through it if they weren't pulled out."

"Yess'um, Miss Kate, and Adam, he say Mama Liz be ailing. Sometime today would you ast de doctor iffen he look in on her?"

"Certainly. This may be a slow thing, and he could go out there in a little while. And, oh, tell Tad to make sure the boys go by the office to tell Priscilla that I won't be there."

Thursday, February 19. This would be a busy day. Cora Beth would be ironing, since they washed the day before, so Selma and Ophelia could cook. They had much to prepare with the doctor and his wife there to eat dinner, and possibly the twins later on, then they all would have supper there too. No doubt, Reverend Bob and Tissy would come up, also. The women loved to cuddle little Bess. She would be one spoiled little girl and now, shortly, another baby to spoil rotten.

At four-thirty that same afternoon, the robust wailing of little John Alyn Russell could be heard all over the house as he made his grand entrance. When Adam was told the good tidings, he left the barn and went to tell Lizzie Mae.

Lizzie Mae was lying on her bed propped up on two feather pillows, cover pulled up to her neck. "Hush yo mouf, Adam! A li'l boy, oh my, I's wish I could get mah han's on 'im. Hep me git up from here, man." She started throwing the cover back but could not raise her bulk. "Come on, gimme a pull."

"Whut yo talkin' 'bout, ole woman? You know you sick and Doc Harris say he be out chere in a little whilst so you jes' behaves." Adam pulled up a chair beside her bed to guard her from falling off the high bed with feather-filled ticking.

"Oh, shoot. I jus ain' good fer nuthun no mo," Lizzie said with disgust. "Now whu you think 'bout dat! We got us a li'l baby boy. I jes' wisht Miss Joyce could see 'im. She sho would be proud, an' Misser Anson, too. Dey be a-struttin' round chere lak dat ole speckled rooster a-guardin' his hens." Then she laughed, something she'd not done in a while.

"See, woman, yo done feels better. Yo be's outten here 'fore long iffen yo jes' take it easy. Yo got dem girls to do all de work yo usser do all by yosef and let dem look affer yo now fer a whilst. How 'bout a ham biscuit an' a glass o' milk? I jes' brang up a bucket full from ole Clementine and, law, she nearly run my bucket over she had so much."

"Well, maybe I just try some, Adam. Ah does b'lieves Selma an' Ophelia is a-tryin' tu run a race tu see which one can make de bes' biscuits. Jes' go on and git me one, ole man."

Adam grinned, enjoying the return of her bossiness. Maybe she'd be up and out before long and holding that baby.

Chapter Twenty-four

BY MID-MARCH, THERE STILL HAD NOT BEEN A HINT OF SNOW, and the old-timers sitting around Ezra's store said that folks had not better be so smug with themselves and certain that spring was just around the corner, for the signs all pointed to a snow yet. The winter had been a cold one, and windy, chilling to the bone. Kate's fussing to David about his going around the mountain area on his mule was all in vain. The older sick folks could not get out to come down to his office in the Gap so there was nothing for him to do except to go to them. He braved the wind once too many times and came down with a cold that soon turned into bronchitis, forcing him to take to his bed.

Lizzie Mae had rallied enough to sit by the fireplace in the little cabin where she and Adam lived out behind the big house. Alyn and Cynthia had taken little Johnny out for a visit one afternoon. This visit proved to be the best medicine Lizzie Mae could have. She rocked him in her arms and said she thought she'd never live to see this day and vowed that Miss Joyce would be walking the halls and rooms of Knollwood watching over this little treasure.

One week later, everyone in the area got up to peer out their windows at a blanket of snow that was the deepest ever seen in the mountains of north Georgia. There was an eerie stillness, no sign of life, no sound could be heard, except for an occasional "plop" from the snow dropping off snow-laden pine boughs. The pines stood tall and somber against the white, not even able to whisper to one another from the snow's weight as a soft breeze played among them.

No one would be about on a morning like this, except for the Kendell Mountain School boarding students, who were already there. Kate and her boys would not be there, neither would Cole and Priscilla Lyles and their children, nor Grover and Jasmine Biggs. So it would be up to Bob Russell to stoke the fires and the other teachers to carry on. The students, with light and jovial feelings, might have a hard time concentrating on schoolbooks. Before classes started, two students (of foreign missionary parents) who had never before seen snow, dashed outside in shirt sleeves to feel the cold white stuff for themselves. They tossed some in the air and soon discovered it could be balled up and tossed at one another.

There was a two-week period that time stood still. Some outsiders might say that time always stood still on Kendell Mountain and down in Union Gap. To Kate's sister, Joan, it was absolutely the most boring time of her entire life. She swore that when the snow melted enough for her to be driven down to the train station, she would return to her home. She would rather contend with her mother than live like a hermit. Bryan was not the only man on earth, and she'd make a new life for herself. Her mother had told her before she left to come to Kendell Mountain, that men were like streetcars . . . there was another one coming by every fifteen minutes. She thought how funny it was that people from the same parents could be so different. She and Kate were very different, that was for sure, but still, how in the world had Kate stood living here in the backwoods like a hermit for so many years? Joan wondered this; it was a mystery to her. Joan thought it was strange that their father had left their mother and then both their husbands had done the same. How ironic! "Oh, well . . . that's life for you, but, Joan, old girl," she told herself, "you are not going to sit around and mope over what fate did to you any longer. I'll just pack up my things and be off." And she did.

David told Kate, after they saw her sister get on the train, "You know, Love, it will be rather nice to have our house back to ourselves for a change."

Chapter Twenty-five

IT WAS APRIL 1930 ON A REMOTE BACK ROAD NOT FAR FROM Laurel, Mississippi.

Little Bear handed the baby back to his mother. "Him fine, grow be big man. We take him home to mountain. Must learn hunt, fish, not carnival ways."

Sassy's eyes widened. "What, Chief! Did you mean what you just said?" She became excited at the very thought of going home and swung around with Moses looking up at her. "See, Chief! Look at him. He's watchin' me."

"Quiet, girl. You want bad people hear?" He leaned forward, speaking softly. "We talk. Time come, we must go."

Sassy sat on the floor in front of him, holding little Moses on her lap. He was a good baby, satisfied and warm; he fell asleep. Little Bear looked around to make certain no one was close by to hear their conversation. He talked in low tones, almost in an inaudible whisper.

"We leave this night. Walk far by moonlight. You put baby things in sack, bring much baby clothes." He pointed to Moses' bottom and Sassy understood. "Bring blanket. Wrap good, warm."

"I understand, Chief," she whispered. "Do I come here? What time?"

"Chief no tell time. No have arm clock. Me come when moon high. Girl be ready. No let baby cry."

"Alright. I'll feed him good ahead o'time."

"You got money? We get on bus when far away. Carnival people no take like soldiers."

"Yes, I have some money and hope it will be enough. We'll have enough to buy bus tickets, but how do you know which way to get us home?"

"We talk people when find bus barn."

"Station, Chief. It's called a bus station."

"Sta-shun," he repeated. "It long way home. We find train maybe? Train goes to mountain."

"Yes, it does, and there's not a bus station in Union Gap. We'll find the way home, Chief, I know we will. I know the train people will help us. Oh, but Mrs. Harris's trains only go from north to south and way over here in Mississippi. We'd need to go east, so we need to find a bus around here first. Mrs. Harris told me that Mississippi is west of Georgia. She pointed it out on a map in my geography book and all the states, too."

Little Bear reached out and put a hand on Sassy's head. "You smart girl. Good you learn." Then he added something he had been thinking about lately. "You talk different. Maybe parents not know. You grow more we been gone, look different, like woman, not girl."

Her beaming face broke out in a wide, satisfied grin. "Oh, Chief, you're kidding me. Of course my folks will know me. The ladies here have been teaching me how to talk better, but I didn't know you noticed. Sometimes, I say things like I used to. It's hard to just start talking different after I've talked my way since I learned to talk."

"You talk better than Chief. Parents not teach. They speak their talk after we come to cave. Not white man's talk. You teach Chief talk good?"

"It's a deal," she answered and held up the hand that was not holding the baby in a truth sign.

One of the men working on some kind of equipment in the barn passed by the two and held up two fingers, signaling the same sign that Sassy had given. Evidently he noticed what she had done.

After the man passed by, Little Bear said, "Girl go now. Get ready. Put on warm clothes. Cold when dark come."

Sassy left the barn walking on air and with a song in her heart that now beat fast in anticipation. She hurried to the house, turning to look all about. Her presence talking with the Indian out in the barn was nothing unusual, except for the late hour. It had become dark while she was there, and she hoped Tony had not been looking for her. For two weeks he had come in nightly, reeking of beer, forcing himself on her, causing some rawness and slight bleeding. Not knowing what to expect or what to do, she confided in Lola and asked for advice.

"You have to get away from here, child, and quickly," Lola said adamantly. "Talk to your Indian friend and the two of you plan an escape with the baby."

The place had become like a prison to Sassy, who had arrived there full of hopes and dreams. Lola told her that she would never be a star if she stayed. That's what Tony had promised her! That's why she ran away of her own free will and choice. Miss Lola also said that at the rate he was going, he would keep her having babies one right after another. Granted, Sassy loved Moses, but she did not want any more babies, no . . . not ever again, and she never wanted a man to touch her again in the way Tony had. It hurt her to the core every time she thought about some of his blood running through the little baby.

"That poor old Indian," Miss Lola said, "could not stand the hardships of being on the move constantly, traveling with the carnival. It was a downright shame the way Tony had him kidnapped! He has to get away from here, Belle, before it's too late and you, too. Tony said that Chief is so old that he'd just die soon no matter where he was, but it's not right for him to die so unhappy. Take him home, Belle, and little Moses."

"What if Tony catch us leaving," Sassy worried. "He'd beat us bofe up."

"Both, Belle . . . not bofe."

Lola told her this only yesterday. Now, back inside the house after Sassy's talk with Little Bear, she was in Lola's room. Lola was standing holding Moses while Sassy sat on the bed. "I'm taking your advice Miss Lola. We're leaving tonight."

Lola stooped to hug the girl with one arm and then she laid Moses in the middle of the bed and sat down beside Sassy. "Belle, you've been like a daughter to me, and I'll miss you. Will you think of me every now and then?"

"Of course I will, and I'll write you a letter when we get home. I just hope we don't get ourselves lost."

"Belle, I want you to take my coat. I know it's warm now in the day, but at night you will need it. You just keep it." Sassy did not see that Lola had placed some money in the pocket because she had reached over to pick up Moses when he began to whimper.

"Thank you, Miss Lola, for the coat. You have been a good friend. I will think of you ever day, honest and I want to thank you for teachin' me to talk lak . . . I mean 'like' a lady. None of my family will care what I sound like, and they wouldn't know the right words either, so they won't care I 'spose. They may think I'm a-tryin' to be somebody I'm not, or stuck-up, like. But I like it and I don't care what anybody say . . ."

"Says, Belle."

"Well, says, and you know what? I'm going to go to school, too, like Miz Harris say, I means 'says.' She be proud o' me, too."

"Atta girl, Belle. Now, I'm here right across the hall so I'll listen out for you. Hurry up now. You'd better go out the window and when you go in the room, push on the window to make sure it will open, but remember to be very careful because you could fall off the roof! What a horrible thought; you could even drop the baby. How will you know when Little Bear has come?"

"He said he'd give his bird call and will throw up a pebble. I'll open the window so I can hear his signal and I've already checked the roof out. You know it slopes down so I'll just lay down and hand Moses down to Little Bear and then throw my bags down." Sassy had thought things out ahead of time.

"Okay, then, but just please be careful!" Lola was as nervous as Sassy. "It's about the time that scoundrel Tony comes in drunk so get a move on. You take care of that darling baby and wrap him up good and don't forget to put some water in his bottle. Get yours and Moses' things all together in a hurry."

They gave each other another quick hug and Lola kissed the baby good-bye. As she took the coat and the baby and had her hand on the doorknob, Sassy turned back to Lola with a serious look on her face and said, "Sophie told me she is gonna make a woman outta Tony if she gets a chance."

"Knowing Sophie, she certainly will," Lola answered, waving Sassy out the door.

The little bedside clock revealed the time to be eleven-thirty. Sassy had their things all ready and had fed the baby who was now sleeping soundly. Normally, he would sleep through the night, and she hoped he would not wake up and cry as they escaped through the window. She sat in the darkened room waiting anxiously on edge for Little Bear's tap on the window with a pebble. Moses was in the little box that served as a makeshift crib. She glanced at him as she walked over to peer out the window into the night. A cloud had covered the moon, making it difficult to see anything or anyone. She was nervous and fidgeting, prancing back and forth. "Oh, what was keeping him? Please, please, Chief, do hurry up before Tony comes." Then she tried to appease her fears by thinking that perhaps Tony was full of beer and sleeping somewhere, maybe in the hay out in the barn. So many ifs and maybes ran rapidly through her mind. The thought now ran through her mind about the night she left her safe bed to flee away into the darkness with the carnival. Would her parents ever forgive her for this? And, what if Moses ever left her like that? She would be heart-broken. At least when her own mother left home it was to get married instead of cutting herself off from her family entirely.

Remorse had set in and the more Sassy thought about it the more she realized with chagrin how utterly stupid she had acted. Why, this man, Tony, had never intended to make her a star at all, he only wanted to use her body! And the more she thought, the more impa-tient she became to get away. Miss Lola was completely right.

The door to her bedroom was locked, and he could not get in, so he banged hard and loud and rattled the doorknob. "Open this blasted door now, girl! You hear me? I know you're in there and I said open the door." He kept hitting the wooden door until Moses woke screaming and Sassy huddled in a corner. Tony raised a foot and kicked the door open. He came in with a hateful scowl on his face, fists clinched.

"Oh, ho, my little flower, what's all this?" He was pointing to the sacks and the coat piled on the floor beneath the window where she'd intended on going out. He looked around at the baby and yelled, "Make that brat shut up or I'll shut him up permanently!" Tony was drunk, without a doubt.

"You're drunk as a skunk, Tony! Keep away from me an' don' you touch that baby," Sassy yelled. Surely Miss Lola could hear all this racket and get help.

"You've got too smart all of sudden, missy," the man said under his breath. "You just don't know what I may do and I asked you a question so gimmie a answer! What's all that stuff on the floor? Plan-ning on going somewhere? Huh?" He staggered over to the baby in the box, who was still crying loudly. "I said shut up, kid!" he yelled in a strident voice and shook the box hard. With fear Sassy lunged toward the box and grabbed the baby up in her arms. His crying changed to a whimper and sobs as he found his thumb.

Tony had on greasy work clothes that smelled of too much use without washing. He had been working on a truck with Lambert. The smell of his dirty clothes and the whiskey breath odor fought each other for supremacy. When Lambert felt the results of too much drink, he left Tony to go to bed. And when Tony, too, could no longer concentrate on the repair job, he decided to go in and visit his little "prize" for a while. Then he discovered that the "prize" was about to walk out on him.

There was a fleeting glimpse of Little Bear outside in the darkness. She saw him! He had come! "Oh, Chief, please don't leave me," she frantically thought with her heart racing madly. She slyly gave a slight nod, hoping that he would recognize the nod as her way of saying "Wait for me." Sassy held Moses tightly and wondered if she could dash past the inebriated man and make a run for it. But, no, she needed the bag of necessities and the coat.

Across the hall Lola heard the commotion and Moses crying. She recognized Tony's loud drunken raving. How many times had she borne the brunt of his fists and cursing words! Never again would she suffer from him and neither would Belle! She ran on bare feet, the full sheer gown flying out behind her down the stairs to Sophie's room. It was now time for Tony's wife to know what was going on. Surely she was not so blind that she had not suspected her husband's shenanigans. Sassy had not been the first. Lola wondered before if Sophie had any idea that Tony had forced himself upon her also. Pounding upon her bedroom door, she called for Sophie to come quickly before he killed that girl. Sophie brushed past, sliding her arms into a robe and dashed out to the kitchen, leaving Lola standing there perplexed. In the kitchen, Jojo, one of the midgets, sat at the table with a mouthful of food. He nearly choked on the bite as he watched Sophie open a drawer, grab a butcher knife, and run from the room, at the same time telling him to go find a doctor at once. Jojo took a drink from his glass before he ran out to obey the orders from Sophie.

As she opened the door to Sassy's room, Lola saw that Tony had passed out across the bed and Sassy was taking the opportunity to hand Moses outside to Chief and now she was crawling out herself with her bag of clothes and diapers. With one leg thrown out, she looked up at Lola and exploded, "Miss Lola! The knife! What are you going to do!"

"You get on out of here, girl! Now! Git, I said. You did not see a thing and I never said one word to you about what I'd do to him if I got the chance. Go, I said, and right now before it's too late and don't look back." She waved the knife in the air with Sassy scrambling hurriedly out to Little Bear and freedom, her heart pounding fiercely. No one saw them walking out into the cold night air. They did not look back even when they heard a bloodcurdling scream from the open window.

Chapter Twenty–six

LITTLE BEAR HAD ON A COAT AND A HAT PULLED DOWN over his ears. He'd found these in the barn hanging on a nail where one of the men stashed them when he'd crawled under his blanket for the night. Sassy was dressed warmly in a long skirt and blouse with Lola's coat and, of course, she'd wrapped the baby in a fuzzy warm blanket over his bunting that zipped up to his neck. She thought when she quickly dressed him that it would be bad when she had to undress him out in the cold for a diaper change. She did think to put in extra bags for his dirty diapers so she would wash them in creeks later. During the day when it was warm and they'd shed their coats, she figured that the diapers could hang from their belts to dry as they walked along.

Now, thankfully, the moon had come from behind the dark clouds and for the time being they were able to see clearly to walk. Both Sassy and Little Bear kept looking back to see if anyone had come out to look for them. So far, they had heard no other sounds. They were walking close to the side of the road to be able to get off the road and find quick cover should a vehicle be heard coming.

Relief washed over the young girl, flooding her body . . . they were actually getting away! She heard a night bird in the shadows that seemed to be serenading the fugitives. The night air smelled invigorating, and Sassy breathed it deeply, filling her lungs. She felt like singing but thought better of it. Little Bear led the way. Many nights he'd roamed the woods of Kendell Mountain, like a prowling bobcat. So accurate were his eyes, he may have been kin to one of them. Over the years, his eyes dimmed so that now he had a hard time picking his way through the darkness. Since he had emerged from his cave and mingled with people, he had noticed glasses on some, Adam for one, and asked about them. One day Adam took his off and offered for

Little Bear to look through them. It made things look so much larger and clearer that the old Indian actually broke out in a smile. Adam spoke to Alyn about this and the two decided that Chief should be fitted with glasses. This was just before he was taken away by the carnival.

Now, the two were walking along vulnerable to whatever this Mississippi back road had to offer anyone brave enough to attack the night. Sassy broke the silence. "Chief, are you feeling all right? Can you walk far?"

"Chief fine. Walk more you."

"But you are carrying all our things. Will it tire you out?"

"Hunt. Take game. Much heavy than this."

"But you aren't young anymore. Do you tire out sometimes?"

"Keep fit. Exercise. No eat much." There was a silence, then Little Bear asked bluntly. "Man, Tony, he hurt girl?"

"Not tonight. He didn't even touch me. Too much to drink I 'spec'."

"Fire water bad. Men on mountain make fire water. Make trouble. Men fight much, make mean."

The two trudged with no vehicle coming in sight—nothing to break the eerie silence except the occasional calling of a night bird and then a distant answer. Now they were walking on the road; Sassy estimating that they had walked for about two hours, and she was tired. Little Bear noticed that her steps had slowed, and he set the packages down and took the baby. She took the packages, commenting that they were nearly as heavy as Moses. They decided to walk on at a slower pace and look for a place to rest. Soon, a house came into view on the other side of the road where a dog came out to bark at them. A door opened; light from an inside lamp shone dimly making ghostly shadows dance across the yard. Little Bear jerked Sassy to the ground in tall grass, with her whispering a prayer that no snakes would be close around. "Shut up, Duke! Git on back in yore house, come on now, boy." The man whistled, and the dog crouched with its tail between its legs, minding its master. Then they saw the door close and the light go out. Duke, as he was called, whimpered, and Little Bear hoped that he was chained to his house. "No like dog," Little Bear said standing up with Moses in his arms still sleeping soundly and not caring what went on. The walking made a rocking motion like a cradle. He was already spoiled so much by everyone at the farm holding him, cooing at him, and talking baby talk that made no sense.

"Chief, let's walk back on the road. We can tell if there are car lights way in the distance. I'm just scared I might step on a snake in this grass."

He agreed with her. "When see barn we stop. Sleep. Girl tired. Little Bear tired."

In another hour, perhaps, they came to an abandoned house. In the moonlight they could see that it was safe to enter—no broken steps and the door was not locked. It reminded Sassy of some of the little cabins on Kendell Mountain. Inside, they looked around as well as they could from the moonlight streaming in through a window. There was no furniture. They would be happy to rest on the floor. As the girl reached in the coat pocket to put her gloves inside, she felt something and drew it out. It was money rolled up with a rubber band around it. As she unrolled the bills, a note fell out. She stooped, retrieved the note, and held it up to the window. Squinting her eyes, she read, "I love you. Have a good trip home and stay there this time." It was signed "Lola."

"Well, I'll be! Look uh heah, Chief. Money! It looks like a whole lot of it too an' all in ten dollar bills! For heaven's sakes alive! Look, here's six of 'em. That Miss Lola is something else. She musta've saved a long time for all this much and here she's given it to us." Little Bear smiled. He knew they could now get train tickets and food.

"I tolt Miss Lola that I had a angel that looks affer me but I do b'lieve she's a-helpin' my angel do her job." She rolled the bills back up and replaced the rubber band, putting them back in the coat pocket. "No, sir," she whispered to herself. "A body just can't have too many angels."

Sassy spread out the coat, laid the baby on it, changed his diaper, and then laid down beside him drawing the coat around them. Little Bear stretched out under the window with one of the sacks for a pillow. He was snoring shortly, but Sassy did not hear him. She was keyed up, tense and began to think, "Oh! What if I roll on Moses in the night!" So she raised up and retrieved his little blanket and wrapped it snugly around him. He was already zipped up in the bunting so he should be plenty warm. Then she rearranged herself on the coat and pulled it around her. What a day this had been! She hoped that tomorrow would be a better one.

In one sense, Sassy still had a morose feeling from her ill-fortune, yet on the other side of the coin, there was a light feeling that she was going home at last. How long it would take, she had no idea, but thinking of home excited her and she felt a deep happiness. Right now there was only the feeling of the unknown that was frightening . . . finding the way home, and she raised up on one elbow, feeling around for the coat pocket to make certain the money was still in it. As long as they had the money for tickets, surely there would be no other problem. She tried not to think of Tony, for when she did, her skin prickled and even the thought that the baby had his genes within him revolted her. But those days with Tony and the carnival would soon be eradicated from her mind as they slipped into the past, and the quicker the better. With this thought, her lips curled into a satisfying smile. She would dream of home.

AS DAYLIGHT PEERED THROUGH THE WINDOWS OF THE ramshackled old weatherboard house, Moses woke, crying with hunger and a wet diaper. They'd have to find a creek or a well to draw water and wash the wet, smelly ones that were being placed in a bag. Little Bear was already outside scanning the place and had found an outhouse in the rear that he would tell the girl about. It seemed plenty safe, and he pulled down some spider webs that were hanging from the corners. He knew she'd be breast-feeding the baby about now so he'd wait a few more minutes before going back inside. He was now wishing that he had told her to go to the kitchen and get a bag of something to eat back at the farm. Anything would taste wonderful right now—cold biscuits, apples, whatever could have been confiscated. He would have earned the food by the meager work that he did around the place. His stomach was growling, and he knew she would be very hungry also.

Soon, they gathered up the bundles, including the coats that would have to be carried on this warm morning, and were on their way again. Surely, this would be the day they would reach the small town where they could get on a bus going somewhere with a train station and then find a train that would take them home.

Stepping out onto the porch, a car was heard coming around the bend in the road, and Little Bear took Sassy by the elbow hurrying her back inside. The car rattled on past causing swirls of flying dust. "Chief, I think we better not pass up another ride into town," Sassy told him, thinking of the long walk still ahead. "Don't you think that we could recognize one of the trucks from the farm? Nobody there had a car. We sho could use a ride. My legs feels stiff this morning."

"Mmm," he agreed. "Chief's back sore, stiff. Floor hard sleep on. Old bones hurt before lay down. Feel bad inside."

"You poor man," she said as she followed him down the steps off the porch. Moses, on her shoulder, burped and spit up. It smelled sour. She wiped it with a diaper that she'd tied to her waist. "Now look at choo, boy. Ain't choo satisfied? At least you had somethin' to eat."

The motley-looking crew started their walk this morning with less energy than the night before—the Indian in the lead with slower steps and the girl even further behind. From a force of habit, she softly hummed a nonsensical tune. This pleasant day made walking much easier than if they'd had to contend with rain. Sassy mentioned this and ended her statement with a "Thank you, God," her eyes turned toward heaven. If it had been a month later, they would have been swatting at gnats and mosquitoes. This would be a good time to go home.

"I sho am hongry," she said, reverting to her old speech. "Wouldn't a hot biscuit and ham be wonnerful? My, my. I does needs somethin' tu keep this baby some milk goin'. When we sees a house, let's ax 'em iffen they will give us a bite tu eat. Now just listen tu how I a-talkin'. I guess Miss Lola would be unhappy if she knew I'd lost all her teaching so soon. It just takes practice, she say. She say I rattles on so that I jes' don' take time tu think about how tu say words." When Little Bear said nothing in reply, she asked, "You hear me up there, Mister, er you already gone def?"

His stomach felt rather queezy this morning so he commented that a cup of well water would suit him just fine, but if they did see a house, she could ask for food for herself. With her carrying the baby in her arms, surely she would not be refused. "Well, I never heard of anybody refusing a cup of cold water to a stranger, but I think your stomach don't feel too good because it's empty and needs a little food. Maybe they could tell us, too, if we're headed in thu right direction to town and how far away it is."

Little Bear shifted the load he was carrying and commented simply, "Need horse."

Sassy answered in a practical fashion. "Since you're wishin' jes' wish for a wagon, too." The old Indian, not being one for wishing, only grunted in reply without looking around to her. She looked up into the clear spring sky. There was not a cloud in sight; the morning air was fresh, and birds twittered in their trees. Sassy noticed how stiffly he was walking. "Chief, why you walk so stiff-like?" He'd already told her before that his legs and back ached.

"Bones old. Girl get old, walk like Chief."

"Does it hurt you to walk? Do we need to stop for awhile?"

"Not walk far yet. When walk much, hurt go."

"Oh, it's like Granny Liz say. She always says to anybody when she gets a chanch, ' I jes' keeps on a-keeping on.'" Then she added, "It must be terrible tu be old."

"Chief live long. Go mountain die. Be with parents. You tell bury Chief in cave, girl."

Sassy drew in her breath in shock at his statement. "Don't talk like that cause we is goin' home, you and me an' baby Moses." She lifted the baby from her shoulder to the cradle of her arm. "Then you will live happy in your cave again and won't nebber haf to go offen thu mountain again. No sirree bobtail." Her thoughts were positive but anxiety mirrored her frowning face. She knew how she would have to keep her spirits light and happy for the old man, so she rearranged her face into a wide smile. "Yes, sir, Chief. We is a-goin' home and my, my, all our folk will dance up an' down when dey see's us a-comin'. My mama, she say, 'Sassy, girl, where you been?' And den she say, 'My, my, jes' look at that fine li'l baby.' An she grab 'im an' hug 'im and Granny Liz, she set us down tu a great big feast. M-m-m, I can jes' taste dem turnip greens and corn pone wit cracklins. Oh, how I does love her cookin', and she make thu bes' cobbler I ever sank my teef into. But Granny Liz, she a-getting' purty old, too, so I 'spec' she kinda slowin' down. But now, Gramma, she a good cook, too. She be a-takin thu load offen Granny Liz 'bout cookin' and canning and stuff like that. My mamma, her name Semma, she haffa teach me how tu cook, too, but I don' wanna jes' stand in thu hot kitchen a-cookin' and a cookin' all day, cause I wants to teach school lak Miss Harris do."

"Girl, talk too much," Little Bear said using one of the longest sentences she'd ever heard him utter. They were walking toward the east, and the sun was now shining right in their eyes. Little Bear stopped and set the bag down that he was carrying with his right hand in order to shade his eyes and look straight ahead.

"See something?" she asked. "I don't hear no car."

"No, Chief looking land. No like . . . no mountain."

The long back roads of Mississippi were flat and dusty with houses far between. The tenant farms were shabby, their dirt yards full of colored children and poor whites. Coming upon one of these houses right now would be a blessing. Had Little Bear not been so elderly and had Sassy not borne a child only two months before, the walking would have been much easier. The terrain was the same no matter which direction they looked, and now trees were few due to plowed fields made ready for spring planting.

Mid-morning and still nothing to eat. "I'm gonna sit down right here and give Moses some water. Now, where did I put that bottle?" She began to search through the sacks for it. "My tongue is so dry I feels like squeezing a drop of water on it. Oh, here's the bottle." She held it up for Little Bear to see. "Look, it is half empty. Maybe I feel better if I says it is half full." She laid the baby across the crook of her arm and poked the nipple in his mouth. He took it gladly. "Chief, when we see a house, there gotta be a well there, too."

Little Bear took advantage of the break and sat down, crossing his legs and watched the baby making sucking sounds. "Chief not see baby. Hear of baby. Not see." He reached out his large hand to stroke Moses' little fingers, and when the baby curled his tiny fingers around Chief's large finger, the old man smiled, "Fine man child. Mother, father proud you bring."

"I hope so, Chief. I jes' hope so."

"We home, you teach Little Bear words?"

"Of course. I told you that I will. Why did your parents not teach you more words?"

"Talk Cherokee. Mad at soldiers. Not do their talk. Tell Chief some words. Boys come cave. Tell Chief words. Say some not tell Chief what mean. Boy, Matt say 'no,' bad word, not say. Say he tell Mama. What mean?"

Sassy smiled, took the bottle when Moses turned away from it, and told Little Bear, "Well, it's like this, see . . . sometimes boys say bad words when they are not with their parents just because they think it makes them more like a grown man. A nice grown man would not use the bad words."

Little Bear had a perplexed look on his face. He just answered, "Humph," and stood up. "We go. Find house. Find creek. Need water. Chief feel bad."

Sassy took the blanket from around Moses, unzipped his wrapper, and felt to see if his diaper was wet. "Yep. Just as I thought." Little Bear had picked up the bags and begun walking on unsteady legs. "Wait!" she called loudly to him. "He needs a diaper from the bag." Little Bear kept walking. "Oh, shoot, Moses, we'll haffa catch up with 'im. Now don't you start crying." She took the baby and stood up, tossing his blanket across her arm. "Wait for us, Chief. We're a-comin." As she feared, the baby started whimpering a wet-diaper whimper. "Hesh up, now. It will cool you off so jes' enjoy the wet diaper." She walked fast to catch up.

Shortly, the road curved and then there was a group of trees up ahead—welcomed trees that produced lots of shade—and Little Bear announced that a creek would be there. Oh, glory be! Sassy yelled and then let out a loud "Whoopee!" The racket frightened Moses, who started crying, and the crying picked up speed and now had become loud bawls.

"Merciful sakes alive, chile, it won't be long, so be quiet. You'll get a dry diaper and some dinner. I wish I had some dinner and a nice outhouse, too. I'll be happy to put my feets in that cool water and wash off some dust." Sassy already had a light feeling. They might catch a fish but who'd eat one raw! "Not, me," she said out loud after having that thought and then wondered how they'd even catch one, if there was any water in the creek.

The girl stopped to kiss and soothe her baby. She placed him in her other arm to shade his eyes from the sun, thinking now that she actually had not even prayed about their situation to ask for guidance. So she dropped to the ground, and with the baby now satisfied and quiet, she bowed her head and prayed.

"Dear Lord, here we are a way out chere in the middle of nowheres and we needs somethin' to eat real bad. That old Indian man is weak from age and he need strength and this here little baby, he need his milk tu keep a-goin. Please hep us and lead us home. Thank you and Amen." She was not praying for herself but for her baby and Little Bear. She was volatile but not selfish.

They had walked quite a distance by now since starting out early in the morning. Little Bear had looked up into the sky several times, noticing that the midday sun was straight up. He felt weak from hunger and thirst and silently wondered if he would be able to hold out until they could find help. When they came nearer, he pointed for the girl to follow him off the road across an open field so as not to have to stop right next to the bridge now in sight. It was an old iron bridge floored with wooden planks. He headed for a group of oaks where coolness would be and where he would find glorious rest. Maybe he could sleep for a while if the rumbling in his stomach would quiet down. He may not ever want to get up again.

Cutting at an angle across the unplowed field made the creek and trees seem further away than when they'd left the road and started toward them. Sassy noticed Little Bear, a good distance in front of her, stagger occasionally. Now, he slowed his pace, set down the bundles in his right hand, removed his hat, and fanned with it. The early spring sun was warm, yet not warm enough for fanning, but the coats

and bundles he carried caused him to perspire. He had always been
used to living among shady tall trees and was adept at climbing the
mountainous terrain; this flatland country was different. Over the past
year of sitting around, his strength had waned.

Walking along, Sassy talked to her son as though he could understand every word she uttered. "Yessir, little Moses, we be on Kendell
Mountain soon an' we won't never go 'way from there and yore
Gramma gonna spoil you plum rotten, I bets . . . an' Joe, he teach
you thangs like how tu swing a sling shot, how tu catch a fish, and
swim and go hunting wit yore Grandpa Tad and Grandaddy Sam and
you is gonna go tu school too, young man." She adjusted the diaper
that she'd placed across the baby's head to shade him from the sun.
She had caught up with Little Bear just as he was picking up the sack
again. "Chief, we have fount us a creek! Do you hear that water
running?" He did not answer but started on with two goals in mind—
a drink of fresh running water and rest. As they came to the sloping
creek bank, they both stood looking over watching the water tinkling
over rocks, falling into a pool which looked like a perfect swimming
hole. The place, serene, cool, and inviting would be hard to leave when
it came time to continue on their trip. Little Bear spread the coat Miss
Lola had given Sassy out on a nice grassy spot and pointed for the girl
to lay the baby down. "You smells terrible, youngun. This diaper has
got tu go." She went down to the creek and wet another diaper to
wash him with and left the bad one there where she would return with
the other wet ones and wash them all. Little Bear went to the creek and
put water on his arms and neck, relishing the coolness on his skin,
then he disappeared behind some trees on the other side. When he
returned, he looked across the creek and saw that the baby was still
nursing so he eased his tired old body down and propped against a
tree trunk and dozed.

Moses held onto his mother's finger as he nursed. She absently
rubbed her hand across his curly brown hair, softly humming a
lullaby, her mind straying many miles away. Soothed by a full
stomach, a dry diaper and her humming, the baby soon fell asleep.
Sassy laid him down on the coat and spread a diaper over him. She got
up to find some bushes or trees for a blind to relieve herself, and then
removed her shoes to walk in the creek. She saw Little Bear leaning
against the tree, asleep, head bent over, and she heard an occasional
snore. She, too, felt exhausted, but the creek was too inviting to pass
up. It called out for her to come and drink and play like she did as a
child Although only a year ago, it seemed now like an eon ago.

She smiled for no one to see but God himself, and she tromped in the water until her skirt was wet from her bending over to scoop up handfuls of the cool wetness and pour it joyfully over her head. Then she saw it! It was sitting on the bank behind Little Bear's tree, in plain sight. How had they missed seeing it? Not believing what she saw, her mouth fell open with complete astonishment. "Well, I'll be!" she exclaimed wading through the water to the other bank and scrambling up the side. The basket was resting on an old tree stump, its lid secured with a latch. Sassy was apprehensive as to whether or not she should raise the lid but lifted it by the handles and gave it a slight shake. Nothing rattled or moved inside so she set it back on the stump and cracked the lid open. Nothing jumped out so she opened the lid wider and saw what she had prayed for . . . food. Astonished out of her wits, she drew in a deep breath and then blew it all out at once. "I wonder if it's still any good, and who could've lef' it here?" She took the basket to a grassy spot and sat down to examine its contents. There were two perfectly good apples, yellow and shiny, a box of saltine crackers, a small jar of peanut butter, a knife and two bottles of orange drink. There was a table knife also. The meager fare looked like a feast right now. Sassy looked around the tree at Little Bear. Should she wake him or just let him sleep until he got ready to get up? She decided to eat her portion of the food, and he could eat after he was rested. She took the basket across the creek, to sit beside the baby as she ate and make certain no ants had crawled onto his makeshift bed. After she placed the basket on the spread-out coat, she sat down, crossed her legs, and bowed her head to give thanks.

"Dear God, I knowed you wouldn't forget about us, me and Little Bear and baby Moses. You knowed where we wuz all along and you sent us a basket of food. If you could feed five thousand men and their womenfolk and children, then surely you hadn't forgotten that us three were hungry, too. Thank you and please help us to find shelter before the night come, if we don't get to town before then. Amen."

With apples being so readily available at the Knollwood Orchards, Sassy thought she would never be so thankful for an apple again, but this apple she was eating was the sweetest, juiciest one that she'd ever had and she relished every bite. And she'd never cared for peanut butter, but these crackers would not have been complete without some. It was delicious, and she licked the stickiness from her fingers when she'd finished. The orange juice bottle had a screw-on lid so she took it down to the creek, rinsed the bottle out, filled it with water, and replaced the lid. Then she thought about the baby's empty water bottle and went back to get it for refilling. She also took the soiled diapers and washed them out and hung them across a bush in the sun to dry. She was not sleepy and had rested sufficiently by the feel of the cool water, the food, and shade from the trees.

This spot was heavenly. Surely people from the area came here for picnics, but then she thought, "What people?" There was just the house they had seen last night where the man went out to quiet his dog and then the empty old house where they'd slept. Despite herself, Sassy relaxed and fell asleep. She was awakened by cries from the baby, who was ready to have his hunger satisfied again. The cries also aroused Little Bear. He raised up stiffly from the sitting position against the tree and at first forgot just where he was. Then, Sassy called out to him and he caught hold of the tree and pulled himself up.

"Look, here, Chief! Look!" Sassy reached over and picked up the basket. "Lookie what I fount! It has food in it, good food, too! Come on over here and get it," she called out loudly. "I've already eaten." He wasted no time in wading through the creek to where she was on the other side.

"Where get?" he asked totally perplexed, raising the lid and peering inside.

"I just saw it sitting on the bank over there," she pointed to show him just where she'd discovered the basket. "I reckon it is just an answer to prayer."

"People leave," Little bear answered, taking the basket and sitting on the ground. "What this?" He held up the jar of peanut butter.

"It's peanut butter and it's real good. Look, I'll show you how to do it." She reached over and took the jar and the knife and spread peanut butter on the crackers. "Here, try this." She watched as he put one into his mouth, and then his eyes lit up with his taste buds responding to the wonderful flavor. Then Sassy opened the bottle of orange juice and handed it to him.

"Humm, good," Little Bear smiled, feeling better already. He ate all the crackers with peanut butter on them and then relished the apple. "Apple not like on mountain."

"No. These are yellow. The color is called yellow. Our apples are red. I like yellow apples." Then she pointed up to the sky. "The sky is called blue and see Moses' hair . . . it is called brown. There are lots of colors." She kept on with her speech while he ate, "And my eyes are blue, too. My mama say my daddy's eyes were blue, too." She held her head upwards for him to glance into her eyes and then stared at his. "And your eyes are brown."

Little Bear was chewing and washing the crackers down with the drink. He did not respond to her lesson in colors. She changed the subject by telling him to be sure and save his bottle and its lid to take water in when they left.

Little Bear looked up into the sky to check just where the sun had fallen to. "We go on soon, girl feed baby?"

"Yes, and I washed the diapers, they're over there." She pointed to the bushes where they were now dry from the warm sun. "I'll just go get them. Keep the flies off of him, please, Chief."

Little Bear threw the apple core aside and reached over to pick up the baby when his eyes opened just as Sassy left. He lifted the baby up and down several times, creating smiles and coos, and then held him in his arms talking directly to him with little Moses watching as though he understood everything that was said. When Sassy came back she sat down and folded the clean diapers, placed them in the bag, except for one which she knew he would need by now. After he was changed, she handed him back to Little Bear and went down to the creek again to wash the wet one. This one would have to be tied to her belt to dry as they walked.

After she returned, they gathered up their belongings, getting ready to resume the journey into the unknown. Little Bear felt stiff and sore and had a time raising himself up off the coat where they'd been sitting. He rolled over on his knees but still could not pull himself up. Seeing his plight, Sassy pulled him by one arm, holding Moses with the other. He came up slowly, and staggering, caught hold of a small tree. "Much old. Bones hurt, food not help that. Need sleep more."

She patted his arm affectionately. "I know . . . and I don't know, but Granny Liz, she always complained about her aching bones. She just plumb too heavy, too." Then, as usual, she flitted from one subject to another. "Chief, we gonna have us one great big reunion 'fore long."

"What 'reunion'? Taste good like peanut butter?"

Sassy gave a resounding laugh. "No, Chief! A reunion means seeing folks that you haven't seen for a long time."

Satisfied with her answer, he struggled to his feet saying, "We not stay here. Must go."

And so they started, reluctantly, toward the road again. The road was level with the field, and they only had to step over some weeds growing between road and field. Sassy carried Moses against her shoulder; Little Bear was burdened with their belongings. He glanced up into the sky again. "Blue, mmuh?"

"Yea, blue . . . and I hopes it stays that'a way, too. We'd have a turrible time if a dark cloud come up. When we gets home I'm a'gonna stay put for a long time before I take off walking. You feel okay now?" He only answered with a nod and a grunt, and Sassy continued with her rambling. "And nobody better not ask me tu go to a carnival wit 'em, either . . . ever again. Do you think that they will let me go to the school on the mountain?" Of course the old man had absolutely no idea about things like that and did not offer an answer. "I'll jes' haffa talk wit Misser Alyn and his Misses 'bout that I guess." They were walking as before, Little Bear in the lead, only with slower steps. The shoes he had on were comfortable. They were wet from the creek, but the wetness helped his burning feet. He was glad that he'd accepted the shoes that one of the men had offered him back at the farm after the man had bought brand new ones. They were a size too large but better that than too tight.

His mind right now was on Kendell Mountain, where he knew the dogwood and rhododendron would be in bloom, trying to outdo each other for supremacy. As a child, his parents had pointed out the plants and trees, teaching him the Cherokee names for them. Now it was springtime, and the dogwood would be looking like snow, covering the hazy-blue mountains surrounding the territory that was the only place he'd ever known as home. Little Bear had savored this sight from one season to the next since his childhood. In his head he could still hear the voices of Running Wolf and Red Bud telling him about their childhoods at Echota. They lived in log houses with their parents, who were farmers and hunters, and fished the nearby river called Coosawattee. It must have been a wonderful life there among relatives and friends. Over the years Little Bear longed for a family. The people on Kendell Mountain had come to be the closest thing to a family he had known.

Chapter Twenty—seven

THEY WALKED AND WALKED, MUCH SLOWER WHILE THE sun felt even warmer than when it was straight up in the sky. If April weather was already this hot, what would the middle of the summer be? Chief's steps now were so much slower that Sassy caught up with him and they were walking side by side. She saw beads of sweat on his forehead and his arm went up giving his head a swipe.

"Tooth hurt," Little Bear said holding his jaw. Sassy scanned the area he was holding when he removed his hand and found that the jaw was puffed out.

"You need a tooth doctor to pull it out," she told him. "I've noticed that you have a couple o' bad ones in front, too. But for your age, it's a wonder that you still have any teeth at all."

"Adam teeth look good. He old, too."

"Yes, he's old alright, but all of his are false ones."

"What word 'false' mean?"

"It means that all of his teeth have been pulled out and the tooth doctor made him some teeth that are not real ones."

"Huh?" Chief looked at her in astonishment. "Girl mean people's teeth not real?" He stopped in his tracks and looked her square in the face.

"Sure. Most all old folks have false teeth because they rot out. Then they can chew anything and not have hurting teeth." The old man shook his head and started walking again.

"Chief get new teeth, new eye glasses. Chief eyes dim. Not see far off. When young, Chief see mountain ranges far, far away. See clouds, mountaintops, see birds high in sky. Not see now." He paused, thinking sadly about missing seeing these things, then said, "Girl look far away, see house, see barn, see wagon come."

161

"I've been looking, Chief, all around. I don't see anything at all except a lot of flat road, but there is a tree up ahead. We just gotta find help soon. I don't know whether there's a town anywhere around or not. My legs is plumb sore." With each arduous step she had become more apprehensive. The enthusiasm that she felt when they had first left the creek was now diminishing. She was worried about little Moses because she'd stopped twice in the past hour to remove a stinky diaper, and now hoped they'd come to another creek before long where she could wash them out. Then, she'd hurried to catch up with Little Bear who had kept ahead even though his steps were slower. Now she was also worried about the old man and wondered just how long he could keep going today. She shaded her eyes with her free arm and searched the horizon in hope of seeing a house somewhere within her vision.

"Chief, do you believe in God?" Her question was honest and to the point.

"Missionaries tell parents is true before come to mountain. Where He now?"

"In heaven, I s'pose, but He sends His Spirit to be with us and angels to help us."

"Tell Him send help now." Little Bear's words showed no enthusiasm at all. They had now come to the tree that was right beside the road, and he stopped in its shade, took out his water bottle, unscrewed the lid, and drank half the water. "Girl sit. Rest. Chief rest." He felt as though he could not take another step, and Sassy welcomed the suggestion. She sat down under the tree, took out her water bottle, had a few sips, and then offered Moses his bottle. He refused and fretted, so she spread out his blanket on top of the coat and laid him down.

A soft breeze rustled the leaves overhead, lulling the trio to sleep on the uncomfortable ground. They had not noticed their discomfort and did not stir until a wagon pulled up and someone called "Woah," to the horse. Sassy thought she was dreaming and Little Bear was still sleeping.

"Weel, whut do we have here? How come you folks er out fer a stroll on this warm day? A old man and a little bitty baby ort not be out on a long walk lak ya'll hadda been on. Whur ya'll bound anyhow?" He'd asked three questions without waiting for answers.

Sassy stood up, relieved to know that this must be the help they needed. She walked over to the wagon, shaded her eyes with a hand, and looked up into the face of the overalled man. He took off his straw hat and fanned with it, then took out a handkerchief and blew his nose, waiting for the girl to speak.

"We not doing it fer fun, mister. You by any chanch a-goin' tu town?" Little Bear woke and struggled to his feet.

The man spat a stream of tobacco juice to the ground before answering, "Town, huh?" then he wiped a grin from his face. "Ain't no town in this here direction, little lady. No Ma'am. Town's direkly tuther way." He pointed behind the wagon to the direction from where Sassy and Little Bear's journey had begun.

The devastated girl looked at the man in the wagon with a shocked look as tears rolled down her cheeks. "Bu-but . . . you means we been a-walking fer haf a night and a day fer nuthin?"

The mule swished his tail and looked around at Little Bear when he stood stiffly to his feet. "I reckon you have iffen its town ya'll are a-wanting." They all were silent and the man sized up the Indian, then said, "How come a Indian, a girl, and a baby together?"

"We're family," Sassy said without hesitation. "We gotta get to town to catch a bus going east."

"I can't turn around and go back there just now, but I tell you whut . . . ya'll climb in the wagon and jes' go on home with me and I'll take you there tomorrie. Maybe my woman'll feed you a bite of supper."

Sassy looked over at Little Bear, who wearily nodded his head in agreement. In seeing the Indian's advanced age, the man climbed down, assisted him up into the back of the wagon, then held Moses while Sassy retrieved their belongings and the basket and climbed up on the wagon seat. He handed the baby up to his mother, climbed aboard, and clucked to the mule. "Gittie-up." The old gray mule slowly obeyed.

"My name's Sassy, and this here is little Moses," she smiled.

"Strange name fer a little 'un. I'm Troy Garfield. My house ain't very fer from here." In a few minutes he said, "Maybe I'd better mention that my misses is kinda stern. She'd do anything fer a body, but she ain't got no sweet disposition. Sometimes she's downright ornery, but maybe you can put up with her 'til tomorrie." He sneezed and reached in a back pocket for a handkerchief. "Been a-doin' that most all day. Sure hope the little 'un don't catch my cold."

"We won't be no trouble, Mr. Garfield, and thank you for your help. It's kind o' you and I'm much obliged."

"Don't that Indian talk none?" Mr. Garfield asked.

"He can talk, but he don't know a lot o' words and kinda talks in spurts. He's jes' tired out right now and not feeling too good either."

The wagon bounced along at a snail's pace. At least the seat had springs under it, but in the back Little Bear was taking most of the bouncing. He rolled up the coat and put it behind his back as he leaned against the side of the wagon holding his throbbing jaw. In a few more minutes, the road rounded a bend where a house came into view. Wet clothes hung limply on a line to dry at the side of the old weather-board house, and four colored children of stair-step size and a dog came tearing around a corner to see who was approaching. On the porch sat two women in straight chairs, one churning and the other fanning. "Hey, Misser Garfield," called one of the children, waving to him. The women stared at the strange people in the wagon as they both stopped their churning and fanning, holding up a hand each in recognition of their closest neighbor.

"'Lo, Miss Bessie, 'lo, Aunt Tandy," Troy Garfield called out, passing on by and then called back to them. "Tell Tate I said 'Howdy.'" Then he looked over at Sassy saying, "Weel, ya'll 'll give them women somethin' tu talk about fer a whilst I reckon," he said and sneezed again.

Moses squirmed, started crying, and demanded to be held up. "Hesh up, youngun. You'll get fed soon and have a dry didee, too. You've been a good boy, yes you have, an' I know you're tired of being josled around. Yore mama am, too."

Mr. Garfield asked, "What's thu Injun chief's name?"

"Just that," Sassy answered. "It's just plain 'Chief.' Actually, it's 'Little Bear' but everybody just calls 'im 'Chief,' and he's got a bad toothache."

"Maybe Ma's got somethin' to rub on his gum. She's a purty good doctor. We about there. See that house up thu road yonder a spell?"

"Well, I thanks thu Good Lord," Sassy said relieved. "My arms feels like they's about to fall off and my legs are so sore, too, and I know Chief is plum wore out, an' this baby's done got thu runs."

Mr. Garfield commented that a good rest would help them all, thinking that his misses would be gracious enough to toss a couple more potatoes, or whatever she had already cooking for supper, into the pot. She came out on the porch with a question mark on her haggard-looking face when she heard the wagon coming in off the road and pull up into the dirt yard. Her dress was dark and plain, covered with an apron soiled from her chores, and her black hair sprinkled with gray was pulled back behind her head in a ball—an austere-looking woman to say the least.

"These people need some help, Ma. I told 'em I'd take 'em to town tomorrie morning and thought you wouldn't mind giving them a little supper," Troy Garfield said as he climbed down to assist his guests out of the wagon with their meager belongings after he first retrieved a handkerchief and blew his nose.

She looked at Sassy and the baby and then her eyes fell on Little Bear as Troy helped him off the back of the wagon. "Surely he ain't thu baby's pa," she said under her breath and came down the two steps to accept the baby as Sassy climbed down. Right away she realized that a diaper changing was necessary, and she handed him back to his mother the moment she stepped down.

"I shore wadn't expecting no company, but ya'll come on in and we'll see what we can do. Supper is ready but it ain't much by no means, but reckon there's a-plenty cornbread and buttermilk if the rest don't stretch very fer." She led the way into the little unpainted, weatherboard house. There was a swing on the porch and a straight chair and a rocker. Inside, they went through a small living room where a kitchen could be seen beyond. To the left of the front room was a bedroom and on the right side was a small bedroom where Mrs. Garfield led Sassy to deposit her baby on the bed to change him. Mr. Garfield was showing Little Bear to the outhouse around to the rear. Mrs. Garfield left the room and returned with a wash pan of water and an old cloth that she handed to Sassy to clean the baby. "It's warm water," she said. Sassy explained about his runs and how he was getting red from rawness. The woman said she'd get some salve and left the room again.

When she handed her the salve, she told Sassy to go out in the front yard and get some leaves, "jes' a few," from the willow tree and bring them to her so she could make a tea for the baby's problem. "Have you got a little bottle with a nipple?"

"Yess'um. It needs fresh water in it."

"You can put the tea in it and give to him. Where'd you get the water from?"

"Outten thu creek."

"Well, no wonder the little 'un has got thu runs."

Helping her with the baby showed compassion, but still, Sassy felt a harsh coldness about the woman. After she'd tended to Moses' needs, she turned him on his stomach and went outside to get the willow leaves.

The supper consisted of field peas (that had been canned in a jar), fried fat back, and corn bread. What there was of it was good to the hungry two visitors. Little Bear tried as best as he could to eat on one side of his mouth because of the hurting tooth. Before he went out to the barn to sleep on the hay, Cleo Garfield poured some turpentine in a small bottle for him to take with him so he could keep some on the tooth.

MOONLIGHT STREAMED INTO THE ROOM FORMING STRANGE patterns on the wall and a tree limb scratching against the house became annoying. Sassy had placed the baby on the back side of the bed next to the wall and placed a straight chair between them to keep her from rolling over on him in her sleep. She drifted off, elated over the thoughts of getting to town tomorrow and on a bus to Birmingham, where they'd catch a train to Atlanta.

There was only a glimpse of light on the horizon when Cleo Garfield called from the doorway for Sassy to get up. "There's much to be done today," she said as she scurried across the room, raising a window after pushing aside the bag of diapers on the floor.

"Much to be done?" Sassy repeated in the form of a question as she sat up in bed. "But, Mr. Garfield said . . ."

Cleo interrupted her statement with, "Well, he won't be going fer awhile because he became sick during the night and you're not going to sit around here while I wait on you and cook your food. There's a washing tu be done and hung out, but first the cow must be milked and wood needs tu be chopped and brought in for the cook stove, among other chores so get your lazy self out of bed," she told the girl angrily.

Sassy sat in bed shocked, holding the cover up around her chest. (She'd slept in her slip.) She was completely shocked at the woman's tone of voice. "Mr. Garfield said it would be alright for us to come here, but since he's sick, we'll just be walking on," she said as she reached over to remove the chair off the bed. Moses woke up crying, wet, and hungry.

"Oh, no you won't," Cleo said in a strident voice, hands on hips as she stood beside the bed facing Sassy. "I know what you are and you oughta be ashamed fer running around with that Indian. Thu very idea! And I'll not have that youngun squalling and botherin' my husband while he's sick. Get up, you hear?"

Sassy swung her legs over the side of the bed. "I'm up, but the first thing I'm gonna do is to nurse this baby."

"You've got a smart mouth, too, girl. How'd you get that baby? . . . Who's its paw?"

Sassy stooped over and picked up the baby and went to sit in a rocker while he nursed, not bothering to answer the unnecessary question. With a snort, Cleo left the room in a huff. "Mr. Garfield was right when he'd said she's not very likable," Sassy told Moses, kissing him, "but don't you cry, 'cause we're not gonna stay here much longer." Then she felt that he was wet and got up from the chair to remedy that before she settled down to feed him.

Troy Garfield lay in bed feeling terrible for two reasons—one because his sniffles had developed into a full-blown cold and two, because he had promised the girl he would take them to town today. Cleo stuffed him with her remedies and rubbed his chest with a horrible-smelling concoction of boiled onion juice mixed with hog lard and turpentine. She was making him sicker than he was, another scheme of hers, he felt certain. Maybe the girl would wait to leave for another day. They should not be walking that long distance into town, and he should have left the field before the sun got up so high on the day before he'd picked them up on the road. That day, Cleo pitched a fit when Troy came in with every stitch he had on wet from sweat, and she'd tried to get him to stay home when he left for town the next morning, saying he had to buy seed. Last night after Sassy went to bed in the small bedroom and Chief out in the barn, Cleo had it out with her husband for bringing the strangers into their house. "They'll probably steal us blind," she retorted, "or kill us, one er thu other."

"What've we got worth stealing?" he asked and then, "Neither one of 'em's strong enough to do anybody any harm. They jes' need a little help, Ma. Be kind fer onest, can't choo?"

Now, Cleo was in the kitchen making biscuits, fuming because she had to feed "those two." "Well, they can jes' work, by crackey," she said and gave the biscuit dough a few punches to accentuate her statement.

When Little Bear came into the kitchen with a bucket of well water, he announced, "Rain coming. In the air."

"Ain't possible," Cleo told him. "Sky's clear."

"Rain by night," Little Bear said again.

"Then you and the girl better get busy. Get that milk bucket over there and go milk the cow an' she's got a washing tu do." Little Bear had milked a cow many times during the night on Kendell Mountain. What little he took was never noticed.

"Mr. Troy in yard?" Little Bear asked.

"Nope, he's sick in bed," she told him as she slid the pan of biscuits in the oven.

The screen door slammed shut as he went out with the milk bucket in hand. Cleo called for him to stop by the well and rinse the bucket out and wash his hands in the pan on the wash stand . . . with soap. Little Bear's mind was muddled with the thoughts of sickness and rain causing a delay in their plans.

BY SUPPER TIME, DARK CLOUDS SAILED ACROSS THE SKY AND rain set in. Cleo glanced out the kitchen window with a disgruntled look, disgusted that she had been wrong and the Indian was right. Now she'd have to put up with them until the rain stopped which, she hoped, would not be another whole day. At least the little 'un was free of the runs, and she had been right about what would cure it. The willow leaf tea worked nearly every time.

Cleo had not always been unkind. She had been a good wife and mother, kept a clean house, and fed her family well. It was three years ago that Bubba ran away with that carnival woman when they came there for the winter. He met the girl in town and carried on with her for a while before bringing her home to meet his folks, and when Cleo showed disapproval, they took off together and had not returned since. Now, here comes this girl and Indian and she'd bet most anything that they had come from that carnival group. The very idea! And here under her roof, too!

Chapter Twenty—eight

ALYN, WILL, SAM, AND THE TWINS WENT INTO THE WOODS down in Hickory Flats to look for the bear that had escaped their previous efforts. Now, the rascal had played havoc worrying the hogs and making them nervous. Before, he had caused them to go off their feed and Adam said nobody wanted a skinny hog. He saw the bear running across the property about daylight and told Alyn that morning when he came out to the barn.

"We'll have to get him this time," Alyn said. Adam preferred to stay at home, saying he was now too old to go traipsing around like he did only a few years ago. Bears usually forage for food at night and sleep in the day so they'd go look for him right before daybreak the next morning. Jasper would only frighten a bear away with all his racket, so he'd be left at home until he got more age on him. They'd take Sam's two dogs, Buck and Cloe, the best dogs with bear. Will had a good hunting dog killed last year, maimed by a bear that the other dogs had cornered. The hunters got the bear but lost the dog. That old bear fed the hunters' families for a while and his skin was tacked up on a wall in the barn.

Ophelia was the best cook of wild meat on the place, having learned all about it from Lizzie. A large roast needed a pod of red pepper cooked with it, in a pot of water, to kill the wild taste. She'd poke it in the pot every now and then to test for tenderness, then salt and pepper it, and brown it in the oven. About half an hour before done, she'd add flour and five chopped onions and some carrots. "That there'll be fine eatin'," she'd say while sliding the pan out of the oven.

Matt and Dan had never been on a bear hunt until now and were anxious to do a lot of bragging about this one. They had not let Alyn forget about his promise to take the boys on a hunt, and now they were actually going.

The men would look for signs right before daylight and wait, hidden far away, for an appearance. The dogs would start pulling on their leashes and barking when they picked up a scent and be turned loose to hold the bear at bay so a hunter could finish him off. Then the work of skinning and cutting up would begin right there on the spot because the bear would be too heavy to drag through the woods. They brought along what they'd need for this job, certain they'd make a kill. Each man would go home with good meat. "I'll bet our folks won't want any of it," Matt said, and Alyn replied that they'd be invited down to the house for a feast one night and wouldn't know what they were eating until they were told later. Both the boys found this funny and said they'd never give the secret away.

Before long, the dogs began whining and straining at their leashes. Then with more intensity, they barked furiously, pulling until they were released to dash ahead wherever their noses led them.

"Let's go," one of the boys called with excitement rising.

"No, wait!" Will called. "We haffa give dem dogs time tu corner dat bear and tire 'im down."

It was completely daylight now, and Alyn caught sight of a tree trunk where the tree had been freshly cut down. "Well, what's this?" he wondered and turned about to discover several more trunks close by with missing trees. "This is strange." Then he asked Will and Sam, "Hey, men, have either of you seen anybody cutting down trees recently?" They both said they had not seen anybody cutting down trees and had not heard any sawing or chopping going on. "Well, I'm going to go down the hill and check around for more." Then he told the boys to stay with the men, and if they returned home before he got there, to tell Cynthee where he'd gone. The boys were too excited to care where he went. They were pulling on the men's coat sleeves to come on and check on the dogs and bear.

Alyn turned downhill, counting ten more cuttings before he'd gone very far. "This is school property," he thought, "and the school board has not brought up the matter of cutting trees. Somebody's stealing 'em. Hardwoods at that!" By the time he reached the outcropping of rock, ten more stumps were added to the count, causing his blood to boil. Here, a stream dropped over rock forming small waterfalls into a pool that Alyn and Luther had called their luckiest fishing hole. Many a time Alyn had taken a string of fish home to Lizzie Mae to fry for supper. She augmented them with hushpuppies, coleslaw, and grits. "A feast fitten fer a king," she'd vow.

He was too upset to pause for long and ponder over memories. At the bottom of the ravine would begin the Pratt property, which entailed twenty-five acres. He wondered what had become of Jake and his wife and children. He'd seen Jake only once or twice around town since he'd been back on Kendell Mountain. It could be he had something to do with cutting the trees. Alyn and Cynthia went to school with some of the Pratt children; there was a house full of them, about eight he guessed. Tissy once told Alyn how she had loved to sit on the Pratt's porch and sing with them while Jake played either his fiddle or guitar or sometimes a dulcimer. It was Jake who taught Tissy to play a guitar when she was only a little child. He recognized her talent. He was away nearly every weekend playing with a group at some gathering somewhere, not only because of his love for music but also to help keep the children clothed and fed.

Because of his now aching leg, Alyn decided not to make the descent to the Pratt property but to turn and cut across and go part of the way by road. As he walked, he was thinking of losing the trees and what a waste, whatever the reason for their being cut down. Back when the big house burned, it was a wonder, or only by the grace of God, that sparks had not ignited the whole mountain into an inferno. The great dangers to trees were lightning causing fires, a careless, thoughtless person, and, of course, tree disease, which caused rot. He wondered what the mountain would've been like in the beginning of time when it was completely covered with forests, but then the flood came and the whole earth was covered with water.

Alyn remembered how he used to sit on the porch of the Tanner cabin watching Hugh, Cynthee's father, whittle little figures or nice carvings of birds and animals. As he worked, Hugh taught the boy about trees, plants, herbs, and such. He said that he whittled with balsa, the lightest wood there is. "Our forest is valuable," Hugh told him, marveling that the child was interested. "In fact, wood is the most valuable thing in the world."

"Even more than diamonds?" Alyn had questioned.

Hugh had answered with a grin and a "Yep."

For a while, Alyn followed the deep-rutted road, thickly wooded on each side. He pealed off his jacket and, making note of the exact spot, dropped it beside a tree intending to retrieve it on the way home. After several bends of the road, he decided to cut back through the woods and skirt the ravine. He came to the edge at Kingston's Cliff that overlooked the beautiful valley far below. The road at the bottom forked; left went to Union Gap and to the right, the road passed the

Pratt property and plowed fields. He could see Rushing Creek, winding in and out among rocks and crevices, looking like a silver snake, brightened by the morning sun. Westward, there was Crooked River crawling its way through the valley.

Alyn was standing, hands in pockets, surveying with his eyes the hazy blue mountain ranges in the distance. He could not remember how many times he had sat on these boulders and gazed out over this valley. To the east he saw tin rooftops of Union Gap's buildings shimmering in the sunlight. He stood for some time, lost in thought. It had not been too long ago that he had stood at this very spot and yelled "I'm home, everybody! Hear me? I'm home!" and his words had reverberated throughout the valley for all the world to hear. Now, he was wishing for the horse that had been with him then, or now, just any horse would do. He noticed a wisp of smoke coming from a chimney that he knew would be the Pratt place back to the right. "Well, somebody must be living there."

When he finally reached the bottom of the mountain, he took the right fork and came upon the cabin that was nestled back off the road in a grove of hickory trees. A flock of hens ran off squawking, wings flapping, and a hound dog came out baying a greeting. The house looked just as he remembered it; logs perfectly aged and none the worse for wear. It did, however, sport a new tin roof that was painted red. A barn had been added across the road and a neatly fenced pasture was home to a few cows and a horse, some of which gazed inquisitively at Alyn from over the fence while chewing their cud, their bells tinkling.

As Alyn stepped into the yard, the dog came up to him with tail wagging, threw his head high, gave a few howls, and then licked the extended friendly hand. He rubbed his head and pulled on the long ears, then looked up toward the house as he noticed the front door open. Seeing that the hound was friendly to the stranger, a young woman stepped out on the porch. Alyn walked to the bottom of the steps with the hound sniffing at his heels and, resting a hand on the Newell post, said, "Good morning, Ma'am. Name's Alyn Russell. Does Jake Pratt still live here?"

She wondered how he had gotten there for having looked around, saw no vehicle or horse. "No, he doesn't." She offered no further information or her name and gave him a skeptical look. Then, curious of what he wanted, she asked, "Is he in some sort of trouble?" She was a beautiful girl, or woman; it would be hard for anyone to guess her age. She had on jeans, a western-type shirt and riding boots, looking as though she'd just stepped out of a western movie. Her long, dark hair was pulled back and tied with a ribbon. She spoke with a northern accent.

"Well, I thought he may be but I'm not sure . . . that is, I don't know. Has he sold this place?"

"He's certainly a nosey cuss," the woman thought. "Do you live around here, Mr. Russell?" she asked evading his question. "You did say your name is Russell, did you not?"

"Yes to both questions, Ma'am." He looked like a little boy standing before a school teacher. "Up on the mountain. Knollwood Orchards."

"I've heard of the place; however, I assumed the owner to be a much older man."

He grinned his boyish grin and instantly she approved his good looks, his clean-cut appearance, and his straightforwardness. "Won't you please come in, Mr. Russell?" she offered courteously. Alyn felt an awkwardness and hesitated. She waved her hand toward the door. "Do come in. It's nice to meet a neighbor. I've found it rather lonely here and wondered if anyone lived anywhere around." She flashed a wide smile, showing a set of beautiful, white, even teeth. He followed her through the open door. She sat in an oak rocker and pointed for Alyn to sit across from her on a couch. The room looked comfortable and nice, so different than when the Pratts lived there with eight children and their dogs tearing through banging doors and chasing one another. The inside had been remodeled completely. By a quick glance he could see through one door to a bedroom and another to the kitchen, where there was floating in the air an aroma of freshly brewed coffee. The furniture was modern, all new, and he saw a floor model RCA Victor radio. His eyes quickly scanned the furnishings and window curtains and then back to the young woman.

"My name is Linda McKnight," she finally offered, "and yes, Mr. Pratt did sell the house and property to me just recently."

"It seems odd that a little place like Union Gap has not been talking about someone new moving in. That happens very seldom and would be the subject in every store and especially the barbershop. Everyone always knows about everyone else . . . there are no secrets here," he smiled slightly.

"Oh, well, the movers came in from the west end of this road," she pointed with a thumb, "you know where it comes out to the highway about eight miles over that way."

"I see. Then you took the short way and saved going over the mountain." She only nodded and offered no other information. Seeing no ring on her finger, he said "Well, Miss McKnight, you have certainly made a cozy home out of this place." He was taking his time getting to the subject of the trees, trying to sort out in his mind just how she could be involved with this at all. "Have you been up the mountain road back to the east side of your property?"

"No. I haven't had a chance to do any exploring around as yet. It's taken all my time getting the house fixed up. My father came and stayed long enough to do the repairs, and then I had unpacking to do." She was just not going to offer any information without his bluntly asking, he could see that.

"There is certainly a beautiful view of the valley from up there on what we call Kingston's Cliff. You can see the Blue Ridge Mountains and the river that runs through the Gap between Coleman and Kendell Mountains. It is quite breathtaking. I used to like to sit there when I was just a kid and daydream about far off places beyond the mountains." Alyn cleared his throat and decided to broach the subject of his visit. "Miss McKnight . . ."

"Please call me Linda."

"'Miss Linda,' then. I don't know where you came from and if you have no family, just how you intend to survive here alone. I can't understand how you even found the Pratts and got them to sell to you. Of course all of that is none of my affair, but what is my affair is your property line back up the mountain behind this house. You see, this property here adjoins that of Kendell Mountain School, of which I am president of the board of directors. Now the problem is that someone has been cutting down our trees without any authority to do this."

She stopped the slow rocking motion of her chair. "Oh, so that's the reason for your visit, and all the time I was thinking you were a congenial neighbor," then without any hesitation asked, "Would you like some coffee, Mr. Russell? I've just perked a fresh pot." Without waiting for his answer she rose from her chair and started for the kitchen. "It'll only take a minute. Haven't even had my second cup." She kept chattering as she entered the kitchen. "Anyone out and around this early probably hasn't even had their first cup." He heard the cups and saucers rattling. "Cream or sugar, Mr. Russell?"

He rose from the sofa and followed her to the kitchen. "No, just black please."

She set the cup and saucer on a small kitchen table with a red-checkered oilcloth and motioned for Alyn to sit. Then she brought her cup and sat across from him. "You see, Mr. Russell . . ."

"Just call me Alyn."

She smiled and wondered if he had a wife. Such a nice-looking man and well educated, too, she assumed or he would not be connected with the school. And look at those broad shoulders and the arm muscles. Yes. He could not have escaped some woman's grasp. She took a sip of coffee, set the cup back on its saucer, and continued. "I'm a writer and this secluded place is perfect for me without all the interruptions of the city life. Here I won't have the distractions that I had there. Here there is peace and quiet and a sense of independence—a feeling you don't have in a city. There are always so many demands there." She paused here, taking another sip and looked at him over the cup, noting that he was waiting intently for her explanation. "As for the trees, I thought there was a marker of some sort across the property or ribbons tied around trees to show the property line. Mr. Pratt showed the property lines to me on his deed but I didn't walk it off. I'll have to go up there some-time; maybe you will show it to me, as well as the ledge with the beautiful view." She flashed a flirty smile. "In a few years I intend to make this into a resort, after all this economy situation is put to rest."

A resort! His mind felt like exploding. He'd not have the woods invaded with vacationing folks frolicking all about invading their land. "But what about our trees that were removed?" he asked. "I counted what would amount to a truckload."

"Oh, yes . . . the trees." She shifted in her chair and looked at Alyn, dead serious concern written on his handsome face. "It's like this, you see, when I started to pay the man who did my moving, Mr. Connor, he's the owner of the moving company . . . well, he asked me if I'd pay him with a few hardwoods since he noticed that the forest back there was so dense."

Alyn felt a red color burn up the back of his neck, and he nearly strangled on a mouthful of coffee as he drained the cup. "Wasn't his truck too small for so many trees?"

"Oh, he didn't have the equipment that day or the manpower or time, of course, so he came back with a large log-hauling truck and two more men."

To this, Alyn raised his eyebrows. "I hope you haven't told them they could get more." He leaned forward in his chair and looked

Linda in the face. "I don't believe you fully understand, Miss Linda. That was stealing."

"Stealing! But I didn't know they were going so far up the mountain. Jake Pratt had made a beaten path-like road up from the west side. He said he had a good fishing place up there, and they went up that way. I thought they were just going to get a few."

"The school could hold you liable, you know, unless you'd like to make a nice donation to compensate for their lost trees. And we'd certainly hate to see a resort come in here. I'm afraid you'd have a fight on your hands. Before you start chopping down trees for that, we'll have to consult with a lawyer for legal agreements." She stared at him with a dazed expression, a stricken look in her pretty eyes that were wide now, and her mouth open in surprise. Alyn rose to leave, took a few steps, then stopped by the kitchen door and said, "Just tell me one thing, Miss McKnight, just what do you expect to gain from all this?"

She made no remonstrance about his leaving and without a conscious thought, shrugged her shoulders and said, "Money, Mr. Russell, money—cold, hard cash." Her wide eyes were as dark as clouds on a stormy day. She looked up at him, a smoldering intensity in her eyes and lips set in a straight line.

"Miss McKnight, our school board meets on next Monday night. You'll be hearing from us." He had reached the front porch, stopped, turned, and said, "I thank you for the coffee." He went down the steps feeling that she was an avaricious person for she'd as much as admitted it.

TWO DAYS AFTER ALYN'S VISIT WITH LINDA MCKNIGHT, Cynthia and little Johnny went in the old Ford (that used to belong to Jim Abernathy) down to ask Tissy if she and baby Bess would ride down the mountain with them to also pay a visit to the new neighbor. The visit, Cynthia explained, was merely to do a neighborly deed and invite her to church. Alyn had attached straps on the backseat to hook around the basket and hold Johnny securely in place.

Now Tissy, holding her baby on her lap, was riding beside Cynthia. They were very curious to meet the young woman who would give up her city life to hide away like a hermit in the mountains. "I'd say she's rather touched in the head," Tissy said, smiling.

"She has ulterior motives, Alyn told me, and he's all up in the air about it."

"Yes, he was talking with Bob about the future resort she is planning. My stars! That's all we need! The very idea!"

"You know something like that would cost a fortune to build and make successful. And besides, how could she do something like that by herself? There's a skunk in the woodpile, if you ask me." The car hit a pothole that Cynthia had not seen as she turned her head to look at Tissy, and the car bounced through it. "Oops, sorry. Guess that knocked the wheels out of line."

Tissy turned to her and suggested, "Maybe we can get her to talking and learn more by listening. If she has any plans, you know she'd like to brag about her project."

"Yes, that's right, and we'd best not say too much about how we feel and just let the school board settle it, or they could think that we've overstepped our bounds."

So it was agreed that this would just be a neighborly visit and now driving into the yard, they saw Linda McKnight across the road in the pasture riding around on her horse. She spied the car immediately, threw up a hand in greeting, rode on to the barn where she removed the saddle, turned the horse back into the pasture, and walked saucily out the gate and across the road, looking sleek and sexy in her riding attire. The two visitors looked at one another with raised eyebrows. "Hummh?" they said at the same time and laughed.

"Good morning, ladies," she said as she approached the car. "Would you get out and visit, or are you only looking for directions, which I can't be of much help, I'm afraid."

"Yes, thank you . . . to the first question," Cynthia answered. "We came to make your acquaintance and welcome you to Kendell Mountain."

Linda McKnight stooped to look into the car and upon seeing the two babies said, "Oh, twins, how adorable, and who is the lucky mother?"

"No, they're only cousins," Cynthia explained, "one for each of us."

"Well, do get out and come in the house. I'm Linda McKnight."

"I'm Cynthia Russell, and this is Tissy Russell."

"Oh?" Linda looked confused. "Which one is Alyn's wife?"

Before she answered that she was Alyn's wife, Cynthia thought to herself, "This woman is very bold to be on a first-name basis with my husband when she'd only met him once."

They were led up the steps and into the living room, making nice comments on all the improvements she'd done to the house. Linda reveled in their obvious interest and led them throughout the house, pointing out all that had been done.

"You must have been in the decorating business," Cynthia commented, "or else you have a natural gift for decorating."

Satisfied with the admiration, Linda smiled and answered that she had worked for an advertising agency but had two books published and now desired to continue with her writing.

"I see," was Cynthia's answer, and Tissy asked if the books would be suitable for their school library.

"Hardly," Linda answered and gave no further explanation about the story line. She offered them coffee after they were all seated in the living room and she had poked and cooed at the babies on their mother's laps, saying that Johnny had his dad's beautiful brown eyes.

"You must be a very observant person," Cynthia said, feeling aggravated with her hostess, and was told that she had to be observant if she were to describe characters in books, but the statement was still unsettling.

When Linda excused herself to get the coffee, her visitors gave each other glances that told the other without words that this young woman had started off on the wrong foot with them. They made small strained conversation while sipping the coffee. Then Tissy explained that her husband was pastor of the Kendell Mountain Baptist Church and that they wanted to invite Linda McKnight to come to church service there. They would be happy to have her attend anytime. She commented that church was of no great interest to her but promised to come soon for a visit.

Chapter Twenty-nine

LITTLE BEAR HAD BEEN ABSOLUTELY CORRECT FOR IT poured rain most of the night. Cleo put a wash tub under the leak in the kitchen, complaining that Troy should have repaired the roof last fall. Little Bear needed to get the cow milked, so between showers, he went and got the milk bucket and brought it out to the barn. Before the rain had started he had led the cow inside to her stall, knowing she would have to be milked this morning. Her gentle lowing wakened him early from his bed of straw.

It was then that he discovered the cat standing by an empty pan begging to be fed. It came to him, rubbed back and forth across his legs, meowing. He smiled, stooped over, and picked up the cat, noticing that she was a new mother. "*E tsi* [mother] *we sa* [cat]," he said, rubbing her fur. She was white with a large black spot on her back and black-tipped ears. "*U nv di* [milk]?" He set the cat down gently and saw a jar lid nearby on the floor which he picked up and rubbed clean. Then he walked over to the cow where she was chewing on hay. She turned her head to look at him, then looked disinterested as he squirted some milk into the lid. Evidently Troy did this all the time, and the cat understood what was being done for her because she was right there when he set the lid of milk on the ground before her. She lapped hungrily. She looked up at Little Bear, her eyes asking for more. He obliged, then took the towel from the nail where he'd hung it at the stall door with the bucket, wiped his hands, and sat down on a stool to do the milking, the cat lying on the floor beside him. He spoke softly to her with some Cherokee words, some English; she cared not which and purred with satisfaction, her litter safely hidden nearby.

The bad tooth had stopped aching. In fact, he did not know when it let up; sometime during the night perhaps, he was thinking as he milked. He had rested and felt better, but how long would it last? Not

179

only had the tooth ached terribly, but every bone in his body. Now rested and the aches and pains having subsided, he felt an urgency for the girl and himself to move on. It was evident that they could not leave until the rain stopped and Mr. Garfield was over his chest and head cold. If the rain stopped, they could walk on but would he be able to go much farther? And if it rained again, the baby could not be exposed to that. They'd have to wait it out. He hoped there was enough food in the house to eat and that the old woman would be a little nicer.

After a breakfast of grits and buttered biscuits doused with sorghum syrup, Sassy washed the dishes, put them away, and scrubbed the kitchen floor on her knees with a brush. Then she was given the task of peeling potatoes to go in a pot of soup for dinner. Cleo was about to assign another task when Sassy said she would have to wash some diapers in the washtub out on the back porch. Knowing this was a grave necessity, the woman relented. When Sassy had hung the diapers on a line draped behind the cookstove, she hurried to feed Moses, who'd already let out wails to be fed again. Cleo had gone to set Troy's bed chamber on the back porch for Little Bear to take out to the outhouse after he had finished churning.

Sassy could hear Mr. Garfield coughing and hoped he would stay in his bed and not expose the rest of them to his illness. "Oh, whut a life!" she breathed as she sat down in the rocker and offered her breast to the eager baby. "Li'l man, ah thinks it about time fer you tu start eatin' some oatmeal an' grits. You'r a-gittin' tu be a mighty big boy." She rubbed her hand across his hair and started singing softly.

Cleo heard her from the thin wall between them where she sat in the living room with her knitting. She decided that the girl was not so bad; at least she tended to the youngun and willingly did the jobs that had been doled out to her without grumbling. Maybe the girl had fallen on to hard times. But, how did she get hooked up with the carnival and that old Indian man? "Well, maybe that's it!" she thought all of a sudden. "Yes . . . maybe they are running away! I wonder if some folks are looking for them?" On and on Cleo thought on this as she knitted and rocked.

She had put another concoction on Troy's chest and had given him some white liquor with a pinch of sugar that she had heated over the fire. This was the only thing that Troy didn't complain about, and it quieted his cough. The more the woman studied the girl, the more she seemed to understand her. "She is a right pretty li'l thang. I know she's shore a lotta hep around here." It would not take much to get used to all that being waited on. All at once, she nearly jumped out of her chair when there came a loud noise from the kitchen. Little Bear had dropped a supply of wood behind the cookstove then gone back out with the door banging on its hinges. "Sakes alive! Just like a man. They're all alike no matter what color, but that one could rightly use a bath." With this in mind, she decided she'd give him some soap and a towel and tell him to take the wash tub out to the barn and have a wash. She found herself thinking that it was like having a family again and maybe she could find it in her heart to be nicer. Without realizing it, the knitting was turning into a baby shawl. She may even offer to hold the little tyke. "Just think, Bubba may have one by now, off somewhere that only God knows where. I just hope that girl he took off with has learned a little gumption. She certainly had a long way to go! Anybody could look at her and see the type she is."

Rain continued for another week. By that time every room had been scrubbed clean, clothes washed, dried behind the stove, and ironed. Sassy washed and plaitted Little Bear's long hair. Little Bear brought the kittens inside to be admired while Mama Cat meowed for them on the porch.

And now, Troy's cold was gone although the cough lingered on. During the rain, he and Little Bear ("Chief" he was now calling him), went out to the barn, cleaned up, straightened up, and sat down. They propped chairs against a wall and had long talks after a checker game that the old Indian loved to learn and play. He never tired of playing. During these sessions, Troy learned all about Kendell Mountain—how the Chief came about living there, the cave, and all the mountain's inhabitants. And he, too, never tired of hearing this story; he now felt as though he personally knew everyone there. Chief told him how the carnival had taken them away and now they were trying to get back home. Troy felt like shedding tears for Sassy and now, like his Indian friend, felt an urgency to get her home to her people.

It was now a June morning, two weeks to the day that Troy had brought the strange trio home with him. All in the Garfield household knew that time was drawing near for the houseguests' departure. Cleo, feeling completely reconciled to the idea of other people living with them, was having reservations about letting them go. She had become attached to the baby and even felt a closeness to the baby's mother. During the rain of the previous week, the woman and the girl sat in the living room on the sofa, heads together, as Cleo meticulously showed Sassy how to knit a shawl while Moses lay on a pallet, inspecting his hands that were held in the air above his face.

"You catch on fast," Cleo told Sassy.

"I like tu learn new things," she replied, pleased with herself and the compliment. "It's actually beginning to look nice. My mama will be proud o' me." Then she looked over at Cleo and added, "That is, maybe she will be after she gets over being mad at me for leaving like I did."

"Why did you leave in the first place, child? And goodness gracious, you are still just a child." She said emphatically the word "are."

"Well, I was lied to by that carnival man, and I believed every word he said but he sure was a low-down-dirty liar. You see, I have always wanted to be a singer."

"Yes," Cleo butted in, "I could understand that. I've heard you singing to the baby and you do have a nice voice."

"That man, his name's Tony, and he's the baby's father. He told me he'd make me a star, but it didn't happen, and he knew I wouldn't become a star singing in his side show."

"So you ran away with them, but . . . what about the old Indian?"

"Oh, Ma'am! Tony had his strong-armed men kidnap thu Chief! He made lots of money on him by selling some worthless stuff in a bottle and telling that Chief had made the Miracle Cure himself. People bought gobs of it."

"I see. That is a dirty shame, but where did he find the Indian?"

Then Sassy laid her knitting on her lap and told Cleo all about Little Bear and his cave on the mountain and how he'd gone with the wagon load of kids and Adam to the carnival. She told about Miss Joyce and her husband, Anson, building the school, about the terrible fire that took their lives, and how Alyn Russell now owned the orchard and the big fine house. And, of course, she named each member of her own family.

Cleo sat mesmerized, knowing that the girl was telling the absolute truth for no one in their right mind could make up this tale! At once, she felt compelled to help her and was sorry that she had been so mean to her in the beginning.

"We'll take you to the bus tomorrow and when we get into Laurel, we will have to telephone Mr. Russell so he can let your folks know where you are and that you and Chief are on your way home."

"Oh, no, Miz Garfield! I won't do that! I just want to go in and be there myself. I want to walk in and say how sorry that I am for being so foolish and not say it on a telephone. Besides, I've never talked on a telephone in my whole life, and I don't know if they have put one in the big house. The school must have one, but it must be terribly expensive to call somebody so far away as that! I need to save my money for the trip."

Cleo felt a sadness already that she, too, would miss the girl and now was wishing that they could stay. The swelling in Little Bear's jaw had nearly gone down from where Cleo had pulled out his rotten tooth with pliers when it started aching again. It was just a hull and came out easily. She told him that the rest of them needed to come out, too. And also, Troy's cough was better. His wife had insisted that he stay in out of the dampness, but today, by mid-morning, the sun came out brightly, announcing a beautiful spring day. There were flowers popping open around the Garfield's front yard, giving evidence of Cleo's previous hard work.

She stooped over and picked up the baby and then sat down in the rocking chair. "I'll certainly miss this little one. He's a good baby. Never cries much. He brings back a lot of memories of when my boy was a baby; seems like only a few years ago. You'd better enjoy him while you can because it won't be long 'til this here 'un 'll be all growed up."

Sassy had grown tired of the knitting and laid it on her lap. Looking at Cleo with interest about her son, she asked, "What's your boy's name, Miz Garfield?"

"We named him Troy Alfred after his pa, but we jes' always called him 'Bubba,' even 'til he left home." She studied for a few seconds and her gaze looked as though she were many years back in time. "He ain't really a boy; your youngun never grows up to you, ya'know? Tomorrow's his birthday . . . forty-two years old, he is. He never married; never found anybody around here he'd have . . . 'til that 'Miss No-Account' come along and he high-tailed it off with her." A tear trickled down her cheek, and she reached up to brush it away.

"Well, he had a good home and good parents no matter what age, and I'd bet you most any amount of money he'll be back home sometime. Did you ever pray about him coming back, Miz Garfield?"

The woman looked at Sassy, startled. "Did I ever pray? Lord have mercy, child, there ain't never a day gone past without us a-praying for Bubba tu come home."

"Reverend Russell, he's Misser Alyn's uncle, he said one time in a sermon that God answers prayers in his own time and not on our time table and that we hafta jes' keep on a-prayin'. I reckon God gets tired of hearing our asking after awhile."

"I know all that, but it is still so lonesome without him around tu do for and he did work hard in thu field with his pa. Have you noticed what is next to the wall in your bedroom with a quilt covering on top?" Cleo asked, changing the subject. She did not want to be sad the rest of the day from thinking about Bubba.

"No'm, I haven't lifted thu quilt tu see, but I put my things on top. I guess it is a chest of some kind." Now her curiosity was aroused; it never took much to pique her curiosity.

"Come and let me show you," Cleo said as she rose from the chair with the sleeping baby in her arms and laid him back on the pallet. Sassy jumped up with alacrity, her heart aflutter, knowing the surprise would be something she would like very much. "It was boughten for me secondhand when I was younger'n you," Cleo told her with a satisfied smile as she pulled the cover off the piano.

Sassy's face broke out into a wide smile, her fingers brushing over the keys lightly when Cleo raised the lid. "Oh! How I wish I could play one of these." She turned to the woman and asked her to please play a tune.

"Well, it's been a long, long time since I've even played anything a'tall. I uster play at church some when I was a girl and that's been a long time ago." She pulled the stool out away from the piano and sat down. It was an old dark colored upright with a round stool that could be adjusted to the right height. She slowly played a few chords, not a song, just chords all across the keyboard.

"Oh, oh," Sassy breathed in amazement. "Please, Miz Garfield, will you show me how to do that?"

"Really, girl . . . I don't even think I could; it's something you feel and you just do it."

"You mean you don't even haffa use a songbook?"

"No, I reckon not. I just play what comes out of my head, but I do have a sister-in-law who is a piano teacher and she plays both ways—with music and without. We'll go by there tomorrow and she can show you some things about it. Do you have a piano at home?"

"No, but I could use the one at the school. Miz Fullman used to teach piano there, but she is old and has quit teaching now. Maybe she would teach me at her home, and I could practice at thu school. I'll haffa ax, I mean 'ask' her. I jes' know I could learn."

Troy came in from the back door followed by Little Bear, their presence announced by the slamming of the screen door. "Here they come, girl. Let's be getting a bite o'dinner on thu table." Cleo closed the lid and stood. Together they spread the quilt back on top of the piano. "I hope them black-eyed peas has not cooked plum dry. With our talking, I forgot about 'em. I'll go put thu cornbread in thu oven, and you can set thu table."

That afternoon they all busied around with the usual jobs, and after supper that evening, Troy announced that they'd set off for Laurel bright and early tomorrow morning. A Greyhound bus left out each day at six o'clock heading to Meridian where they could board a train to Birmingham. They'd spend the day doing some shopping, and he'd also like to stop by his brother's to let him meet Chief.

LAUREL WAS A SIMPLE VILLAGE; A LINE OF UNPAINTED cottages that were the homes of country folk who kept their dirt yards swept clean and who sat on their porches exchanging talk with their neighbors. Smoke curled from chimneys, evidence of dinners being cooked early on stoves that heated up kitchens and made beads of perspiration on faces of the cooks. A few dingy white picket fences held honeysuckle and morning glory vines; hollyhocks, standing tall and straight, gazed over the fences like children that had been told not to leave the yard. From porches heads raised and conversations ceased as curious eyes followed the strange group riding in Troy Garfield's wagon. People would gossip and conjecture as to who the strangers with the Garfields might be. Someone said they were seen passing Tate Johnson's house in the wagon with Troy over two weeks ago, and Tate told Ely Gordon, "My wife and younguns seen 'em when they went by and Troy called out to 'em."

Troy's mules rambled slowly past the row of houses, a whiteboard church, and the grocery store, where the proprietor stood in the doorway talking with a customer out front and threw up a hand to the Garfields. Troy raised a finger as a way of recognition to someone propped against a porch post, who flicked a cigarette out on the dirt road and called out "Howdy," when they passed. Troy called out "Woah," in front of Laurel Feed and Seed, climbed down, wrapped the harness straps around a post, and said to Cleo, "I'll just go in and check on thu bus, but you come on in, Sassy, to get your tickets. Let Ma hold thu little 'un." She handed Moses to Cleo, saying, "I thought we were going to a bus station."

"This here is the bus station," Troy answered, giving Sassy a helping hand down from the wagon as she murmured that Laurel was not as big as Union Gap.

Inside, they were told that the bus would leave promptly at six and even though they'd bought the tickets early, they must be there on time or it would leave without them. After some discussion, Troy and Cleo decided it would be best if they spent the night there with Troy's brother and his wife because it would put them so late in getting home. The chickens would need to be fed and the cow milked, so he asked Ely if Tate happened to come in to tell him to please go over and do that for him. Even the Evanses on up the road from him would do, whichever happened to come in the store. "Be obliged to," Ely told him. Then Troy and Sassy went out, with Sassy carefully placing her change and the tickets in her bag.

She looked nice today after having washed her hair and put on the outfit that had been washed and ironed. The dress she'd worn to do the daily housework was one of Cleo's old ones that the woman could no longer wear after she had put on some extra pounds, and Sassy was happy to give it back to her. The wagon now rolled past a movie show, and Sassy longed to see what was playing, at the same time wishing she could stop there.

"That place is a den of sin," Cleo said knitting her eyes together and pursing her mouth. "Them movie stars are all sinners." This statement startled the girl in the back of the wagon. She had enjoyed going with Aunt Nellie and saw nothing wrong in what they had seen. She decided to let the subject drop or Cleo would know that she had been to a show before.

Little Bear was propped against a box with a pillow to his aching back. Sassy sat on an old quilt beside him. She placed a hand on his shoulder and said, "Chief, at last we are on our way home." Then her matter-of-fact voice gave way to excitement, and she squealed with delight. "Aren't you excited, Chief? You haven't said a word for a long time. Just think! In another day we'll be on the mountain."

These magic words were like music in the wind to him, and he smiled and nodded his old head sagely. "Chief not have strength to walk up mountain."

"Oh, come on now! Of course you will. Everyone will help you. We'll all go to the cave with you and someone will come each day to bring you food and whatever you need." Her arm went around his shoulder and she thought about how she had come to love the old man. Then she thought that if she had not run away with the carnival and the men had kidnapped Little Bear, none of them would ever have seen him again or known what had become of him.

"Eyes go dim. No hunt. Maybe Chief live at school."

"It might be better if you do. They would look after you real good and remember, Mr. Alyn said he is gonna get you some eyeglasses and then you will see much better." She patted his shoulder with her left hand and laid her head on the other shoulder. No one had ever done that before, and now he, too, felt love for the girl as though she were his own daughter—the family he'd never had.

Chapter Thirty

THEY MADE THE STOPS THAT TROY INTENDED TO MAKE, AND then he guided the mules toward Edward Garfield's house. His brother and his sister-in-law lived at the northwest edge of town, the opposite direction from where they had come in to Laurel.

Little Bear wet a finger on his tongue, held the finger up in the air and announced, *"dv ga na ni."*

"Speak English words, Chief," Sassy told him. "What did that gibberish mean?" she questioned.

"Rain," he answered simply.

"Rain?" Troy asked. "With not a cloud in sight anywhere in the sky?"

"Don't doubt him," Cleo said. "The last time he said 'rain,' it did just that for days and days."

"Well, I'm just glad we are here before it starts or we'd get soaking wet," Sassy added.

The wagon bumped along, soon reaching the long, narrow road up to Edward and Mary Sue's house which sat back off the main road, fenced off from a pasture full of cows down front. Edward recognized the two people on the wagon seat and wondered with curiosity who the two were riding in the back. He threw up a hand, then went inside to tell Mary Sue that there'd be company for dinner. She was stirring a pot of soup and commented that she'd just throw in some more potatoes and tomatoes.

Sassy enjoyed the visit in the cozy house with Troy's friendly relatives. After dinner, Little Bear went outside and sat propped against a tree and slept. Of course, Sassy was compelled by their hosts' questions to tell the story of how she came to know the Indian and why they were traveling together. Mary Sue's eyes widened when she heard about their being with the carnival and tossed a glance at her sister-in-law across from her. Cleo pressed her lips together in disgust and nodded.

After the women had washed the dinner dishes and the men had gone to gaze over the fence at Edward's cows, Sassy excitedly asked Mary Sue if she would please play her piano. Moses was fed, diapered, and laid down to sleep when the piano lesson began, with Sassy relishing every minute of it. Before long, Cleo stated that she was tired of all the racket and went out to the wagon to fetch her knitting.

AT A QUARTER AFTER FIVE, TROY'S MULES PULLED THE WAGON up in front of the feed and seed store/bus station where several people had already gathered to wait for the arrival of the bus to Meridian. With the people having bought their tickets in advance and the seats sold out, the store was closed. There was an old lady who was holding the hand of a small boy, a man and woman, two young girls, and a lone man.

The lone man stared with interest at the Indian and the young girl holding a baby. The gaze of his dark, beady eyes intensified as Sassy felt his stare and glanced the other way when their eyes met. He saw that she was uncomfortable and grinned with satisfaction. She changed her position by switching the baby to her shoulder, patting his bottom, and tickling him under the chin. In a minute or two she glanced back at the scroungy-looking man in overalls and an unkempt shirt. Dirty, stringy brown hair hung limply below a beat-up hat. He was still staring, but this time his look seemed more of a warning. It was all she could do to keep from looking at him another time, but when Troy announced that he saw the bus coming in the distance, she had forgotten the man and started gathering her belongings. Cleo had given her an old suitcase that held everything, except the bag she needed to take some baby items from often. The shawl and the knitting she'd started with Cleo's help was in the suitcase.

Little Bear slid off the wagon from the back and held out his arms for the baby as Troy came to the back, took the suitcase, and helped Sassy down. She came around to Cleo's side, giving her a big hug and bidding her good-bye, promising to write just as soon as she got home.

"Thank you for everything, Miz Garfield. I don't know what would've become of us if you and Mr. Garfield hadn't a helped us, and I'll never forget you, and you jes' keep on a-praying for Bubba." She saw a tear run down the woman's cheek as she held the baby up for her to kiss good-bye.

The bus pulled up and nosed against the front of the building right beside where Sassy and Little Bear were standing, making them first in line to board. The rest of the passengers fell in behind them. The doors opened and the driver stepped off, saying in a loud voice, "Step back, folks. Step back and let 'em get off. Move right along, please," he told the people who were getting off as he helped them down the steps. Sassy stood waiting with their tickets in her hand.

The last person off the bus was a nice-looking man who was smiling as though he was happy to arrive in Laurel, and just as he stepped down Sassy heard a peal of shrill laughter and the words, "Bubba!" coming from Cleo, waiting in the wagon. She scrambled down without any help and ran to her son, again calling his name and exploding with laughter, throwing herself into his open arms. Troy already had his handkerchief out of his pocket wiping his eyes and blowing his nose. "Sassy!" Cleo exclaimed, waving her arms, "Sassy! Look! It's Bubba!"

The girl threw up an arm and blew her a kiss as the driver helped her up the steps, followed by Little Bear. Someone leaving had vacated the seat right behind the driver so Sassy plopped down in it with Moses, motioning for Little Bear to sit beside her. The driver had ticketed her suitcase and kept it to place in the compartment under the bus. Troy's wagon pulled away with all of its occupants waving to the girl who was waving back at them. Sassy drew a long breath of delight, telling Little Bear that this was actually happening; they were on the way home at last!

The driver was placing suitcases under the bus when the scroungy-looking man stopped right beside Sassy demanding indignantly, "You, girl! You an' that blasted Injun git on to thu back of thu bus wher ya'll belong! Hear me, or are you deaf or somethin'?"

Sassy gave the man a cold glare and replied as loudly as he had to her, "I'll have you know I have as much right to sit anywhere I take a notion to. I am French, and is this the way you treat foreigners?"

"Yeah, French . . . you ain't no more French 'n I am. What's your name?"

"My name is Belle LaMont, that's who I am."

"Let's hear you say something in French, Miss Smarty." He placed his hands on his hips with assurance that she would fail his test.

"Va te faire cuire un oeuf!" she answered with the words that Miss Lola had taught her to use in case someone else confronted her. Lola had learned a few choice words from a Frenchman she knew. These were not nice words, but at the time he thought it would be funny to teach them to her. Then Sassy came along saying she was French. "Someone might doubt you, girl, so you learn these words to tell them."

"That don't cut no ice. I still know what you are," the man said loudly right in her face. "You just made that up!"

The bus driver hopped quickly inside. "Hey, you! What's going on here?" Everyone was gawking and consulting one another.

"Ah tolt 'em tu git tu thu back wher thu likes of them belong." Then facing toward all the passengers, the man yelled, "Folks, are we gonna stand fer this!"

Little Bear had no idea what the man was talking about, but he knew this character was up to no good. "Leave girl alone," he said softly.

"You know who you're talking to, old man?" He leaned over in his face and looked at the old man with a cold ruthless gaze. "You ain't no better'n her and ya'll are gonna set in thu back and I'm setting here, that's a fact."

At this point, several passengers left their seats and moved back for fear they would be caught up in the ruckus. He then reached over and grabbed the belt holding up Little Bear's pants. Sassy turned sideways with her feet out in the aisle so the Chief would not fall against the baby. In doing this, her feet struck the man on an ankle. He yelled and slapped the girl hard across the cheek with a stinging blow that left a red imprint. Little Bear gave the angered man a shove, and he fell across the aisle into the lap of a big, heavy woman. "Get off me, you monster!" she screamed. He struggled to his feet, lunging at the Indian, giving him blows with his fist.

Little Bear staggered and fell to the floor. He looked up in astonishment at his enemy. His dimming eyes saw a soldier standing over him with his hands on his hips. "Man, mean soldier," he said, fear clearly showing on his wrinkled face as he tried to scramble to his feet. Somewhere way off in his head he heard Sassy calling for him to stop as he crawled toward the open door; the arrogant man laughing loudly. He was a big, rough-looking character with an ugly scar on one cheek.

The driver closed the door just as Little Bear was nearly there. Too late, the driver had stood intending to help the old man, but Scar Face got to him first and threw him a blow that sent Little Bear against a metal corner of the platform that supported the driver's seat. He lay still and silent where he fell with the man standing over him, fists curled, and his face full of anger and hatred. Just then, the driver, standing behind the attacker, opened the door, tapped him on the shoulder, and when he turned, gave him a swift shove that sent him sprawling down the steps and out the open door to the ground. All the passengers clapped and cheered as the door closed. A passenger helped the driver move Little Bear back into his seat, and the bus took off with the attacker pounding on its doors, using foul language at the driver and swearing that he'd get him fired.

Little Bear's head was swimming, and he reached a hand up, rubbing the knot that had risen on his forehead.

"Ma'am," the heroic driver said, "when we reach Meridian, you'd best have a doctor look at the old man. A hard blow like that could be serious and cause repercussions."

The small crossroad towns became fewer and farther apart, all deserted. Even through the darkness the countryside was made known by the wet, damp smell blowing in through the half-opened window beside Sassy. There had been little traffic on the road as the bus roared on through the darkness. Sassy stopped thinking of actually being at home; now her thoughts were only of this present night, which was suspended alone in time.

Little Bear slept, but the baby was fussy and restless. Sassy took out his bottle of milk from the bag between her feet on the floor, knowing that this would satisfy him for a while, and maybe he would sleep. She hummed softly as she usually did when he nursed, and she hoped it would not disturb others around her. Her mind hopped from one thought to another like a bird in a tree trying to decide on which limb to build its nest. It was very kind of Miz Garfield's sister-in-law to give her a teething ring and two small baby bottles (one for water, the other for milk), saying they belonged to her grandbaby and had been left there only a day or so ago. She even filled them with the milk and water before they left for the bus station.

Now, Sassy was thinking of the knot on Chief's forehead and wishing she had some ice to hold on it. Once, when she'd fallen and bumped her head, her mama had held ice to the place and a knot never did come up. "Dear Lord," she whispered to herself, "I've got so much tu learn about raising this little boy. I didn't know Mama and Pap were so smart."

The driver pulled over to a filling station where a man was standing beside a suitcase flagging the bus to stop. There was only one seat left—the one that would have belonged to the man who had been kicked off earlier. He fumbled in his pockets for his money and then with a thumb, the driver pointed toward the back and waited for the new passenger to be seated before he took off again.

About two miles on up the highway, another stop was made in front of a small grocery store where a woman stood anxiously waiving. As the bus pulled up, Tim Taylor, the driver (so a nameplate up over his head revealed), opened his window and told the lady that no seats were available. "Hey, driver," a man two seats behind Sassy spoke out, "I want to get off in another mile. Could I sit on the steps and let'er have my seat?" This arrangement was agreed upon, and they pulled away with another passenger.

"At this rate we'll never get there," Sassy was thinking when the bus took off belching fumes. She looked over at Little Bear, who still had not stirred. He'd pulled his hat down over his face. "At least he's able to sleep," Sassy told the baby. "And your bottle's empty so you go to sleep, too, and don't wet your didee yet." She placed him on her shoulder, patting his back. He burped with milk running out his mouth and down her back. She wiped it with the extra diaper she was holding.

After the passenger was let off, the driver began to talk to Sassy, seated directly behind him. "Where you folks headed to, Ma'am? Ya'll staying in Meridian?"

"No, Sir. We're gonna get a train to Atlanta."

Curiously, Tim Taylor asked, "Who's the Indian?"

"He's family," Sassy answered.

"I heard you tell the redneck character that you're French."

"Well, we're all sorta mixed up."

He let her explanation go at that except for saying that we're all mixed one way or another and that his family had come to America from Germany. "When we get in to the bus station in Meridian, Ma'am, I'll go in to the office with you and make out a report on the old man's accident . . ."

"Twern't no accident," she interrupted.

"I know, but we'll have to report the incident and then we'll call over to the train station about their schedule to Atlanta. I'm afraid it will be tomorrow sometime before a passenger train will be going out, but it will go to Birmingham and you'd have to change trains there going to Atlanta."

"Oh, my goodness!" the girl worried out loud.

"Or," Tim continued, "you could take a bus from Meridian on to Birmingham."

"I just want thu quickest way. You see, we have to take a train from Atlanta to north Georgia."

"Why not take a bus from Atlanta?"

"No, sir, thu bus don't go through where we live a way up in thu mountains."

"Well, don't you worry; we'll work it out some way. You need to get your uncle there to a doctor as soon as possible."

"However you can help me, I'll be much obliged. I'd get us lost for sure if it were left up tu me. We've been trying tu get home for a long time."

"Couldn't we telephone your people?"

"No, sir. Can't do that." She offered no further explanation.

True to Little Bear's prediction, the sprinkles on the windshield now got harder, and Tim reached over and turned on the wipers. Their steady rhythm soon lulled Sassy to sleep. It was a fitful sleep filled with dreams of trains and busses racing one another up the highway. Bubba Garfield was driving the bus; his dad was driving the train, and they were waving to one another out the windows as all the passengers were yelling for them to stop. When Sassy opened her eyes, Tim Taylor was trying to get control of the sliding bus as it turned sideways across the road after a tire blew out. They were in the middle of nowhere. When the bus came to a stop, Tim hit the steering wheel in complete disgust with his fists.

"Just sit calmly, folks. I'm going to steer us straight over to the side and if someone will hold my umbrella and several men will give me a hand, we'll have this here bus rolling in no time."

It took them exactly two hours. The men got back on the bus all wet in spite of three umbrellas. It was now eleven o'clock. Without the incidents, they should have been in Meridian no later than nine. The driver was the last to get back on, and as he was closing his umbrella, Sassy stood to her feet holding Moses and the noise that emanated from her turned into a piercing scream. She had reached over and shook Little Bear; his hat slid to the floor, revealing his mouth gaping open and his eyes rolled back above the lids.

"He won't wake up!" She shook him again. "Chief! Wake up! We're on our way home, Chief. Don't do this to me. Don't you die on me!" Tears ran down her face as she hugged Moses closely, and he woke up squalling loudly.

A lady came up behind her and gently took the baby. In desperation, the girl sat down and fell across Little Bear sobbing her heart out. "Oh, Chief. What'll I do now? We were going home. Just one more day." Her plans had gone strangely awry. "That's all we needed," she said wistfully. "One more day." Her thoughts galloped like her Grandpa Adam's old gray mule when he got in sight of the barn. She knew she had to pull herself together and think more clearly about what she needed to do. She felt as though she'd come to a brick wall. It would do no good to panic, for it would only make her ill and then who would look after Moses? Still, she was in a state of dark depression, trying to accept the truth of what had happened. Her face was drawn with anxiety. She decided that life is full of injustices, and she wished that she were a child again, free of decisions and worries.

ALYN RUSSELL AND HIS WIFE AND BABY WERE SITTING ON the porch enjoying the late afternoon sun. Cynthia, holding little Johnny on her lap, commented that she was so happy that spring was here at last. They had been walking out among the apple trees, with the blossoms now giving way to greenery. Alyn had always loved each stage—from blossom to greenery and tiny apples appearing and soon maturing to large red ones. He loved the harvest season as well; the hustle and bustle of picking and crating and getting the apples down to Union Gap and on the freight train.

The baby, gurgling and laughing, looked up at his mother as he finished the bottle she was holding. She placed the empty bottle on the floor beside her chair and held Johnny up on her shoulder and patted his back. Alyn had been saying that he was pleased Tad had taken to gardening so well. He seemed eager to learn everything from Grandpa Adam, who was teaching him about bee-keeping as well. The old man was finding it hard to keep up with all his work; his steps were becoming slower. Even though he'd always taken great pride in all his work, not wanting to be bothered with anyone helping, he now was happy to have Tad pitch in like he'd been doing lately.

When they first had come on the porch and sat down, Alyn was talking to Cynthia about the new apple trees that had been planted where old dead ones were taken out as well as the business in general. She needed to learn, too. It could fall on her shoulders one of these days to carry on. "For crying out loud, Alyn," she said, "Let's not sound pessimistic! Not on this beautiful day. Why, I learn more about this place every day whether you realize it or not." He smiled at her, admiring her beauty, thinking how much more beautiful she was sitting there holding their child. Life had become complete for him. He could not ask for more.

"Selma has offered to tend to Johnny for me when school starts back in the fall," Cynthia said.

Alyn only grunted and commented that he'd rather she would stay at home. "I don't have to do any housework and I won't grow stale," she replied with determination. "And besides, you know the school needs me."

He stood and gazed down the road. "I hear Doc's car coming up the hill. I'll wave 'im down, and maybe he'll come sit for a spell."

Doc saw them on the porch and stopped the car out front on the road, leaning his head out the window and calling for Alyn to meet him out on the driveway. "Must have our mail," Alyn said as he rose.

"Well, I'll just go in and change the baby's diaper and get him a sweater," Cynthia replied.

Alyn came out the front door, past Cynthia's flower garden and under the arch where her cherished climbing rose was showing off a display of buds. As he leaned over with hands on the open window ledge, he noticed that Doc's face was solemn. "Hi, Doc, what's up? Get out awhile. We're just enjoying the porch and the fine weather."

"I have some good news and some bad news, Al."

"Oh? Well, let's have the good news first," Alyn grinned.

"The good news is that Sassy is walking up the road."

"What? You don't mean it!" He knew that Doc did mean it, and that was good news indeed. "Then why didn't you give her a ride?"

"I did from town to halfway up the road, but she insisted on walking the rest of the way up. Here's her bundles and suitcase." He pointed to the things on the backseat and the floorboard. "She's carrying another bundle that she wouldn't turn loose."

"Oh, my, let me go tell Cynthia and get Sassy's folks on the porch. I'll tell them that we need to talk to them so the surprise won't be spoiled." As he turned away, he turned back, asking if she knew anything about Little Bear.

Doc cleared his throat, still not smiling and replied, "That's the bad news. You see, well . . . the Chief is coming home tomorrow in a box on the freight train."

"Oh, no!" Alyn was stunned and hurt. "No wonder you didn't seem happy that Sassy is coming. I'm sad to hear that, but the old guy must be ancient. I'm surprised he has lasted this long. Just wish we could've found him years ago. Did Sassy just show up or were you contacted about the Chief? And where did they come from?"

"Mississippi. The station in Meridian called me down at my office at six o'clock this morning saying they had put Sassy on the train to Birmingham. She transferred in Atlanta to our line. They wanted to see if it was alright to bill the shipment to us. Of course, I told 'em by all means, and Chief will arrive tomorrow at two o'clock."

"I'll go tell Cynthee and gather the folks on the porch. Thanks, Doc. We'll settle up with you." Alyn opened the door to the backseat and took out Sassy's things, leaving them on the walkway for the time being.

"No settling to do, Al. He was our friend, too, you know." Doc drove away as Alyn hurried to tell Cynthia.

Lizzie Mae sat dozing beside the cookstove with a dishpan of potatoes about to slide off her lap. Selma came through the kitchen door just in time to grab the pan; the paring knife had already dropped from Lizzie Mae's hand and lay on the floor. Selma shook her head and spoke in a low tone to Ophelia, who was stirring stew in a cast-iron pot. "Some day dat woman jes' gonna sleep her way on into heaben." Just then Alyn rushed in behind Selma and took her by the arm. "Come, Selma, and you, too, Ophelia." He helped Lizzie Mae to her feet. "Come on, Mama Liz. We need you, too." The women could tell by his smile that everything would be alright, whatever it was, and they followed along behind him as he guided the old woman along through the long hallway to the library and out on the porch where Cynthia was waiting.

"Whut choo wone us outten here fer, Misser Alyn baby?" Lizzie Mae asked, using the pet name she'd given him when he was just a child.

"You'll see in just a few minutes, Mama Liz. Here, you sit right here, and we're gonna watch down thu road. In another minute or two we should have a surprise." Adam and Tad, who were hoeing in the flower garden with Joe running around close by, heard the women's chatter on the porch and came around front to see what was going on. They never stopped their work to sit and chat. Shortly, Joe said in his high, shrill voice as he pointed, "Lookie, somebody's a-coming up thu road." Everyone looked over the rail, seeing a lone figure carrying a load. Now, the late afternoon sun cast shadows and silhouetted the form of a woman with a baby on her hip.

Cynthia was standing, holding her own baby in her arms. "Look, Selma! Look! Who do you think that could be?"

Then it came to her at once and she shrieked "Sassy!" so loudly that the girl trudging up the hill bearing the load on her hip, stopped, looked up, and then threw up her free hand as a wide smile broke across her face. Jasper and the two hounds bounded across the yard and down the road, with tails wagging, to welcome the girl who was struggling to speed up her pace. Selma was the first off the porch, hurrying as fast as she could; Joe was close behind. Tad saw but waited at the edge of the flower garden to give his wife time to reach the girl. Even from a distance, Selma could see that her daughter was a woman now, the childish look of innocence gone. She was a woman carrying her baby. Before she reached her daughter, Selma could not contain the tears that were flowing freely.

Seeing her mother, it all came together at last for Sassy. She was home at last, and for a brief moment she felt ten years old again. Both their eyes brimmed with tears as they rocked in each other's arms, Moses squeezed between them. "I'm so sorry, Mama," Sassy said now sobbing, her dark lashes wet with tears of remorse. "I'm so sorry for causing you so much grief."

Selma wiped her eyes on the tail of her apron and took the baby from her daughter. "You home now, chile, and all grief has gone . . . an' look at choo," she said to Moses, kissing her grandson for the first time and holding him close. Moses laughed, looking up with his shiny blue eyes (like his mother's) at his grandma. Joe hugged his sister as she told him, "Boy, you sure have grown!"

"You, too," he answered. "What's thu kid's name?"

"His name is Moses William Jackson."

"Dat's too much fer somebody little like him; I'll jes' call 'im 'Mo.' Let me holt 'im, Ma."

"He's heavy, boy. Don you drop 'im. Now be careful." Joe took the baby and held him tightly as they walked on up the road.

Sassy took a deep breath, drawing in the fresh mountain air, feeling the knot in her stomach relax as she exhaled. Sated with the fresh air and the thought of being on Kendell Mountain and with her family at last, she threw her arms heavenward and yelled, "Thank you, Jesus." She did a joyous twirl in the middle of the road, something she had not done in a while.

She saw Ophelia and Tad coming to meet her and waited for them with outstretched arms. Up on the porch she saw Mr. Alyn standing with an arm supporting Mama Liz, and there was Miz Cynthee holding a baby in her arms. Grandpa Adam was in the front yard, leaning on a hoe. Sassy's lips curled in a smile. She looked up into the late afternoon sky and felt that Little Bear was home, too, with the "Great Spirit" and also his parents, Running Wolf and Red Bud. Memories of Tony and the carnival were now stored in the back of her mind, where they would be hard to remember. They were now just like a bad dream.

All was now well on Kendell Mountain.

PART TWO

Chapter Thirty—one

IN THE SEVENTIES, THE COMPUTER AGE WAS A TIME WHEN science fiction came true, a time of spacecrafts and astronauts. It was the time that young boys had read about in comic books and dreamed about as being way out yonder in another century.

A president had resigned when impeachment was evident; and another president was shot to death. Three wars had been fought; the young men just now coming home from Vietnam. People were protesting and rioting; young people were leaving home, living in communes, and earning the name of "hippies" or "flower children," and smoking pot and experimenting with LSD. Indeed, this was a turbulent era.

The town of Union Gap, Georgia, far removed from hippies and riots, was still slow and backward, but they were feeling very modern since electric wires had been strung there about ten or twelve years ago and a few people had put in telephones. The telephones were mainly three-party lines except for the doctor's office, the mayor's office, and the railroad station. Union Gap and Kendell Mountain were places where children learned values. Most of them stayed at home until they became adults, and then the majority chose to remain in the town and raise their families. Over the years, since our story ended in 1930, some of the area people gave birth to more children, but as the law of God would have it, some went on to meet their Maker. Those who met that fate will be revealed during the second half of the book.

PENNY RUSSELL WAS DEFINITELY IRRITATED! SHE RAISED HER eyes heavenward, blew out her breath in disgust, and plopped down

201

on the stool beside the telephone table. "You know full well, Rusty, that I told you more than a week ago I could not go." The girl pursed her lips into an unhappy pucker. She let the irate young man rave on before explaining again for what seemed like the hundredth time just why she could not go to the school party with him. School had just opened for the fall term and this would be the first football game and dance afterwards. How could he possibly go without his girlfriend there, he had asked and went on by saying that it was very selfish of her to knock him out of going . . . didn't she have any feelings for him at all? It was expected of her to go.

"What? Expected! Well, what am I to do while you are playing in the band and I have no one to dance with? Am I suppose to be a wall-flower or what?"

"No. I don't expect you to be a wallflower or anything of the kind, Penny. If anyone will be a wallflower, it will be me if you go away and I don't have a partner."

"Rusty Morgan! How could you be a wallflower and play in the band like you do with all those silly girls falling all over you all the time? We only get to dance when you get to take a break, which isn't often. I'm the one who has to stand around and talk to the nerds who couldn't get dates."

"Now, you sound jealous, sweetheart. Does that mean you love me just a little bit?" he crooned into the speaker.

"Well, of course I do, silly, but they just make me sick to my stomach, like I want to throw up or something awful. But you certainly seem to enjoy it!"

"What about David Adamson?"

"I told you this afternoon that Al was just trying to get you riled up. I thought you understood that."

The two teenagers had been arguing at length into the telephone until the girl's mother called from the kitchen. "Penny, darling, please get off the phone. Your father may have tried to call a dozen times."

"Yes, Mother, just a second please." And she turned again to hear what Rusty had asked. "I told you before, Russell Morgan," using his given name, showing that she was furious with him, "that we are going to my grandfather's on Kendell Mountain and we'll be there all weekend." Then as an afterthought she added, "Why don't you come along with us? We'll ride horses and have lots of fun."

He explained that the band could not do without their lead trumpet player so it would be out of the question. He'd just have to mope around after the party as an extra, or go on home or something.

It certainly would spoil everything for him. The voice called again from the kitchen. "I'm coming, Mom. Listen, Rusty, I've got to hang up now or I'm going to catch you-know-what if my dad has tried to call. I'll give you a ring when we get home, okay?"

There was a short pause, then she whispered softly into a hand cupped around the receiver. "I can't talk now, Rusty . . . oh, of course I do, but I can't say it out loud. Gotta go now," then she hung up and trooped off into the kitchen that smelled of pound cake and baked chicken. Just then the back screen door banged shut, followed by the banging of the wooden door, and the tornado entering was promptly sent back outside to scrape his shoes before walking upon the spotlessly scrubbed tile floor.

"Al, I have told you a thousand and one times to please not track mud into the house. Where in the world did you pick that up anyway?" Beth Russell frowned, stirring a pan of giblet gravy.

"Oh, I cut across the empty lot," he answered as he swiped a cupcake from the cabinet and crammed nearly all of it into his mouth.

"Gross, Al," his sister said. "Mom, why does it take boys so long to grow up?" She was taking out plates to set the table, her regular mealtime job. Continuing her disgust with younger brothers, she said, "Do you know what Al had the gall to do to me today! And right in front of everybody! I mean practically the whole school even."

"Aw, dry up," Al said, wiping his mouth with the back of a hand. "I just wanted to ride 'ole Pucker Lips' a little. He gets ruffled up at nothing." It did please the mischievous brother to aggravate his sister and her boyfriend.

"Now, Al, why do you torment your sister so? It does look to me like the two of you could get along as well as your little brother and sister. They don't quarrel and carry on so." Beth carried the steaming pan to the sink to rest it there while she took a hot pad from a drawer and placed it and the pan on the counter.

"But they're just babies, Mom . . . do you know what he did! He told Cathy Reece right in front of Joan Davies and Rusty that I said I like David Adamson a lot and want him to ask me for a date! Now, that's what I call uncouth!" She placed the plates on the cabinet and turning to her brother told him, "A fine brother you are, and since I can't go to the party, Rusty is doubly mad at me." She stood close to Al, looked him square in the face, placed one hand on her hip, and shook a finger at him. He brushed the finger aside.

"Oh, I'm sure, Penny, darling, that Rusty did not take Al seriously and . . . oh, there's the phone. Al, be a dear and get it." When he started through the swinging door from the kitchen, she called after him, "And if it's you father, I'll be right there." Al banged into the door as he exited with another cupcake in his mouth. Wiping her hands on a towel, Beth turned to her daughter and told her to go in the den and tell the younger children to turn off the television and go wash their hands for supper.

This had been a very trying day for Beth Russell. Now she was glad she had finished getting the supper ready and could soon sit down in a relaxed atmosphere with her husband and children, hearing each of them give an account of their exciting day. It was exciting for Susan because it had been her first day in the first grade. Peter was happy to see some of his old friends now in the second grade with him. They both had related some of the exciting day to their mother in the car on the way home, but the excitement would spill over into supper time when their father would be there, telling about landing the largest contract ever for his company. This would be the construction of a large office park in Atlanta for the New York tycoon, B. J. Thrower. This B. J., Charles told Beth, had the foresight to realize that Atlanta was due for a building growth and had offered him an opportunity to get on the bandwagon! And already they were on a first-name basis. Now, three days of her husband's time had been demanded to go over the contract, and he was due back home this afternoon. The family was going to Kendell Mountain tomorrow—Saturday. Charles had left his car in the airport parking lot when he left for New York City and now was due home any minute. He promised he'd call from the airport.

Beth wished they lived on Kendell Mountain so the children could go to school there. However, she would not consent for the older brother and sister to stay up there with their grandfather, Uncle John, and Aunt Teresa, in order to go to the school where she and Charles both had attended and graduated. She would not split up her family. It was enough that their father was away from home so much of the time! They had a beautiful ranch-style home on the affluent north side of Atlanta. Beth was active in her church and did not lack for friends, and she would be active also in P.T.A. this year. She also had been taking oil painting lessons, but all this did not suffice for her husband's only interest—his business. She felt as though the business were another woman, or what it would be like if there were another woman. He was a workaholic. One would think they needed the money desperately. She could not think of anything they actually needed; in fact, she'd told him only recently that it might do the family good if they lacked for something. The children needed to learn some priorities and values. Whatever they wanted, they got. When Charles was seldom there for them, their grandfather and uncle lavished their attention on them; their Aunt Teresa doted on them.

The Atlanta Russells spent every Christmas on Kendell Mountain, and during summer vacation from school, the children took turns there on the mountain. Teresa said she'd rather have them one at a time in order to devote all her time to one. She could spoil them to the hilt that way, and they loved their aunt dearly. She was the youngest of Alyn Russell's three children, and her entire life was wrapped up in all her family and the running of the house. Teresa, so like her lovely mother Cynthia, was the apple of her father's eye. Johnny was five and Charles three when Teresa was born. Her brothers drug her around until she could keep up with them and hold her own, then they learned early that girls were not as soft and weak as they seemed on the surface. Pretty, yes, but inside, Teresa had a definite determination that the two boys had rather leave alone. She never knew her mother. No one ever realized how she daydreamed of her, gazing at a photograph of her holding little Charles in one arm and Johnny by the hand but never seeing a photograph of her holding baby Teresa. She could only feel that her mother had been a real person when she visited the cemetery at the overlook. As a child, she felt that her birth was the cause of her mother's death. When she was a teenager, she asked Doc about it. When he saw her concern, he was more than anxious to set her straight. No! Her birth was not the cause of Cynthia's death, but it was an infection that set up during the ninth month. Her temperature had risen to a dangerous level. She went into convulsions and labor started. She could not be saved. Doc assured the girl that she should not ruin her life worrying about something that was not her fault.

The house still held its dignity and status as it had back in Joyce Abernathy's time. Teresa Russell had not known that time. She loved to hear her father tell about it, and when the children visited, they always asked questions and were thrilled to be carried back into a time that seemed so foreign, so unreal, like stories from a book. They never tired of these stories and knew that what their grandfather was telling was the absolute truth.

John Russell had never married. He occupied the upstairs floor of the Knollwood house to himself. After he returned from the Korean War, he entered medical school at the urging of Dr. David Harris. Neither of his boys had the interest—a great disappointment to both their father and their mother, Kate. For ten years now, John had been the local doctor. Doc and Kate were happy to be free at last to travel and to visit their boys' families without the worry of their leaving someone back on Kendell Mountain who needed their attention.

"Mom," Al called from the next room, "It's long distance; Dad says to hurry." Al asked his father a number of questions about New York until Beth got there and took the phone from him.

"Charles, what is the matter? I thought you'd be home from the airport by now. Where are you?" He recognized the worry by the tone of her voice.

"I'm still in New York, honey. Listen, I'll be tied up here 'til tomorrow night. You and the children go ahead and drive up to Knollwood in the morning, and I'll come on up Sunday morning."

"Oh, Charles, you'll miss Teresa's birthday party Saturday night. And it's just too much driving up for a few hours when we'll just come on home after dinner Sunday. I know she'll have several folks invited." Her disappointment was evident. "Well, nothing else has gone my way today so this is just par for the . . ."

"What went wrong, Beth?" he broke in.

"Oh, just to begin with the washer broke down and I had to go to the laundry mat and then was late picking up the kids from school and forgot to get your sister's birthday gift." Before she could say another word, Charles broke in saying he had to run along and for her to drive carefully around those mountain roads. She looked into the phone when he hung up as though she could actually see him there. This was so typical of Charles, always in a hurry. She pictured him in her mind as a runaway truck on a downhill grade. Someday there would be an inevitable collision. Two years ago a slight heart attack had slowed him down but only for a short while.

Yes, they would go ahead tomorrow for she'd not disappoint the children by backing out. This was not the first time Charles had changed his plans at the last minute. Beth shoved the door open a little harder than was necessary when she returned to the kitchen. "And I put an extra effort on this dinner, too," she told herself in disgust. "Drat that B. J. Thrower guy. I don't like him, and I've never even met the man."

As she was putting the finishing touches on supper before the children came in, Beth was thinking about her conversation that same morning with Connie Roland, wife of Charles's business partner, Gregg Roland. The two women had met in an aisle at the grocery store and sat down afterwards for a cup of coffee at a little shop next door. Connie, a talker by nature, went on about their husbands' different personalities—how likable and outgoing Charles was and how quiet Gregg was, to the point of almost being secretive. "Maybe when he comes home at night he'd rather forget the day's problems," Beth had suggested to her friend. Gregg kept to the office, ruling it and the personnel with an iron hand. He kept the job foremen on the run with one hand and the other hand on the checkbook. This was not Charles's territory. Being an expert salesman, he brought the jobs in and carried them to completion.

Now in the kitchen stooping to take bread from the oven, it was Beth who decided that Charles was the silent one. Yes, he actually was distant to her tonight. "Come to think of it," she thought, "his coolness has not been only lately." They seemed to have lost close contact with one another in the past few months . . . since he started on the Thrower contract and was away so much. She knew his father would be disappointed because of Charles's absence. Like herself, Papa Russell had grown accustomed to these absences but refused to show his disappointment outwardly. His daughter-in-law was very dear to him and the children, his very heart.

Then, there was John—good, faithful, homebody John. There was something fundamentally different about the two brothers, as though they were not brothers at all, even made from a different mold. Beth had always been fond of John, his warm and gentle smile and so sure of himself, as any doctor should be. She knew that at any time she could depend on John if ever there was a need.

Her train of thought was abruptly interrupted by two arguing teenagers, the clatter of two younger children, and the yapping of Sally the dog as she skidded across the kitchen tile floor to her feeding bowl. Peter came through the door, took out a sack of dog food from a cabinet, and poured some into the dish. "Come on, girl, here's your supper," he said as he rubbed his hand across the little dog's back and then returned the sack to the place he had taken it. He got down on all fours and talked to Sally as she ate, looking at Peter while she chewed and wagged a thank-you.

"Peter, wash your hands and come to the table now," Beth called from the dining room where the others were already seated. The boy dashed some water on his hands, gave them a cursory wipe on his pants, and was in his chair in a matter of seconds.

"Mom, are we going to eat before Dad gets home?" Susan questioned.

"Yes we are. Your father won't be home tonight so we are going up to the mountain tomorrow and have a nice birthday party for your Aunt Teresa."

"Oh, goodie, I want to ride on Uncle John's horse," Peter exclaimed.

"And Penny wants to see Preston Thompson," Al said in a singsongy voice, rolling his eyes, "And I'm going to tell 'ole Pucker Lips.'" He laughed with satisfaction in getting a rise out of his sister.

"Mommm," the girl pleaded, "Please tell Al to be quiet."

"Now, let's all be quiet," Beth demanded. "We'll ask God to bless our meal, and I think I need to ask Him also to help my children be kinder to one another."

And so their excitement peaked while they packed a few things and got ready for bed early. Beth called out in the darkness before anyone had gone to sleep, "Everyone, don't let me forget to pick up Aunt Teresa's present in the morning." She had been secretly working all year on a portrait of the children's grandmother, Cynthia Russell. She'd taken the photograph from a dresser in Teresa's room and was hoping that it would not be missed until she could replace it. The painting turned out beautifully, like a carbon copy of the photo, and she had left it at a shop to be framed. So Beth was as excited as the children about going up to north Georgia.

Chapter Thirty—two

BETH'S GREEN CHEVY STATION WAGON STEAMED INTO THE only gas station in Union Gap. "Stay in the car, kids," she told her crew as she stepped out to talk with Earl Fletcher, who was coming out from the garage side of the station, wiping his hands with a dirty rag. He recognized Beth Russell at once. "Morning, Miss Beth, when's that husband of your'n gonna buy you a decent automobile? 'Peers like this is the way you make a grand entrance to our town ever time you come," he grinned, revealing a bad tooth in front. Beth returned his greeting with a smile and a nod. "You're right about that, Earl, and on both counts, too."

Al got out of the car and came around to have a look under the hood when Earl lifted it, gazing underneath. Shaking his head, Earl told Beth, "Must be another radiator leak. Sure hope the radiator won't have to be replaced this time because I don't have one on hand and being Saturday, we couldn't get one delivered here 'til Monday, maybe even Tuesday."

"Oh, dear," Beth worried, "what will I do? Charles may not get to come this weekend."

"Whoopee!" Al exclaimed. "We get out of school on Monday!" His statement was ignored.

Then, Susan yelled out the window and pointed, "Look! There's Uncle John getting in his car!" Each of the children called to him as they piled out of the station wagon. John had emerged from his office, and when he saw the group he got back out of the car, threw up a hand, and then came striding across the road swinging his black bag in the other hand. John was tall like his dad, with dark hair like his mother's side of the family and a quick smile and winsome personality. Today, he was dressed in a dark suit and tie, his usual neat attire when seeing patients, except for the white jacket that was worn in the office.

Upon reaching the children, who had met him halfway, he hugged the girls and shook hands with the boys. "Well, here's my favorite family in all the world," and turning to Al, said, "Man! You're tall as your mother!" Then he punched Al in the stomach and tousled Peter's blonde hair.

"But, I've grown, too, Uncle John," Susan said tugging at his coat. "Look at me and guess what?" she asked, not waiting for him to guess, "I'm in the first grade now."

John handed his bag to Al and stooped to pick up the little girl. "Yes, my pet, you certainly are getting to be a big girl like your beautiful sister." Penny beamed when he said this. Sally added to the excitement by barking loudly to be let out of the car. Peter opened the door and took the squirming little dog in his arms. "Don't let her down, son, she may run in front of a car," John told him. Then turning to look at Beth on the opposite side where she was talking with Earl, he said, "Now let me see what we have here. This dragon seems to be letting off some steam." He put Susan down and walked around the station wagon, the kids following behind.

"'Lo, Dr. John," the station proprietor said, a wad of tobacco evident in one cheek. "Picked up any more nails lately?"

"Nope. I've steered clear of those roofers up at the school." Then turning to his sister-in-law, said, "Hi, Beth, good to see you. Charles not along again?"

"Hello, John," she smiled. "No, he's out of town, up north in fact." She breathed a sigh of relief now that John was there for Earl had said nothing to buoy her spirits about what could be wrong with the "gas-eating dinosaur." The last time she came, it had stopped running and John said then that Charles should have better sense than to allow his family to ride around in "that thing," especially around these winding mountain roads. In her heart Beth agreed, knowing that nothing would be gained by placing all the blame on Charles. She could have just stayed at home until he could come with them in his new Buick. At any rate, she'd always placed all the confidence in the world in dependable, faithful John, whom her children adored.

"I'm sure you realize, Miss Beth," Earl ventured hesitantly, "uh . . . that you'll be without a vehicle this weekend. The parts place is already closed and it'll be Monday 'fore they'll open up again."

"But," Beth frowned, giving him a quizzical look, "how do you know it needs a new radiator when you haven't even had it on the rack? Dr. John examines people before he operates."

John gave a cackle. "Smart woman here, Earl," he said still grinning.

Earl turned his head, spat tobacco juice, and replied, "Well, now, I figger I've seen this here happen enough to know what it'll be and you see," he turned pointing to a vehicle up on the rack where he'd been working, "I'm tied up with that one right now. That there's Reverend Sellers's car and he's having fits for me to hurry up with his 'un."

John knew that there would be no hurrying Earl come either hell or high water. "Don't fret, Beth; we'll figure something out. Let's put your luggage in my car, and we'll check back with Earl later."

"Dr. John, if you're on your way to make a call I'd be happy to take Miss Beth and her kids on up to Knollwood," Earl said.

"No, but thanks, Earl. I was just on my way home." Turning to the children he told them to get their luggage and put it in his trunk. Al handed him his black bag with John calling to them that their mother gets the front seat.

"Oh, John, I have to get a package out of the station wagon myself. One of the kids may drop and damage it."

"I'll get it for you, Beth."

"That's okay," she said. "I'll just get it," not that she thought he would damage the precious painting that took her months to do, but it would be like John to hand it to one of the kids and they'd throw a suitcase in on top of it. Last year, John had asked her to do a painting of the valley as seen from his upstairs bedroom window. She had photographed the scene and painted it exactly, and now it hung in his office where all the patients could admire the beauty and feel the soothing effect it had on viewers. Teresa's painting, although now wrapped with brown paper, did not conceal what it was. She'd found just the right ornate gold frame that set off the portrait and now she was anxious to see her sister-in-law's face when the paper was removed.

Dear Teresa. This painting would be a lifelong treasure for her—a painting of her mother whom she never knew. She treasured any belonging that had been hers and now the little photo in a frame that sat on her dresser was missing! She searched underneath the dresser for it in case it had been carelessly knocked off by one of the women in dusting, and she had searched under the bed. Maybe Papa had taken it, but when questioned, said that he had not seen it either. It was such a mystery!

Teresa taught ninth grade English at Kendell Mountain School. Since graduation from college, she'd plied herself, her whole being, in fact, to the school, the students, and the studies. And last year, when

Alyn Russell resigned as president of the school's board of directors, the board as a whole elected his daughter, Teresa Ann Russell, to fill his empty chair. During each trip to Knollwood, Beth was hounded to allow Penny and Al to attend the school. Last trip, Teresa felt that Beth had wavered somewhat because of her pleas. Time and time again she'd commented to Teresa that if the two were allowed to stay there, it would seem as though she were abandoning her children for others to raise.

John's Buick took the mountain curves smoothly on the road that had been paved only ten years ago. The young people in the backseat were busy petting the dog and talking among themselves. Susan, sitting between John and Beth, felt drowsy. She leaned against her mother and fell asleep quickly.

"Everybody okay up at the place?" Beth asked.

"Yes, all's well, that is, except for Papa's fuming and fussing because I brought him a walking cane and insisted on his using it. His leg gave way recently outside, and he had a nasty fall."

"Oh, I'm so sorry to hear that. Is he alright now?"

"He got over it and luckily there were no broken bones, but there could be another time, you know. His old injury has weakened the leg so he needs to take every precaution. Stubborn old cuss. He just doesn't want to admit that he's getting older."

"Now, who would want to admit that!" Beth smiled.

"What about Charles? What's up with him lately? I suppose he's still running around like something crazy."

"You've got that right. If he does get up here tomorrow, I hope you can talk a little sense into him, too. With that spell with his heart before, I fear that all the stress he allows himself to be under will take its toll someday. But, he's so proud, you know. And I'm happy for him that his business is growing. He's just going to have to depend on Gregg to do more or get someone else to help him out. This trip he's taken to New York to finalize a big job may prove to be too much for their small company."

John thought about this for a few seconds, then looked over at Beth, and feeling concern for his brother, said, "That's Charles for you. He could bring the business in, if the company can produce." There was a short silence, then he added, "Maybe we'll have a chance to talk. I'd like to listen to his ticker, too."

"Oh, I wish you would, John."

"Look, Mama, look!" Penny exclaimed. "They've finished the new building. Oh! Isn't it big, and it has large columns on the front. It's so beautiful!"

The new addition had been given the name of "Russell Hall" in honor of the longtime president of the board, Alyn Russell. It would house classrooms on the second floor, a gymnasium on the first floor, and a cafeteria and kitchen in the basement. The giant building was brick, and across the front at the top were these words in Gothic letters, "OUR AIM—GOD'S WORD AND INTELLECT."

John slowed the car and turned onto the school's driveway that circled in front of the massive building. Charles's family had visited Knollwood all along during the past summer as the construction was going on. They had not been up, however, since it was brought to completion and now school had actually started. Out front on benches sat some boarding students; some studying, others milling around talking and laughing with friends. Some threw up a hand in recognition of Dr. John, as he was affectionately called. New students had not as yet had an occasion to come to know the school's doctor.

"This is a dream come true for Papa," John said. "He said that he wished Aunt Joyce and Uncle Anson could see how their hard work turned out." Beth was quiet as she tried to imagine what all they went through in getting the school built. The solid buildings still stood, just as they had been erected in 1913, the wood cut from trees on the land here. Papa said that he and our mother sat for hours each day watching the carpenters work."

Penny broke the silence by saying, "Mom, I believe I would like to go here for my last two years of high school where my grandparents went."

"Do they have a football team?" Al asked. They had only played softball among other schools up until now.

"Yes, Al, they'll have one this year and are hard at work practicing. The good thing is that they must have above average grades in order to play."

"Well, if Pen comes here, 'Ole Pucker Lips' will want to come, too, and play in the band."

"Now, Al," Beth turned and told him, "don't start up again with your sister." Penny had already jabbed him in the stomach with an elbow.

John drove on around the paved drive back to the road, turning left past the marble monument with the name "Kendell Mountain School" engraved on it, and on up the steep road toward Knollwood Orchards. It was a brilliant autumn day with a warm sun that caused the oaks and maples to try to outdo one another with their orange and yellow colors. Even the dark green pines seemed to glow when sunrays peeped through the dense forest and fell on them. Black-eyed Susans and golden rods nodded in a slight breeze as little blue gentians struggled to make a showing underneath Queen Anne's lace that swayed as the car passed.

Susan sat up, rubbed her eyes, and looked out to see if they were nearly there. "Mama, the little flowers are pretty along here. I want to pick some for Aunt Teresa," Susan said, her dark brown eyes pleading. Before Beth could object, the little girl touched her uncle on the arm asking, "Could we, Uncle John, just a small little bunch?"

"How could anyone refuse such a little sweetheart as you? I know Aunt Teresa would be so pleased on her birthday to be given such a beautiful bunch of flowers." He pulled to the side and switched off the engine.

"John! I'm certainly glad she didn't ask for the moon!" Beth laughed and just as the back door flew open, she told Peter to hook the leash on Sally's collar. The two boys decided to walk the rest of the way with Sally, who was very obliged for the romp. "You guys stay on the road and don't go into the woods," their mother demanded when they darted off. Soon, with a large bouquet in Susan's hand, the car overtook and passed the boys and dog. John honked the horn without even asking if they'd rather get back in. Everyone waved. "Let 'em walk. It will do 'em good," Penny said, glad for the silence from her pesky brother, Al.

John turned to Beth and told her that the place would be buzzing with the apple harvest. "Dad is always right in the middle of it, you know. He shipped out most of them last month, but this year the newer trees have outdone themselves. He's provided the school's Home Economics Department with an abundance for the girls to learn preserving and so on. The school will make good on having them sell apple pies, tarts, and bread, too. The stores in town sell a lot of them."

"Maybe I need to go to that school, also," Beth smiled down at her little daughter. "What do you think about that Susie-Q?"

"Oh, Mommy! You're too old to go to school," she laughed.

"How would you like to have Mom in your class, Susan?" Penny asked, causing her little sister to giggle.

"She's too big and wouldn't fit in my desk!" Susan answered with giggles intensifying.

Papa Russell was on the back porch washing his hands at the sink there when his son's automobile drove into the yard with his daughter-in-law and two granddaughters. The questioning look on his face was very profound and instead of smiling and throwing up a hand, he stood there wiping with the towel, anxiously waiting for an explanation about the boys and also her automobile. Susan jumped out in a hurry still holding the flowers in her hand. "Papa! Papa!" she called loudly, holding the flowers up high. "Look! These are for Aunt Teresa because it's her birthday. Aren't they pretty!" She scrambled up the steps and into her grandfather's waiting outstretched arms, her golden curls bobbing down her back as he picked her up and smothered her with kisses. "You know what, Papa?" And before he could ask "what," she continued on. "The boys are walking up the road with Sally and we stopped at the school and saw the big, big new building, and you know what else?"

He laughed at her childish excitement. "What else, my pet? What else?" His dark brown eyes, like her own, twinkled as he waited for more of her chatter.

"Well, Penny says she wants to come up here to school next year, and Mama said she'd better come, too, so she can learn to make all the good stuff that the girls learn to cook. But she can't do that 'cause she has to take Peter and me to school."

"You don't have to worry about your mother going to school because we don't let old ladies do that." He gave Susan another peck on the cheek. Then she whispered in his ear, "You'd better not let her hear you call her an old lady."

"No. I won't because she'd spank us both." Still holding Susan, Papa Russell walked to the steps as Beth, Penny, and John were coming up. Papa put the little girl down and hugged his other granddaughter, kissed her, and then hugged his daughter-in-law. "So, that scoundrel, Charles didn't make it again . . . and did your car die on you at last?" Susan followed her sister inside calling for Aunt Teresa.

"Yes, on both counts, Papa. John rescued us down at Earl's place where my station wagon could have been mistaken for a steam engine, and Charles got detained on a trip. You can deal with him; he doesn't listen to me."

"Doesn't listen to anyone . . . never has. Come on in. Teresa's in there somewhere. Sounds like they've already found her. She'll be happy to see you and the kids, and I'm glad you came on anyway, Beth."

"We all would have been disappointed if you had not come," John said, meaning every word he said.

Beth loved this old house. Everytime she came it became dearer to her. This was where her children's grandfather was raised . . . not the same house, but one just like the other house that had burned down. Papa Russell said that it seemed the same to him. He and the children's grandmother had tried to duplicate it in every way.

"I'll just go back for the luggage, Beth," John told her.

"No, don't; please let the children get it, but if you'd like, please see that they don't touch Teresa's present . . . oh, here they come now. Would you help them, Johnny?" Sometimes she called him by the name that he was called when they went to school together. She and Charles and Johnny were a trio.

"We'll put your things upstairs, and I'll bunk in with Papa," he said going down the steps.

THE NIGHT WAS STILL WITH A QUIET LANGUID BEAUTY. Bullfrogs down at the creek tuned up their drums, and, from the pasture behind the barn, sounds of a cowbell tinkled gently. The evening air, pervaded by the fragrance of a jasmine bush that grew at a corner of the porch, was heavenly as Beth drew in her breath and relaxed completely, letting go of all her hurried daily schedule down in Atlanta. She looked up and saw stars sprayed across the now darkened sky and commented that it would be like heaven to live right here all the time. The others around her could not begin to imagine what she was feeling.

There was a plethora of chairs lined around the porch rail like sparrows on a telephone pole line. After the lovely birthday supper cooked by Selma and served by her daughter-in-law, Beula Mae, the party guests were ushered to the porch for an evening of relaxed conversation. The guests were Cole and Priscilla Lyle, their daughter, Jamie, and her husband, Tim Langston, and their son and daughter Bobby and Martha Jo. Then, of course, there was the family—Papa Russell, Teresa, John, Beth, and her children. Tissy Russell begged off with a cold, and her daughter Bess and husband, Mike Bledsoe, were away for the weekend.

So the group on the porch were enjoying themselves with a hum of desultory conversation. "Too bad Charles isn't here," Cole said. "Haven't seen him lately. You must be working him to death, Beth."

"Afraid not, Cole. He's doing it himself."

"Well, come to think of it," he added, "We haven't seen much of our son and his wife either. Charles and Gregg must be keeping Brad on the run."

"One of these days they'll all wish they'd sat down and enjoyed doing absolutely nothing," Alyn spoke up. "Too bad most folks don't know how to enjoy life 'til they get my age and then it's too late. These aches and pains sure stop creeping up but gather more speed as the years fly by." He reached over and rubbed his leg as he said that. Tim laughed at what Alyn Russell had said, then was told that he, too, would find out one day in the not too distant future.

Jamie changed the subject by asking anyone who might know, "How does Miss Tissy like her little apartment in the new building?" It was Teresa who spoke up saying that she loved it but doubted seriously if she would stay at the school more than another year. She continued on, saying, "But haven't we been blessed over the years to have new ones as well as our very own to step right in when someone was needed to fill a gap."

John spoke up, grinning, "You betcha, like my lovely sister who just might get the job of principal when and if Miss Tissy steps down."

"Now, Johnny," Teresa said in embarrassment. "Don't be talking too quickly. After all, Miss Tissy may not have any intention of stepping down." Teresa carried the marks of confidence accrued from her ten years of teaching. She'd secretly already had aspirations of being principal some day.

"It's true, though. My sister is smart . . . I taught her everything she knows, especially how to make the best mud pies and even how to put a wiggly worm on a hook."

Everyone laughed to hear this coming from John, until Papa Russell broke in saying, "Oh, just let me tell you about the time . . . ."

"Now, Papa, please! Don't you get started," Teresa pleaded. She was saved further embarrassment by Beula Mae poking her dark bushy-haired head out the door announcing, "Joe, he say dee ice cream freezer won' turn no mo. Ever body come git a dish uv it fo' it melts. It all be puddles 'fore ah kin git it out 'chere to ya'll."

"Okay, Beula Mae, and will you please call the children in to get theirs and take it out under the oak tree."

"Yas'um, sho will."

Martha Jo and Bobby, (Jamie and Tim's two), the same age as Beth's two oldest, had been enjoying the company of the visitors. They all had been playing kick the can. Although far below Penny and Al's dignity, here now at Knollwood it was somehow different. Penny was glad that Rusty Morgan was not around to see her playing like a child.

Back on the porch enjoying the peach ice cream, Teresa said with one hand pressed over her heart, "Beth, I'll never stop thanking you for my lovely painting. It will go right over the mantel in the living room. I'd like to have it in my room, but it needs to be where everyone can enjoy it, especially Papa. Besides, I do have my small photo back that 'someone' stole from my dresser." Teresa's delight warmed her father's heart as it always had. So like her mother, Cynthia, he could see her in Beth's painting as well. Beth smiled, feeling a great satisfaction with her first oil portrait as well as satisfaction that the others were so pleased.

Peter, about run down from his activity outside, came on the porch and sat beside Papa Russell, whom he idolized, giving a run-on report of his second grade class, his teacher, and a number of friends he had also known last year in the first grade. The little boy was still baby chubby and cheerful and, as Teresa had said a hundred times or more, "the spitting image of his Papa Russell."

In a few minutes, Susan came in and climbed up on John's lap. It was evident that her eyes were drooping with sleepiness as she rubbed them and yawned. "She'll be out shortly," Beth said just as the sonorous old hall clock struck nine.

Priscilla Lyle glanced at her wristwatch and said, "My, how time does fly when folks are having fun." Then she turned to her husband, Cole, and said, "Babe, we'd better be getting on home."

Cole agreed with, "Yep, I 'spec' so. Time to turn in."

They stood to make their "good-byes" and "ya'll comes" when Alyn held up a halting hand, "Oh, wait. We forgot to mention that in two weeks the Thompsons are having their annual barbecue, and you know the whole neighborhood is expected to be there, as usual. They don't send out any written invitations." He looked toward Beth. "We'll have to work on Charles, you know."

ON SUNDAY MORNING AFTER CHURCH WHEN JOHN'S CAR pulled in the driveway with the family, they saw Charles's Buick beside the shed where Alyn's truck was parked.

"Look! Look!" Susan pointed. "There's Daddy's car!"

Peter echoed his sister, "Daddy's here; Daddy's here!"

"Wonders never cease," Beth said under her breath, yet loud enough for John to notice as she got out of the car.

Chapter Thirty-three

THEY WERE WALKING OUT IN THE ORCHARD AMONG THE trees now divested of their crop. "It does look like Papa would be tired of all this by now and want to retire," Charles told his brother.

"Retire to what?" John answered as he followed behind. "His rocking chair? Most people work a lifetime to buy a mountain home and retire there, but I'd say in Papa's case he's already here. This is like a hobby to him; it keeps 'im busy and going. I think able-bodied people are foolish to sit down and fold their hands. Look at old Doc Harris, for instance . . . he's eighty-seven and kept at the old grind well past retirement age. Now he and Aunt Kate are enjoying life. Papa has no one to travel with him and he says he's seen enough of the world anyway; not to mention that it's all corrupt and 'going to hell in a hand-basket.'" He grinned, thinking of Papa's words, but Charles only looked disgusted at the logical answer he was given. He had hoped that Johnny would agree with him for his own ulterior motives.

Charles Russell, always immaculately groomed, tall like his father, his dark brown hair now streaked with gray, was nobody's fool. He always knew what he wanted and went out to get it. The main problem with Charles was that he was in too big a hurry to get whatever it was he wanted. That was the way it had been when he won Beth from John during high school. John and Beth had not been dating for long when Charles turned on his charms. He usually wanted whatever big brother had. From a pause to collect his thoughts, Charles turned loose of a tree limb and faced John.

"Don't you think it would be wise to put this land to good use?" He spread his hands out to emphasize the territory. His expensive watch and diamond ring sparkled in the sunlight. "It's a shame that these puny apple trees are taking up so much space for such a pittance of a profit!"

John showed his shock that quickly changed to annoyance with his brother. "You're borrowing trouble, you know. There'll be an explosion when you even drop the slightest hint of this to Papa."

Undeterred, Charles went right on. "Don't you see, John, we could make millions here! And that cave," he pointed toward the direction of Little Bear's cave on up the mountain, "would attract thousands of people. We could play up the Indian theme and . . ."

"What in heaven's name are you talking about, boy! Where did you get such a tomfool notion?"

The younger brother paused, collected his thoughts, and then said, "This contact in New York asked me to find some land that could be bought and our firm would be hired to build a resort on it."

"And you want our land? Mine and Teresa's inheritance, as well as yours? You may as well put a gun to Papa's head, Charles! That's the most ludicrous thing I've ever heard in my life, and if you even mention it to Papa, I swear to you I'll . . ."

"You'll do what, John?" He walked closer and punched a finger in John's chest. "What? Tell me what you'll do?"

"This," John answered as he doubled his fist and socked Charles so hard the blow sent him sprawling to the ground. Completely shocked and caught off guard, Charles held his throbbing jaw and looked up at his brother. "Wow! You still punch a mean blow! I thought we'd grown out of our fighting stage a number of years ago. Am I bleeding? I may be in need of a doctor." He got up, dusted his clothes, never offering to return the blow; however, John was not finished with him just yet. He glared at Charles eye-to-eye. "And another thing, little brother, all this out-of-town stuff! Are you playing around?"

Charles ran his hands through his hair and grinned. "Are you still jealous because she married me and not you? . . . not that it's any of your business at all, but since you asked . . . you could call it 'just bringing in business,' you know. The ladies like attention, rich ladies, that is. You should try it sometime, Johnny; might even do you good." He gave a sideways grin. "I'm pretty good at giving out prescriptions, too."

"You'd do this to Beth? And the kids?"

"I'm not hurting them. They have a nice home and good food on the table. Just let me tend to my affairs. Oh, incidentally, I was talking to Mo a while ago, and he's agreed to come work for me."

"Why should he leave Knollwood after all these years? This is the only business he knows; besides, Papa needs him. He's big and strong—in fact, the best worker on the place. What brought this up?"

"Well, he could live down there with Sassy, his mama. She teaches at Brown University, you know. The thing is, since this integration mess, the coloreds are a problem to work with, and we need a forceful colored man to be their foreman."

Moses Jackson, a big man, solid as a rock, as strong and resilient as a horse, possessed a deep commanding voice that held one's attention when he spoke. He would be a good foreman. The men under him would work or be kicked off the job without warning.

"There should be plenty of 'em down there without picking on our man. He'd be lost and helpless."

"That's a laugh! Moses helpless? I well remember the time he beat the tar out of you because you took his steelie marble." Charles had hoped John would agree with him about Moses going to work in Atlanta.

Charles dusted his pants again and laughed as he turned to walk away leaving his older brother mulling over all he'd said. There had always been and would always be a deep chasm dividing the brothers.

IN THE CAR GOING TO ATLANTA ON SUNDAY EVENING, Charles talked on endlessly explaining the rudiments of the job and just what would be expected of Moses. At first he would work under Ned Crawford to learn the ropes and later be given a crew of his own to supervise. "It may take awhile," Charles said, "but you are bright and quick to learn, so just hang in there, get along with the men, pay attention, and do the job right. Our business has no room for sloppiness; there are codes and inspections to be met, but I know you'll catch on pretty quick. Oh, I meant to congratulate you on the nice job you did repairing and adding on another room to Tad and Selma's house."

"Thank you, Charles. I think they like it." He had an inborn ability for building. Moses had done well under the eagle eye of Teresa's tutoring back when she first finished college, and his scores won him the equivalent of a high school diploma. She also coached him to speak properly. With his determination, inherited from his mother, and this opportunity being offered him, he should do well.

"Uh, Mo . . . down there in the presence of the workers you'd best call me 'Mr. Russell.'"

Mo looked at him with a question on his face. "Okay, then, if that's the way it has to be, but they must be uppity folks."

"No . . . well . . . just different from Kendell Mountain people. Oh, you'll see. They just don't like coloreds getting too friendly with the bosses. Like maybe they are trying to butter them up or something like that."

Moses frowned, wondering if he'd decided on this job too quickly. Those people would not understand that he had run the woods with both John and Charles when they were kids—fishing, trapping rabbits, camping in the cave. Why, they were more like brothers to him, and now he has to call him "Mister Russell"!

Charles looked over at Mo and saw him deep in thought. After a few minutes, Mo said, "I'm sure Beula Mae was right in saying she and Scooter would stay on Kendell Mountain until I'm pretty certain this job will work out." The little house they occupied there at Knollwood once belonged to Adam and Lizzie Mae, and Mo's wife loved it there. He'd made various repairs and replacements to the house, and with its solid timber, it would be there for years to come. He had added a room also for eight-year-old Scooter. "Beula Mae's awfully upset," he continued. "This was sprung on her all at once. But another way to look at it, Mama has a nice size house and Beula Mae could do all her housework and cook, too. Mama's got plenty of room for us and some to spare. She rents out the basement apartment so it would be all the same if we rent it from her. Before long, maybe Beula Mae will see it my way."

Charles felt this would be a good opportunity for Mo, and he too hoped Mo's wife would soon agree.

Chapter Thirty-four

THE ROAD FROM UNION GAP THAT LED UP KENDELL Mountain forked where the grade became steeper. To the right, the road led past the school and on to Knollwood, but if one took the left fork they would go by the Thompson's farm. In 1937, Jeremiah Thompson bought this land from Linda McKnight, who had been shunned by Alyn Russell and laughed at when she suggested marriage. She sold out and left the area as quickly as she had once appeared. Now, Jeremiah's son, Jud, owned the land. Jud raised, bred, and sold horses. The original old house had been remodeled and added on to so much that no one would ever know it was at one time so small. A wraparound porch and an upper story had been added to the house as well as the massive family room with a cathedral ceiling and rock fireplace. In this room, Penny and Al Russell were visiting with Preston Thompson.

Penny admired Preston who, in her mind, was much more mature than Rusty Morgan. Preston was home from military school for his first weekend since going back for the new year that had started in August. He had been going there from his freshman year, and since the school was not too far away, he came home often. The two Russell teenagers had come along today with Papa Russell, now out in the barn with Jud Thompson.

"Please come to the barbecue, Penny," tall, lanky Preston urged. "I'll bet your mother will drive you back up Saturday week. It's going to be great fun, and you can help me with the decorations on Saturday morning." He had not mentioned anything about Al coming along as well, probably assuming the whole family would be back.

That would be another Saturday night to turn Rusty down, Penny was thinking. He would be upset with her again. Al thought of this at the same time and grinned, picturing in his mind "Ole Pucker Lips."

"Yeah," Al agreed, "if Mom can't bring us, then we could ride the bus."

"Were you invited, Al?" his sister asked smugly. Preston smiled, turning aside to hide his amusement.

Charles and Beth's family had attended these affairs before, but not last year, for they had made a trip to the Bahamas at that time. The year before that Penny was a skinny thirteen year old with bird-like legs and pigtails, and Preston had not even looked at her twice!

Edna Thompson, Preston's mother, came into the room with a plate of brownies still warm from the oven and a tray of soft drinks, which she set on a low table before the young people. Al's mouth watered as he reached out to be the first to sample one, noting his sister's quick glare but too late to do anything about it with a mouthful. She gasped and felt horrified at her brother's atrocious manners, thinking that Mrs. Thompson may like to retract the invitation for them to attend the barbecue. Edna Thompson, an enthusiastic woman with an infectious laugh, only appreciated Al's appetite. "Your folks may already be planning on coming to the barbecue," Edna said. "Beth certainly enjoyed herself the last time you all came. Your grandfather, John, and Teresa have never missed even one. Mr. Alyn is always here on the Friday night before helping with the cooking." She was walking out of the room as she was adding the last few words, "Hope ya'll can come, Honey."

"Thanks, Mrs. Thompson, I certainly hope we can, too, and these brownies are wonderful."

Al got up, going across the room with the last of the brownie in his mouth. He stood before the massive fireplace gazing up at the deer heads above the mantel. Preston had been sitting on the arm of the couch beside Penny. "We're gonna have a square dance this time, and old Dr. Harris is to be the caller. I suppose he and his wife will have a lot to talk about. They're just back from Europe, you know."

"Yes, they were gone when we came up the last time," Penny answered, turning her head up to Preston so that it made her long hair swing. He looked down on her hair, thinking how shiny and bouncy it was and how he'd like to run his fingers through it.

"My brother and his wife and their little monster are coming next Wednesday from Nashville. Roy's band is coming in on the day of the affair, sometime during the afternoon."

Penny now felt greatly impressed. It sounded as though the Thompsons were going all out for the affair. "I certainly wouldn't want to miss it for the world!" she exclaimed, then took a sip of cola.

The brownies were too sweet for her liking, and she only took one bite to keep from being unmannerly.

Preston had already downed one and finished off his drink. "I'll play some of Roy's records for you," he said as he strode across the room to the record player with Al following behind.

"What kind of music does Roy's band play?" the boy questioned, also feeling impressed that he would get to associate with a real, live Nashville band. He liked the popular music that the school band played rather than country but would not for all the tea in China let his sister know that he admired Rusty Morgan's trumpet playing.

"Country mostly," Preston answered. "His band played and he sang on the Grand Ole Opry show recently."

"Wow! You don't say! That's great, and we'll get to meet 'em."

"Yeah, sure . . . but Roy is just a regular guy, no put-on at all about him. He's just my brother." Preston selected a record, placed it on the player, and turned up the volume. "Come on, Pen, let's dance." He pushed a chair aside and taking her hand, they fell right into step to the slow you-done-me-wrong type slow song. Penny felt flattered getting this attention from an older boy, and the thought crossed her mind that if Rusty knew, he'd be insanely jealous.

"Ole Pucker Lips would be jealous if he could see you now," Al said as he licked the chocolate icing from his fingers. They had a way of catching each other's thoughts. It was uncanny at times.

Al was disgusted and went out to the barn to find Papa and Jud Thompson when Preston asked, "Who was Al talking about, Pen?"

"Oh, just a kid I know who has a crush on me," Penny answered smugly. Al had recognized that his sister was relishing this new attention from Preston Thompson, but he also knew that their father would not like her being attracted to the older boy.

"You turn me on, doll," Preston stooped and whispered in her ear.

She flushed from her cheeks to her ears and purposely made some steps away from him. "Don't talk like that. You embarrass me."

He grinned at her recklessly and was thinking that she was pretty but still just a kid. "You'll be back for the party," he told her with assurance. "I'd like to show you around our place. We have a lake and boats, too, and we could go horseback riding . . . just you and me. Come over on Saturday morning but slip away from Al."

"Won't you be awfully busy getting things ready for the party?" The music had stopped, but he still stood holding her in the dance position.

"Well, after that then. You could come over and help us with the decorations and then we could go."

"Maybe," she said, not wanting him to feel too sure of himself. "I may. We'll see." Then she thought, "This has been Rusty's problem all along. He's always treated me as though he owned me," and she decided it was high time she acted like a woman of her own. No man was going to push her around . . . not Penelope Elizabeth Russell!

Chapter Thirty-five

ON THE MORNING OF THE THOMPSON'S ANNUAL BARBECUE, Tad was sent down with some extra folding tables and chairs and was to inform Preston Thompson that Penny would not arrive until noon. Her father was delayed returning to Atlanta until Saturday morning so they must go to the airport first to pick him up. Why he had not left his Buick at the airport, Beth did not understand; but she was to drive there in his car with the kids and they would leave from there for north Georgia.

Selma also went down to the Thompson's place to assist Mrs. Thompson and her hired woman, Effie, with the baking. The whole Thompson property now buzzed with lively activity. Roy's band had arrived and were setting up in the barn where new sawdust had been scattered. Tad was instructed to drive the truck around to the barn and open out chairs against the walls and place two tables together where the drinks and cakes would be served.

Outside, Preston struggled with a string of lights he was hanging from the veranda along a manicured walkway down to the barbecue pits. "Stop pulling on the cord!" he crossly told his niece, Tammy Jo— cross no doubt because Penny would be late and the six year old had given him too much help this morning. She had tagged behind him all morning deluging him with questions, sticking fast beside him like beggar-lice, and now he had hurt her feelings.

"You just don't like me, Preston," she pouted, her eyes clouding up. He saw a tear run down her cheek and, climbing down, he stooped beside the little girl with long blonde curls, putting an arm solicitously around her shoulders. "I'm sorry, sweetheart, that I was so cross with you. I do like you, in fact, I love you, but I'm much too busy to play this morning. There's a thousand things to be done."

She pulled away from him. "I can't even count that high, and you can't do that much stuff in one day!" she exclaimed and stamped hard on his foot and fled. Preston felt sorry he had hurt his niece's feelings but only shrugged and climbed back up the ladder to finish his light-stringing job. He didn't have time to bother with the kid. Where was her mother anyway? She should be watching out for her. Everytime they visited, she left Tammy Jo to follow after him. "She wouldn't do that this time," he decided in exasperation, "for Penny will get all my attention. LeAnn could stay out of bed and watch out for her preco-cious child. LeAnn was just lazy as all get-out! And I can't see why Roy idolizes her so," he was still thinking. Then, shrugging, Preston said out loud, "Oh, well . . . everybody has different likes," and left it at that.

The large barbecue pit down near the creek was now sending a wonderful aroma into the air, permeating with steaming meat, and it made Preston's stomach growl with hunger. He put away his tools and ladder and followed his nose to the creek. Just as he helped himself to a morsel of tender meat, he spied the two horses and riders cantering along the road to the house. His face broke into a broad grin and then fell as soon as Al's horse pulled alongside Penny's. "Rats! Can't she go anywhere without him?" Preston threw up a hand and called "Hellooo," as he started up the bank from the creek. When they drew near he told Penny, "I thought you'd never get here." Then pointing, he said, "There's your Grandpa and Uncle John and Tad down by the pits with the others."

Al dismounted and handed the reins to Preston, who was eating the last bit of the meat he'd pilfered off the grill, and walked away toward the pit intending to do the same thing Preston had done. "He doesn't know it, but he's heading down there to be put to work, the dummy."

"I'm sure they won't get much work out of him," Penny smiled. "And, just how did you get out of it yourself?" she asked cheerily.

"I'll have you know I've been working all morning stringing lights, among other things, and trying to dodge my brother's kid, Tammy Jo. What took you so long?"

"I didn't know I was supposed to hurry. Besides, it takes a woman awhile to get dressed and do her hair and so on, you know."

"I'm sure you are just as pretty when you crawl out of bed without doing a thing." He looked at Penny with longing eyes, wanting to put his arms around her and plant a long, romantic kiss on her perfectly formed lips. The guys at school were always talking about their conquests, and Preston had made up some juicy tales since he had none to top the ones they told. Penny was a lot younger than the girls his friends talked about, but he could say that she was a couple of years older. She was certainly a lot prettier than the girls in the photos that he was shown.

Preston, a good-looking young man, had impressed Penny more lately than anytime she'd seen him before. He had become so grown-up, so sure of himself, so different from Rusty Morgan, who now seemed like a juvenile to the girl. She felt like a butterfly that had just come from its cocoon, ready to spread wings and fly.

"How about that ride around the place, my fair lady?" he made a theatrical swooping bow. "Looks like we're free of the brat brother for awhile." Penny flashed a white-tooth smile and answered, "Okay, but go down there and whisper to Papa where I'll be. If you tell him out loud, Al will be along."

Preston did as told, came back, and mounted John's horse that Al had ridden, and pulled against the reins. He led up the bank and out across the worn path, through the upper pastureland where a few cows were sleepily grazing. They did not lift their heads until the two passed, then one cow gave a soft low, answered by the bleating of her calf. Penny, on the chestnut-colored mare with a long, full mane, followed close behind. Preston turned every now and then and smiled or made a witty remark. The path divided into two paths. "Jeep road," is all he said. Penny did not know where it led, but right now she felt that she could follow him to the end of the rainbow. "Oh, Rusty," she thought, "you silly adolescent child." Then she pushed him far back into the recesses of her mind where he wouldn't seep out again today. She deliberately turned her head to look straight ahead at Preston and smiled to herself as if to defy Rusty.

"My folks are coming over at six-thirty. I must get back in time to get myself dressed for the party and return with them."

"You would be the belle of any ball just as you are," he told her.

"Oh, silly! In these old jeans!"

"You'd look pretty to me in anything." Preston had pulled the horse over to let Penny ride alongside him in time to see her face flush with embarrassment. "Most girls this day and time don't flush at anything. You're pretty that way." This made her flush even more, and she decided to change the subject.

"This is a beautiful place, Preston. Does Mr. Thompson farm any of the land?"

"Only feed for the stock and a family garden."

"I see. Has he always raised horses?"

"Yep. I guess that's all he knows." He pulled on the reins for the horse to go right and took the lead again. "There's a creek at the bottom . . . the same one that runs down behind our house but down here it's pretty deep. I used to go skinny-dipping here as a little kid."

The horses turned across pastureland and walked leisurely down the slope to the creek. At the bottom, Preston dismounted, held up his hands to help Penny down, and tethered their mounts to a nearby bush. On the far side of the creek, the land jutted upward into a dense forest where birds were twittering and chirping in the trees. "Oh, how heavenly this place smells, like wet moss . . . kind of a woodsy smell."

"Come on down here and let's jump the rocks to the other side," Preston said.

"Just let me take off my shoes so I can wade." Penny sat down on a rock and began taking off her shoes and socks. "Where's the deep part you were talking about?"

"On down yonder. We certainly don't want to wade there! In fact, you'd be wading on bottom with water over your head," he laughed.

"Why do people always want to cross a creek to the other side?" she asked feeling silly as she reached out her hand to his.

"Same reason a chicken wants to cross a road I suppose . . . to get to the other side." She let him help her jump across the jutting rocks and now wished she'd left her shoes on. Rushing water sounded loudly requiring them to speak up to be heard above it.

"Papa Russell says that people always cast to the other bank to fish and then after they cross over they cast back to the side right where they were to begin with."

"Oh, don't you see what he was doing?" Preston asked but answered before she could say anything. "He was just using child psychology on you meaning, things are better right where you are instead of running off to another place. I see right through these adults. My father tries to use it on me all the time." Penny was right; she felt sure Preston was completely adult to figure all this out.

The rocks were fairly flat now so he let go of the girl's hand and jumped on across. Turning back, he warned behind cupped hands, "Hey! Watch that big rock there; it has some slimy moss. Don't fall on it." Water poured over the nearly submerged rock and just as Penny's foot touched it, it went flying out from under her sending the startled girl into the water. "Oh," she yelled, "Preston! I'm soaked!"

"Get up, you ninny," he laughed uproariously and splashed out to give her a helping hand. She laughed good-naturedly at herself, all the time feeling embarrassed and then angry that she had skinned her ignorance when she wanted to act like a refined lady. On the bank, he impulsively put his arms around her waist, still laughing, and planted a kiss on her forehead. She looked up at him from under dripping wet hair and caught her breath. Only Rusty had kissed her . . . well, maybe a couple of others, brotherly like on the cheek, but none had meant anything or made her feel butterflies like just now.

"Preston, don't."

"Why not?" He gave her a confused look.

"I'm all wet. I'll get you soaked, too."

"I wouldn't mind. I've been wet before." He took her hand and pulled her to a soft grassy spot where the sun beamed down through the trees. "Sit down here for a minute and catch your wind and then we'll go hunt up some dry clothes for you. Think some of my jeans might stay on you? I could hunt up a belt, too." She laughed, picturing what she'd look like.

"Oh, I'll dry out soon. I'll have to get on back to Knollwood anyway to get ready for later on."

"Not anytime soon, I hope." Then he pulled her down beside him and put his arms around her. This time he hoped she did not recognize his tactics. He had used sneaky tactics on girls before and now feeling quite sure of himself, he subtly stole another light kiss.

Penny Russell, fifteen years old and budding into womanhood, was indeed flattered that this handsome man, three years older, was attracted to her. "Oh, Preston, I'm just a clumsy ox! Now my hair will be a mess! I must go now and get it dry."

"Not just yet, sweetheart." Preston drew her tightly to him in a passionate kiss that took her breath away. At first she resisted, then, relaxed, and Preston laid her back on the soft green moss. "I love you, Penny," he lied. "You know that, don't you? I loved you the first minute I laid eyes on you. You do have some feeling for me, don't you? I think you do. I've noticed how it shows on your face, in your eyes . . . your actions."

"I . . . I . . . I'm attracted to you, Preston, but really, I hardly know you. You're usually at school when we come up."

"I know all I want to know about you, beautiful." He kissed her again and gradually eased himself on top of her, all the time working with one hand to undo buttons.

Penny was frightened, and a mixture of emotions churned around inside her. She had to stop him before this went any further, and for a moment, she was stricken with panic. With all the force she could muster, Penny shoved and kicked Preston. Her teeth bit into his wrist causing him to turn her loose just as she slapped him hard across the face sending him sprawling into the creek. He stood up, and with water pouring off his head and his entire body soaked, he wiped his face and called, "Wait, Penny, please come back, I'm so sorry. Please wait!" She was already scrambling up the bank when Al's voice was heard calling his sister's name. He was riding one of the Thompson's horses, coming across the pasture nearly to the creek's edge. Penny was pulling at her clothes, trying to recover her decorum and feeling humiliated. Al had seen the horses tethered to the bushes, and now he saw his sister coming up from the creek, waving to him and smiling. She'd never been so happy to see her brother in her life. Scurrying to her horse as fast as her legs would carry her, Penny mounted and fled away. As Al approached she called to him, "I'll race you home, little brother!" Then she pressed her legs into the horse's sides, and it took off with Al standing there saying, "Well, I'll be a monkey's uncle, if that don't beat all. Hey, wait, Penny; I'll have to change horses. Preston had John's." When he discovered Preston all soaking wet coming up the bank, he laughed and said, "Hey, Preston . . . ain't it too shallow for swimming!" Then he laughed again, and changing horses, he took off like the wind.

Preston was left standing on the bank unwinding the reins and hating what he'd done. She was a pretty kid, and he liked her. Now he was hoping she would not tell anyone about his advances. He swore and doubled up a fist and rammed it against a tree. The pain was not as great as the pain he was feeling in his heart for letting his actions get the best of him. He walked back down to the creek. Stooping, he dipped his hand into the water, watching the blood dissipate in the ripples, and vowed that he'd not tell the guys at school, nor anyone else, about this.

The sun was disappearing over the mountain range that surrounded the green fertile valley where the Thompson ranch sprawled. The fields were still and quiet, but this time Penny didn't notice. She was still shaking inside from what could have happened and ran the horse out the gate onto the road and faster until the grade became steeper up the mountain to Knollwood. Al pointed his horse toward the barbecue pits to inform Papa that Penny had gone on home.

She made the horse carry her to Knollwood with breakneck speed where she surged immediately upstairs to the bathroom and feeling sick to her stomach, threw up. Her face was pale, and now her whole body was shaking. She'd managed to get in without meeting anyone until her mother heard her retching and came rushing in.

"Penny, darling! What in the world has made you so sick?" she exclaimed. Before Penny could answer Beth felt her forehead remarking that she had no fever.

"I'll be okay, Mom. It must've been something I ate over at the Thompsons', and then I rode Uncle John's horse so fast it just shook up my stomach. I'll feel better in a little while."

Beth put her arms around her daughter's shoulders, hugged her, and kissed her on top of her head. "I certainly hope so, dear. Maybe you should just lie down for awhile and have a rest before we go back for the party. You don't want to miss all the fun and the dance." Holding her out at arm's length she added, "You look rather tousled, and I do believe your jeans are damp. Heaven's sake, what have you been doing?"

"My foot slipped off a rock, and I fell in the creek."

"Well, get into something dry before you catch a cold." Then Beth left the room, hearing the back door slam, the two younger children run in calling for her, and Sally barking loudly.

Chapter Thirty-six

AT SEVEN O'CLOCK, CHARLES, BETH, AND THEIR OLDER SON stepped from the Buick and emerged into the crowd already assembled. Penny and the younger children rode down earlier with John, Papa, and Teresa. Someone nearby remarked to Alyn Russell when he got out of the car and turned to give his granddaughter a hand, that he had brought a pretty young woman as his date for the evening. He placed an arm around her as he drew her from the car, hugged her, and remarked that she was the "spittin' image of her grandmother." Penny's new apple green dress made her large brown eyes seem even larger and the youthful face beamed with satisfaction. She knew that she was pretty and that heads would turn to gaze after her. But when she spotted Preston Thompson among the milling crowd, she held her head high in defiance and quickly joined her mother who was walking toward the veranda where a group of ladies had gathered.

Charles Russell joined the men down at the pits, shaking hands with old acquaintances, and at once becoming the center of conversation. His laughter, light and carefree, rang out above the others. Cain Watson walked up to Charles offering his hand and said, "Haven't seen you in quite awhile, Charles. What's all that gray stuff on top of your head!" Everyone laughed at his remark, and then he continued. "I was down in the big city this week and seen this here big sign in front of some construction that read 'Architect and Engineering by Russell and Roland.'"

Charles was pleased with the attention that Cain Watson's statement aroused as others within hearing distance turned to join in the conversation. He smiled affably and answered, "Well, you must have been on Highway 41, Mr. Watson. For awhile now we've had a monster of a shopping center under construction there. It's going to be quite an innovation in shopping with lots of stores offering most any kind of merchandise you could name."

"Sounds tu me like it will put a lot of other places out of business, too," Mr. Watson announced.

"Maybe, but then those stores just might like to rent a space in this shopping center instead of going out of business." He lit a cigarette while some other comments were being made. One man suggested that this is what Union Gap could use, while the rest of the men laughed at this statement, knowing that it was preposterous. "Also," Charles continued, "we are about to begin building a very large industrial center. Both of these projects will put us well out front as construction leaders and at last out of the red." After a few more questions and comments, Charles made a startling suggestion. "Union Gap could spring forward if some of you old reprobates would turn loose of some of this land! What's the use in paying taxes on unused land?"

"Well, son, it's like this," one man said, "I was born on my land and so was my Pa. That land is going to my kids when I'm gone. It's all paid for, and I don't owe a dime. If I solt it, just wher would me and my wife go? I certainly wouldn't want tu live in thu city!"

Then someone else spoke up in agreement, adding that they didn't need a shopping center around these parts. Charles answered, "I wasn't speaking of a shopping center, gentlemen, but a resort where people could come and spend a weekend or a vacation. This would be a great boost for the area and bring business into Union Gap."

Jud Thompson's brother, Buford, whose field was adjoined to Jud's, commented that Charles needed to start with his own father's land. "That would be the best place for something like that."

"Land lying idle is wasteland," Charles said.

"Somebody else's might be," Watson told Charles irritably, "but mine ain't! Ever last bit of it's been planted and harvested. My land works for me."

"This is a tomfooled notion you've got in your head, Charles! I suggest you put an end to it right now!" This was his father speaking. John looked up sharply from his cooking in time to catch Charles's gaze. Evidently John had already told their father he may be approached by his younger son about his idea. "Why don't you go over yonder on Coleman Mountain and get some of those folks to sell you some land. Over here on Kendell Mountain you're batting heads with a bunch of stubborn men, and I reckon I lead the pack." Charles saw a smile on his father's lips and knew that he was shooting for the last word about the matter. He'd always been that way. Alyn Russell put a hand on his son's arm. "Don't fret yourself, son. You'll get all worked up. These folks would fight to hold onto their land." He pointed to the plate of steaming barbecue in Charles's hand that was just passed to him by John, who was helping to put food on the plates. "Stop up your mouth with this. Now this is good eatin'!" Then the dinner bell on a pole in the yard sounded, calling everyone down to the pit area where tables had been set up, laden with coleslaw, baked beans, and the wonderful-smelling meat.

Cars and pickups, loaded with neighbors from all around the area, had been pulling into the yard for the past hour. Some arrived on horseback. Those with cakes and pies were directed to the tables where these would be served later during the dance. In the food line, as Penny reached John serving the barbecue, she held out her plate, telling him not to forget that he'd promised her a dance later on.

"My fair lady, how could I ever forget?" He reached a finger out to touch the end of her nose. She wrinkled it at him and turning around, bumped straight into Preston, upsetting her plate and sending food down the front of her new dress.

"Oh!" she wailed loudly with everyone around turning to see the girl's distraught expression.

"Oh, no, Penny! I'm so very sorry." Preston grabbed a napkin and brushed at the mess on her dress, smearing it even more.

Her eyes blazed at him as she hissed under her breath, "Don't touch me, Preston."

Edna Thompson saw what had happened and hurried to her side. "My dear child. Please come up to the house with me." She took the girl by the hand, and as they walked away said to her son, "Preston! How could you be so clumsy!" In the house, she found her daughter-in-law, LeAnn, still dressing for the occasion and asked her if she might have something that Penny could wear. They came up with a lovely top and a pair of jeans that fit nicely. To Penny's surprise, she was quite pleased with the outfit that fit her just perfectly. "Leave the dress, dear," Edna said. "I'll get the stain out tomorrow, and Preston can bring it up to you."

Quite an evening of festivity it turned out to be with the big-time band and singers and the dancing. Old Dr. Harris proved himself to be the square dance caller he'd always been, clapping his hands and stomping his feet, keeping time to the music. Roy Thompson shook Doc's hand, pumping it up and down and seriously offering him a job in Nashville. "Back on thu stand, boy! We'll have to talk later. We got 'em in thu mood so play us a tune for a Cartwheel Turn." Then he clapped his hands and called for everyone to form a circle and started his call.

> "Turn that wheel around to the left
> Look at thu gal you got yourself.
> Pick 'er up and set 'er down
> Trot around and paw thu ground."

The group obeyed his commands as folks on the sidelines clapped, keeping time to the music. Doc's wife, Kate, was sitting with some other older ladies on chairs pushed against the wall. She said that all this jumping around was a thing of the past for her, but she loved the lively music and seeing her husband having such a good time. They would not miss this affair for the world. The ladies began to talk among themselves about all the square dances they had attended in the years past.

> "Now move that circle back to thu right
> And hug that girl with all your might!
> All join hands and center go,
> There's lots of cotton yet tu hoe.

> "Turn that wheel thu opposite way
> And send your partner on today.
> Pick 'er up and set 'er down,
> Trot around and paw thu ground."

Alyn Russell was sitting with a group of men talking more about what Charles had said about their land, agreeing with them that it was a foolish idea. Alyn told them that his son need not broach the subject with him about his land, but when he "'kicked the bucket,' there'd be no telling what he might do with his inheritance." The music seemed to get louder and even the dancers' laughter and shouts drowned out the talkers as they leaned closer in toward each other to make out what was being said.

> "Now swing your partner 'round a whirl
> And pass her on, get another girl,
> Well, here's a cute one, I declair
> With a pretty flower in her hair.
> Kiss her lightly or she may fret
> Prettiest gal that you've had yet."

Just as this happened, Beth wound up in the arms of John who was more than happy to get this lovely creature for his partner, and he planted a kiss lightly on her lips. "John! You cheated! That was supposed to be on the cheek."

"I didn't hear Doc give any such instructions," John smiled.

"Well, he'd better give some stopping instructions because I am about done in," Beth answered breathlessly.

"You're just out of practice, maybe," he answered.

"Now move that circle back to thu right
An' hug that gal with all your might!"

"I can certainly say that I'm glad I got you for a partner," John laughed down at Beth. "I've seen a lot of women here tonight that . . ."

"Oh, John, for heaven's sake!" She felt embarrassed.

The dancers followed Doc's instructions until Penny inevitably wound up with Preston. "I think Doc deliberately did that for me," Preston told his partner.

"You must have paid him," she answered unsmiling.

"Penny, please. I've got to talk to you. Let's go outside." Without an answer he pulled her from the circle and outside where he found a bench. "Please sit down and just listen." She opened her mouth to speak, but he placed a finger against her lips and said, "Pen, truly, I mean honestly, I am so sorry about this afternoon. Really I am. I don't know what got into me. Could you ever, ever forgive me? If you don't care anything at all about me, could we just be friends? I swear to you on my knees," then he got down on his knees. "I will never get out of line again. I promise you this." The moon bathed her hair in shimmering silver. She lowered her eyes, gazing at her green shoes that now did not match her outfit. "I do love you, Pen, honest I do. Please be my girl."

"Not like today," she said softly. "If you ever try to get fresh with me again, I'll . . ."

"Don't worry," he interrupted, "with an iron fist like yours, I would be plumb crazy." She couldn't help but smile when he said this.

Tammy Jo came bouncing around the building and discovered Penny on the bench and her uncle on the ground in front of her. "For pity sakes, Preston, what are you doing down there! And why aren't ya'll in there dancing to my daddy's music? I know, Preston . . . you're just jealous because you don't have a band, aren't you?"

Preston got up and sitting beside Penny, answered with irritation, "Oh, go away, pill. Wait, on second thought, why don't you go find Susan and Peter and show them how to hunt for snipes like I showed you one time, remember?" That should certainly keep them occupied for a while and out of their hair!

The child's face lit up like a lantern. "Yea!" she squealed. "But I never did find any before. What did you say they look like?"

"I told you that they're cute little bitty furry animals that make nice pets."

"Oh, yeah. We were playing hide-and-seek, and they are hid somewhere. I'll go find Susan and Peter so we can hunt for snipes!" Then she took off again but came back shortly asking if they would need a cage. Preston smiled as he told her she would not need anything to put them in because they would just follow along.

"What was that all about?" Penny asked.

"Just a little game I showed her . . . all in fun, but actually I thought it would keep her out of our hair for a little while. Before long they'll come running back saying there must not have been any snipes out tonight."

Fearful that Penny had lost the words he had asked her before his niece interrupted, Preston took Penny by the hand and said, "Just tell me you love me, too, and that you will wait for me to finish college and then we can be married."

"But what if . . . what if . . . you feel different later?"

He understood what she was feeling and answered, "Don't worry, Penny. There won't be anything to worry about as far as I'm concerned."

"By the time you finish college, you won't want to marry me. By then you may have met someone else and think that I am still a child." Tears began to form in her eyes and slide down her cheeks. Turning aside she tried to wipe them so that he would not see. He took a handkerchief from a pocket and wiped them himself, kissing her cheek lightly.

"Will you wait for me, Penny?"

"Only if you promise me that you'll respect my upbringing and my Christian beliefs. Either that, Preston, or leave me alone. My mother would drop dead if she knew about this afternoon and Papa Russell, too, and John . . . he'd kill you." She did not mention what her own dad would do.

"John wouldn't kill me if my father found out first. He'd skin me alive." Penny smiled at his answer and began to feel better about the situation. Yes, maybe she did love Preston Thompson.

It was quite awhile later that the party began breaking up. Cars lined the road from the house out to the state road; headlights were blinding in rearview mirrors and friendly "good nights" were being called from windows. At the foot of the front steps, the Russells gathered and expressed their thanks to Jud and Edna Thompson for such a wonderful evening, and then Charles told Al to go round up the two little ones.

"I haven't seen them lately, Dad," Al said.

"I haven't either," Penny put in, looking around without seeing the children.

Jud Thompson then suggested that they may be inside the house with Tammy Jo and asked Penny to go look for them. He told Preston to go see if they were watching the band dismantle. Then he called after Penny to find LeAnn and see if she knew where they'd gone.

After a thorough search of the nearby party areas, the remaining group began to be concerned for the whereabouts of the three small children. "Where did you show her to look for snipes, Preston?" Penny asked when they both had returned from their search of the house and the barn. Thinking that surely one of them would return with the children, the rest of the group had remained out front talking, but now hearing what Penny had just asked, Jud Thompson exclaimed to his son, "Don't tell me you told them to go snipe hunting, Preston! How could you?"

"Well, Dad, I just . . ." His mother cut in with, "So that's why they asked me to borrow some flashlights. Oh, no! Where are they?" Jud was now shouting into cupped hands to some of his hired help down near the stables to search that area, and then John dashed inside to telephone the sheriff's department just as LeAnn was coming outside to see what all the commotion was about. Edna was next to Beth with her arms around her shoulders, both women caught up in a feeling of great despair. Papa Russell suggested that the women wait inside the house in case the children showed up there, and he'd wait for the sheriff and his men outside. Already, the men there had spread out over the property and down toward the creek.

Penny, still dazed by the day's events, watched her mother who stood by a window gazing out into the darkness, unable to see anything at all. She tried to put herself into her mother's body, to imagine what she was feeling at this very moment. "It's strange," she thought, "how things can change in a twinkling of an eye—how tranquil lives can become turbulent like a whirlpool of troubled waters." Take this morning, for instance . . . Penny was a child, and tonight, with this . . . this terrible thing that could turn into a tragedy, she was a woman. This experience they were going through now was one that the world could keep! She wanted her little sister and brother back safely at home. "They were just babies," she thought with a shake of the head, and her lips trembled. Beth came to her daughter and placed her arms around her shoulders and together they sobbed.

Wiping her eyes, Penny said, "Oh, Mom, what will we do?" She was grasping for words to assuage her grief. Beth kissed the girl's forehead answering, "I don't know, dear. Truly, I don't know that we can do anything but pray." And then together they did just that.

LeAnn Thompson sat on a couch and bent over the coffee table drumming absently on it with her fingertips. "That child," she said. "I told her a dozen times to calm down and behave. She's so devilish lately that I just can't control her. Always getting herself into something, and when she gets with a crowd she just gets wilder." Tammy Jo's mother continued babbling about her daughter until Penny wished she would be quiet. She wanted to listen for every sound. The children may come running up at any moment. They could open the door and come in, but Penny wanted to hear them from the first possible moment when any sound could fall on her ears. In LeAnn's nervousness she talked on and on. The sheriff had arrived and deputies in a truck brought their hounds that were now being given articles of clothing to sniff. Mrs. Thompson brought out something of Tammy Jo's and then found Susan and Peter's jackets on the porch swing where they had been playing "train." As the dogs went off baying with the men into the darkness, Papa Russell came in to sit with the women. John insisted that he not attempt the search of the woods, telling him that one of the men should stay with the upset women and he was appointed to do that. "They're my grandchildren," Alyn Russell protested at first, feeling he was being treated like an old man, "and I know these woods like the back of my hand. Do you think I'd sit around for one minute and not look for them!"

"But, we need you here, Papa," John imparted, finally talking him into staying.

Penny asked Edna if she would accompany her to again search through the large, rambling rooms. Three children most likely would not be hiding, but it would not hurt anything to look anyway; she could not just stand wringing her hands. Going up the staircase, Penny told Mrs. Thompson that six years ago on the day her family moved into their own large two-story house, Al was missing for several hours. Back then he was nine years old and there were many places in the uniquely built house for a child to lose himself. He was finally discovered up in the attic fast asleep in a packing box.

Down the long hallway of the Thompson's house were bedrooms on each side, with a linen closet and a bathroom at the end of the hall. They searched each room, opening every door, and from one of the closets there was a room opening up to the attic which they also searched, to no avail. Coming back, Edna opened the door to her own mother's bedroom, and there was the old lady down beside her bed, praying incoherently in a consistent pleading tone. At this moment, a pang of fear rushed through Penny's whole body that maybe God was punishing her for not being the big sister she should have been—more loving, helpful, and attentive. Maybe they would never find the children! Right this very minute they may be lying at the bottom of a crevice or perhaps washed down into the river! There were so many "maybes" that she could think of. Suddenly a chill knifed through her, and she felt alone in the whole world. Then she heard Granny McClelland's voice loud and clear, "He is my refuge and my fortress, my God in Him will I trust."

By this time, neighbors had returned. They had gone home from the party and heard the news from a jangling telephone as word was passed along. The group in the living room spoke quietly with no false hopes being raised. That was the way among country folk. They were a circle of dear, determined friends whose very presence in a time of need spoke their feelings. Someone went to the kitchen and made a pot of coffee and some hot soup for the searchers who would be coming in and out from time to time.

It was around 3:00 A.M. when heavy footsteps were heard on the porch, and Charles came through the doorway followed by John. Beth's hopes soared. She nearly smiled. "Charles!" she exclaimed, "Have they been found?" Her husband looked extremely haggard and his jacket was torn. He combed his fingers through his hair and then put his arms around his wife, feeling for the first time like he had been missing out on her life. His white face was fixed in grim lines.

Sensing his loss for words, John answered for him because their dad had also risen stiffly to his feet, waiting. "No, Beth, no sign of any of them. Have any of the men returned?"

"Several have been in and out to see if we'd had any word."

"It is past time that the National Guard should have been called in," John said, heading toward the telephone. They heard him tell the operator to connect him with the governor's home, and while he was waiting, he turned to his brother and told him that it would be a good idea if he stayed there with Beth. He was thinking more of Charles and remembering that he shouldn't be climbing through the forest exerting himself since he was still under the care of a heart specialist.

Time passed slowly. Everyone in the house had glanced at their watches or the mantel clock countless times. More neighbors had returned to sit with the Russells and the Thompsons, and the pastor of the Kendell Mountain School, Reverend Chester Lawton, and his wife, Karen, were among them. Reverend Lawton held a prayer service and then others joined in praying. This went on throughout the long night until around four o'clock when Charles talked Beth and Penny into lying down in one of the bedrooms upstairs. Neither had shut an eye, watching Charles pace from window to window, gazing out into the black night.

Charles remembered these woods of his boyhood where his children were now lost. He remembered the snakes in October. Folks always said October was rather late for snakes, but there were always some stragglers about. He remembered the gypsy colors of the sweet gums and hickories, the chatter of working squirrels dropping acorns and hickory nuts from overhead limbs. His mind drifted as his eyes were transfixed on the beauty of the autumn woods, and for a few moments, he forgot about the grave problem at hand. Autumn on Kendell Mountain is a season of somber beauty when sunrays penetrating through the pines turn the landscape into a pattern of intricate color like a patchwork quilt. Browns overpower the evergreen pines, and the dark reds of sour woods painted a masterpiece. Then Charles was thinking about Rushing Creek, deep in some places, and then, there was the river, wide and cold, falling here and there over boulders that had rolled down from the mountainside. The woods were beautiful this time of year . . . until his children became lost; now they were nothing but treacherous. The black bear of north Georgia would not bother anyone, he assured himself. They kept away from people unless they were hurt or their cubs were being endangered. "Don't bear go into hibernation by this time of year?" he questioned himself, still thinking that all children have had an innate sense of adventure from the beginning of time to explore the unknown. Then a little voice from within gave him some consolation by adding, "But not at night."

It was not yet daylight. Charles rubbed his crossing eyes and bent over in the chair in which he was sitting, with his arms resting on his knees, wondering who John was searching with. "Oh, John was a strong one alright, strong with will and in body . . . and here I am sitting by the window like a woman," he thought, "a weakling, not even able to hold out to look for my own kids." His mind flashed momentarily to three terror-stricken children thrashing helplessly in a cold, white torrent of the tumbling river. His thoughts were broken by the sound of the front door opening downstairs and then the murmur of voices from the front room. The noise aroused Beth. She jumped off the bed and brushed past her husband who had started out the bedroom door at the same time.

"Who is it!" Beth exclaimed hurrying down the stairs. Someone answered that it was John and the sheriff. She saw that none of the children were with them as they entered and hopes fell as her heart sank.

"Anything at all, Johnny?" Charles questioned.

John only shook his weary head and rubbed an arm across his solemn face. Someone shoved cups of coffee into the tired men's hands. "The mountain's working alive with searchers," Sheriff Williams said. "Every inch is being combed. Don't see how them younguns can be missed this long . . . they're bound tu turn up. It's a-gettin' light, and we'll be able tu see better." He turned toward Beth and Charles and then toward the Thompsons, saying, "We'll find your children, folks, you can bank on that."

Behind Beth and Charles's backs coming down the stairs was Granny McClelland. She stared straight ahead toward John. "John Russell," she said, rolling her Rs in her Irish accent. "I've got a message forrr ye."

"Message for me, Granny? Who from?"

"Aye," she answered in the thick Irish burr. "A message from the Lord Almighty." He sent an answer to me pleadings . . . plain as day it t'was." She pointed an arthritic finger at an angle towards the door and said, "Go look up on North Ridge behind Doc Harris's house. That's where them angels be. One of em's hurt bad. Go now, Johnny boy." Granny McClelland saw John Russell as the little boy he was when she came straight from Ireland to live with her daughter, Edna Thompson, and her husband Jud. Edna fell in love with Judson Thompson the first time she saw him during World War II in Britain.

The men looked at one another in bewilderment. "What's there to lose?" John shrugged as he downed the last drop of coffee. "We've searched all the area on this side down here and completely missed that area up on the mountain. But I just don't see how they could have wandered so far!" John pressed on his hat, saying that he'd always felt Granny McClelland had a straight line to heaven. The two men went out the door and met some more of the searchers returning for a report and some hot coffee. They turned on their heels and followed when

John repeated what they'd just heard from the old woman. Sheriff Williams already had his car's motor started when John got in the front side and the other two men in the back. They roared off into the predawn light just before the National Guard unit arrived, followed by a truck with a television crew.

"I just cannot see how little legs could climb steep terrain and cover so much ground," John said, and Sheriff Williams answered, "Particularly in darkness." They rode on in silence until they passed the Knollwood entrance, then John said, "Granny said behind Doc Harris's place, so let's go on up there and park." Then he told the sheriff to stop. "Let's go by here and awaken the colored men and get their hounds."

"Of course, John, I should've thought of that. Just tell 'em to bring the dogs on up because they know how to handle their own dogs, and we'll go on ahead."

When they arrived, the sheriff knocked loudly on the door to Doc and Kate's place. The old couple would still be in bed at this early hour, but would no doubt awaken to find the sheriff's car in their yard and become alarmed, so he'd best let them know what was going on.

On up behind the old house, the men all spread out in four different directions, John heading toward the waterfall, hoping with all his might that the children had not come this far. He discovered strength he did not know he'd had since he was much younger, scrambling on all fours at certain places and stopping every few seconds to call out the children's names through his cupped hands. John now had a feeling of desperation and urgency. Each turn of the path looked the same; he thought he'd never forget . . . so many times he and Charles had hunted this neck of the woods. By mid-morning he was watching an angry sky now boiling overhead; in the distance, rumbling thunder could be heard warning that nature waits for no one, not even innocent little children. The dark sky warned for an hour before the rain broke through, peppering down in straight lines.

Al and Preston Thompson were the ones who found little Tammy. She was nowhere near the place that John and the sheriff were searching. She was lying scrunched up on a table-like ledge that jutted out about six feet below the cliff's edge. Preston tied a rope (that somehow he'd thought to bring along) about his waist with Al securing the other end to a tree. Preston reached his niece and bent down to lift her in his arms, with Al calling down, "Is she alive, Preston? Feel her pulse."

"I . . . I can't tell. Just pull me up, hurry. I've got her." Preston felt his own heart pulsating and throbbing over his whole body. It had pulsated when he was dancing with Penny until he thought he would burst but not with the frantic fear that he was now feeling. Slowly, inch by inch, Al was pulling the rope up, rain falling on his bowed-over head, and Preston was holding the little girl by one arm and the rope with the other. The boys did not have a gun to fire as an announcement; they just hurried as fast as they could manage down the slope. Al stopped, thinking that there was no use in his going with Preston. He needed to search for his brother and sister. The forest was now so full of sopping wet men that as soon as Preston came upon the first man, he fired his pistol. Al propped his arms on a tree, bending his head across them and sobbed. "Oh, Susan . . . Peter . . . where are you? Dear God, please help us find them." Then he yelled with all his might, "Susan! . . . Peter!"

Papa Russell had not been able to stand the waiting any longer and had joined the men on the mountain. He was a healthy, strong man in spite of his bum leg, so defying John's instructions and nature itself, he had been searching all morning, carrying a gun that he took from his car when he rode over with one of the men. He had heard the gunshot just before he found his grandson standing against the tree sobbing. He walked up to Al, placing his arms around him, pulling him away from the tree. "Maybe someone has found them by now. Come on, son. Let's go home. We'll call over to the Thompsons."

"Papa, do you think we'll find them?" They were walking down the trail now that would lead them into the apple orchard.

"Of course we will. They're around here somewhere, the little imps. Probably laughing at us. I'll skin 'em alive."

His statement made Al show a flicker of a smile. "I prayed and told God that I wouldn't ever fuss at 'em again."

"Well, I didn't make any such promise. After I hug and kiss them, they'll get their bottoms tanned." Al knew he actually would not lay a hand on them except as he said, to hug them up close and love on them.

Together they took a worn path (that had been stomped down long ago by hikers or perhaps hunters) on to the big Knollwood house.

Chapter Thirty-seven

THE PART OF THE NORTH RIDGE WHERE JOHN WAS SEARCHING now belonged to Alyn Russell. He had purchased it several years ago from Doc Harris for no earthly reason at all other than the shear pleasure of saying it was his. It was twenty acres that lay between Knollwood and Doc and Kate's place. Just over the ridge from their house was the cleared pastureland where Beth and John had brought the children on picnics many times. It was the same spot that Alyn and his wife, Cynthee, loved and where Alyn had first told her that he loved her. It always held a special meaning to Alyn both as a young boy and in later years. "Papa's trying to hold onto the past," Charles said to John one day after he had been severely reprimanded for asking Papa again to let him have his portion of the land. "All old people look behind," Charles told John. "They don't seem to look ahead at all."

"There isn't much for them to look to in the future, is there?" John had answered.

No one else was searching close by John. He could hear the dogs baying in the distance and hoped they had found the children. He decided to sit down for a moment to catch his breath. Thankfully, the rain stopped, and the sky was beginning to clear. When John sat down on the wet log, he heard a squirrel in the tree overhead chattering, no doubt fussing because John had sat down on his acorn burial ground. He gazed up overhead when the little animal scurried to another tree and then John heard another sound . . . like a grunt. He didn't want to run into a wild hog or anything else. Then he heard the sound again, but it was more like a moan. As he looked all about him, an arm reached up from out of the leaves where he was sitting, and scrambling to his knees, John frantically brushed the leaf pile aside and there was Peter! "Peter! Oh, thank God!" He picked the little boy up and held him close, rocking him in his arms.

"I'm so c-c-cold, John." The child's faint words trailed away and John kissed him tenderly. Peter moaned, not opening his eyes. Not wanting to lose this place for fear of missing the girls, John called out for help in the hope that someone would be close enough to hear his cries. "Help!" he called again. "Over here! Is anyone near?" He placed the little boy gently upon the bed of leaves so he could fire his pistol, giving a signal to the others, and momentarily a return shot rang out echoing across the mountain. He sat down beside his nephew to wait and taking off his coat, he wrapped it securely about the boy, rubbing his hands. Peter stirred. His eyes flickered, and he spoke softly to John. "Please don't be mad, John. We got losted." The words came almost too faint to make out.

"I'm not mad, Peter. If anything, I'm most thankful. Where are the girls?"

"Don't know. I'm s-s-so cold." He drifted off again as John picked him up to hold him close for warmth.

Peter was rushed to the hospital in the sheriff's car the moment they brought him down, with John still holding the sleeping boy. For the next eight hours, he slept almost like death itself as both Charles and Beth paced the hospital hallway.

COMING IN THE BACK WAY, PAPA RUSSELL AND AL HUNG their wet coats on a nail by the back door to dry. They let the back door slam and made tracks in the hallway with their wet boots. "Dry clothes for you and me, boy, and we'll start a fire in the grate. We'll be having a house full of people shortly."

"To heck with people; I just want the kids back." Al disappeared into the bathroom near the back door, and Papa Russell headed on toward his room to get out of his wet clothes. There in the middle of his big oak bed was a curly-headed doll. A live one!

"Susan!" Papa exclaimed.

The child sat up, rubbing sleep from her eyes. "Hello, Papa. I'm not lost anymore." Her grandfather, now overwhelmed with relief, felt hot tears form in his eyes, clouding his glasses and streaming down his face.

"Grandpas don't cry, Papa. My goodness."

Al heard the talking and came flying into the room. "Hey, it's Susan! Well, a fine one you are, Miss Smarty! Where've you been?

Worrying us all nearly to death!" Papa looked at Al with a reminding look, who caught the message and remembered his promise. "It's a long time before she grows up, Papa, and how can a feller teach his sister anything if he doesn't scold?"

The old man shrugged his shoulders and smiled. "It was your promise, not mine." They both looked down at her pixie face, the pink upturned mouth curved slightly at the corners.

"How long have you been here, sweetheart?" her grandfather asked.

"Oh, simply hours and hours. I'm all slept out, too. Peter and Tammy got lost."

Alyn scooped his granddaughter up into his arms, forgetting about his wet clothes. He headed to the parlor where they'd build a fire. Susan hugged her arms around his neck and told him that he was so much smarter than all her friend's grandfathers. They all just walk around in the park or sit in front of stores and stuff like that. "I've got the best grandfather in the whole wide world." Then again, she thought she saw tears glisten in his eyes and said, "But I told you that grandfathers aren't supposed to cry, you know."

"These are the happiest tears anyone could ever have, my sweet," he answered.

THE REUNION AT THE THOMPSONS' RANCH WAS NOT A joyful one. Little Tammy's neck had been broken in the fall, and the whole house, now full of people, were sadly trying to console one another. Outside, television crews with their cameras were on the scene and many people milled around dolefully. Charles's partner phoned, the governor phoned, and when J. P. Thrower's office phoned trying to get in touch with Charles, that office official had been informed about the situation and said he'd pass the word to on to J. P. Then telegrams poured in. Penny sat beside the hall telephone in the Thompson's house talking very efficiently to the callers . . . until Rusty phoned, then she broke down crying. "Oh, Rusty," she sobbed into the phone, "How sweet of you to call. I wish you were here. You wouldn't believe it, Rusty . . . all these people . . ." her voice trailed off as she was unable to say more.

"Golly, Pen. I couldn't stand not calling, but I've tried all morning and the phone was busy. We've seen the news flashes on television, and I saw you and your mother in one scene. I just hope they find Susan real soon." Then he added as his way of assurance to the girl he loved, "I'm sure they will, Pen. Try not to worry yourself sick. I just wanted you to know that I love you." And at this time, she felt that he truly did. He sounded like he was growing up . . . his voice even sounded deeper.

A pervading sense of guilt racked the girl to the very core when she thought about riding off with Preston and not watching her little brother and sister at all. She wished that she had been the one who was lost up on the mountain and may never come back. Right now she wished that she could die, except for the fact that it would make another hardship to add to her parents' grief. She sat still (as the Henry Grady monument in the middle of Marietta Street in Atlanta), looking at the telephone after Rusty hung up, until it rang again jostling her back to life. This time, she walked away from it. Someone came in with the news that Peter had been found and rushed to the hospital. The phone call that Penny walked away from was her brother saying, to the one who had answered, that Susan was safe inside the Knollwood house with her grandfather and Al.

A FEW DAYS AFTER CHARLES AND HIS FAMILY RETURNED TO Atlanta, Alyn Russell decided he would go down to the cemetery. He'd not been in a while and today he felt low, concerned for Charles and the repeated attempts he'd made to get his father to turn loose of some Knollwood land. Also, the recent events of losing the little neighbor girl and the near tragedy of his own grandchildren, had left him with a morose feeling.

He pulled his old truck to a stop on a little dirt road that led into the cemetery and went to stand beside Cynthia's grave. He had stood thus many times through the years since she was laid to rest here, talking to her as though she could hear every word he said but knowing full well that she could not. It was rather like therapy for him alone. Today he held a bunch of daisies that he'd picked along the roadside and now placed them in a vase on the headstone. Always, standing here he sensed a presence of calmness and peace, as though Cynthee was right there beside him. At times he could even feel her arms around him and her head on his shoulder.

When he was a boy, Alyn told the great oak tree his troubles, sitting for hours on end and leaning against the tree trunk working out in his mind anything that could be of trouble to a young boy, with his dog waiting faithfully at his side. Now, he went to Cynthia's grave.

"Well, Cynthee, I'm here again. Feel kinda low today . . . needed you to sorta prop me up. It's that boy again. We figured out what to do that time when he got expelled from college, didn't we? It was a boyish trick that time. I left here chuckling about it that day, remember?" He sat down on the low concrete wall around the grave, thinking for a few minutes. "I'm using this stupid cane now like an old man. But I find that it does come in handy. John insisted that I use it. Then, there was the time that Charles ran off with that little Smithfield girl to get married. They came back, though, on their own after thinking about it more. That was before he took Beth from John. I know he's basically a good boy, Cynthee. I'm sure the Lord knows he is. I did the best I could with 'im . . . and John . . . remember the time John had to bail him out of jail for drunk driving? That was awfully embarrassing to John . . . and little Teresa, she hadn't never been any trouble. None a'tall."

Alyn stooped over and picked a blade of grass, stringing it through his fingers. "I'm afraid, my pet, that Charles isn't doing right by Beth. Can't rightly put a finger on it, but it just isn't exactly on the up and up. She's a dream, that Beth. You two would've loved one another. She's so much like you were . . . like I remember you, my Love. If only that Charles would wake up." He sat there for a while hunched over thinking, then sighed. "John loves her, too, you know. I ache for that boy. I haven't told this to anybody, Teresa or anybody, but I just know. And that's not all, either. Charles is wanting his share of the land. Wants it now. Can't say as I blame him any, but he'd just ruin it . . . mine and your land, honey. I'd soon have to move and John and Teresa. I couldn't bear to have all those people tromping all around our hills, turning every leaf, and throwing their beer cans and pop bottles among the bushes . . . not going to have it, I tell you. But, do you know what he's doing now? He talked to David Harris a-trying to get him to sell his land. I wouldn't ever have dreamed it! No sir, not in a million years. I hope Doc doesn't give in to 'im. Nope. I just don't know what to make of that boy anymore. He's not the sweet little boy I used to know. 'Course he and John always did get into brawls and I was always separating 'em."

Alyn stood and shaded his eyes with a hand, looking skyward. "It's gonna rain, Sweetheart. Guess I'd best be getting on back. Don't mean tu trouble you none with my worries. Guess it'll work out. Usually does . . . but, if you get a chance, please speak to thu Good Lord about our boy. Like I said, he's basically a good boy but he does make me so gol-durned mad and hot under the collar. I feel like turning 'im across my lap with a paddle!"

He sighed deeply and turned to retrace his steps to the truck. "Be back again before long, my Love."

Chapter Thirty-eight

BY THE MIDDLE OF OCTOBER, ABOUT THREE WEEKS AFTER the never-to-be-forgotten barbecue at the Thompsons', there had been a little frost during the night and in the early morning dawn a mist still lingered over the pasture below Knollwood. Daisy and Prince were feeding in the bottomland when John appeared by the fence at the top and whistled for them. The horses snorted and galloped eagerly up the slope to receive the sugar cubes they knew would be in their master's outstretched hands. He stood waiting for them, dipping into the bucket for the treat that they had come to expect when called up to be saddled for a ride.

Teresa telephoned Beth the day before asking if they would come up, telling Beth that she had someone who wanted her to paint something special. It would be a paying job. "A paying job!" Beth exclaimed through the speaker. "I've never charged anyone for one of my paintings! Do you think I could actually get paid for something that I enjoy so much?" Teresa told her that a teacher gets paid for teaching and she enjoys helping the children to learn, and a doctor gets paid for making people well. He certainly enjoys having happy patients, and of course she should be paid for she was an excellent artist.

"Well, of course, we can come. You know the children are always happy to come up there, but Charles is working every hour he can before bad weather sets in and slows the builders down, so you know how that goes."

"Yes, yes, I do understand and really didn't expect him to come anyway, but you and the kids come on . . . and sweet little Sally."

"You know that dog has to go everywhere the children go."

Teresa laughed into the phone and said that it was settled then, and they would be watching for them on Saturday.

John patted the horses gently and gave Daisy some extra head rubbing, which she loved. She flung her mane and shook her head, nudging him teasingly for another treat after she'd finished the two he had handed her. "That's all, old girl," he told her. "Today we go for a ride and when we return, you'll have another treat." He turned to Prince and told him, "Today we're taking Beth and her children riding, and I want you both to be on your best behavior." The horse neighed at once as if he understood his master's instructions. John opened the gate, and the horses followed him inside the barn where he found Tad puttering around with unimportant little jobs. "Give 'em some oats, Tad, and saddle 'em up for our ride in about an hour. The folks got here early, but we'd better give them some time with Papa before I go dragging them off."

"Yes'ah, Dr. Johnny. Missy Beth gon lak dat Daisy. She one fine mare and gentle as a li'l ole colt."

John and his dad enjoyed riding the bridle paths they had made through the woods and had done so for years. Papa Russell insisted that the exercise kept him young. He'd been riding since he was five years old when Adam first set him up on a horse. John whistled his way back to the house, smelling Selma's scrumptious breakfast cooking. The aroma of ham floated gently on the cool morning breeze, tantalizing his nostrils. He had worked hard all week. His office was full each morning when he arrived. He then made home calls, seeing those too sick to come into the office. If this kept up he'd need an assistant before long. His office secretary and assistant, Emily Phillips Tatum, told him that at the rate they were working, she would need an assistant as well. So now, John was ready for a relaxing day of lazing around playing with his younger nephew and niece. Teresa told him that he need not include the older two in with his plans as she already had made plans for them.

Beth, John decided to himself, certainly needed this outing as well. He felt certain that she needed her spirits lifted after putting up with his brother all week. He could not recall when she had last ridden over the land. One time (before they'd sold off the other horses) she had been along with Charles and himself . . . but that was a number of years ago, oh, and Papa was along, too. Teresa had never been one for enjoying being on a horse. At that time Papa had wanted to show Beth the acres of timber and the meadow up beyond Possum Ridge, where a stream poured along over the rocks on its journey down the mountain. This meadow held a special meaning for Papa Russell. John wondered why he was so interested in taking Beth there. He thought of her exclamations over the enchanting spot then and how she had wanted to come back to it later and bring the children for a picnic, but somehow they'd never gotten around to it. John decided he'd ask Selma to fix up a basket of food. An outing always made one hungry, especially the kids.

At ten o'clock Tad brought the horses up to the house, all groomed and saddled, ready for the morning ride. Susan and Peter dashed off the back porch full of energy and excitement, pleading with Tad to help them up into the saddles. Doing this, he told them to sit still and not fall off or he would be in big trouble; then he held the reins until John and Beth came down the back steps.

"Now, what do we have here?" John questioned, at the same time handing the food basket to Tad until he could mount in front of Peter.

"We be your Indian guides," Peter piped up with seriousness on his face. "Me 'Brave Sneaky One.'" Then pointing to his sister he said, "And this my squaw, 'Princess Tagalong.'"

Beth said, "I'll say you are certainly a sneaky one, and you both are tagalongs!"

John came over to assist Beth up on the mare's back. The job took several tries, and finally Beth suggested that they move over to the porch steps where she could get on much easier. He looked up at Susan telling her that she looked nearly as pretty this morning as her mother . . . but not quite.

"She not my mother. Me Princess Tagalong."

"Oh, have it your way, Your Highness," he shrugged, conceding and swinging himself into the saddle with Peter. He reached over to take the basket from Tad and instructed Peter to hold it carefully or there'd be no lunch today. "If you two Indian guides get us lost, there's enough food and drink in this basket for only two days, then we have to live off the land."

Beth sat erect in the saddle, unafraid of the gentle mare that led the way without any nudging at all. They crossed the backyard, leading into a path that rambled around beyond the dormant apple orchard, then ascended the slope, which gradually led up the mountain to Possum Ridge and beyond. "There must have been a lot of activity going on around here recently," Beth turned and said to John.

"Yep, always is this time every year. I've managed to escape it since college days, but when we were at least eight, we were expected to pull our weight."

"Don't tell me that Charles had to work picking apples?"

"And packing them, too. It was either that or suffer the wrath of Papa, who believed that hard work never hurt anyone."

There was incessant jabbering up the way and plenty of giggling. The children were having the time of their lives. Beth said to Susan, "Listen, what do you hear?"

"Oh, it's a creek. Please, Mama, let's stop and wade! Please, please!"

"The water is too cold," John spoke up. "Keep going until we come to a clearing, and then you will see something very pretty. And that's where we will stop."

"I'll certainly be glad," Peter grumbled. "This basket is heavy. We'll have to eat up everything inside it so it will be light going back."

Before long, the group came to the clearing, and at once Beth remembered the place even though it was a number of years since she was up here and had not thought of their outing there since. None of the children had even been born. "Susan, Papa says this is a fairy meadow with a little fairy living under every rock."

"Oh, let me down, quick," the child squealed. "I want to see."

"You just hold on for a second, and when you get down, remember . . . you two are to stay within sight."

"The fairies had better not be like the snipes!" Peter exclaimed. John didn't know whether to laugh or be sad when he mentioned the episode that got the children lost.

"How utterly beautiful!" Beth exclaimed. "I need my canvas and brushes. What a painting this would make. We should have brought a camera."

"Ta-dah!" John exclaimed in a singsong way as he drew a camera from a jacket pocket waving it up in the air for her to see. He seemed to think of everything.

"It is even lovelier than I remember before . . . and look, the meadow is filled with black-eyed Susans. See, honey, they are named after you . . . and there's golden rod . . . and, what's those little blue flowers?"

"Don't ask me," John shrugged as he dismounted, taking the basket from Peter and then helping him down. He went to assist Susan, who ran off with Peter to gather flowers, and when he helped Beth down she said, "Thank you, Johnny, for bringing us here. You always seem to think of everything." He only mumbled that maybe he was thinking of himself as well.

The horses went off to munch on the lush green grass. "Won't they wander away?" she asked.

"No. Why would they with all this nice grass all around them?" He thought of Charles when he made that statement and thought to himself that he needed to stay in his own pasture as well. John spread a blanket on the grass for them to sit on and watch the children. He reached over and picked some clover, handing Beth some. They made clover chains like little children. She laughed when he encircled a chain and laid it on top of her head like a crown. "My mother showed me how to make the chains. She used to bring us up here often, and I remember one time she brought our little Sunday School class here on an Easter egg hunt."

"I wish I could have known your mother. She must have been a wonderful person."

"Yes, she certainly was. One time when we came up here the whole place was covered with patches of wild flowers. They had not mixed with other flowers, causing a field that looked like a patchwork quilt . . . here a splotch of yellow and there a splotch of golden brown," he emphasized with a hand. "Mama said that the fairies had spread out their wash on the ground to dry." He smiled but with a faraway look in his eyes as though he were seeing his mother right here on that day a long time ago. Beth could not imagine Charles talking about sentimental things like this. Why couldn't he be more like his older brother?

Peter pointed a finger up towards a tree at the edge of the forest. "Look, Susan. Look up in that tree." A squirrel was sitting on a limb eating a nut, chucking at the intruders below. "He's cheating because he's supposed to be burying the nuts and acorns now for the winter."

"I guess he has to eat some of them, too, Peter. You know he gets hungry like we do sometimes," his sister answered sensibly. The squirrel dropped the empty shell and scampered to another tree.

No rock was left unturned in the meadow that morning; no fairies found; no nook left unexplored. They brought their mother pretty-colored leaves to save for them to take to school. Susan's class was doing a project of waxing them. John took out his camera and snapped a photo of this scene, and others, too, but the one of the children with the pretty leaves they had gathered would be a treasure. When they tired of chasing one another and rolling down the hill in the grass, they lay on their backs and gazed upward into a buttermilk sky. Peter discovered a hawk circling far, far above, and then he made out another speck circling with him.

"That will be his mate," John told them. "The male will court his mate by showing off with long dives and swoop back up to her."

"Just like a man," Beth joshed. "Always showing off." Her lips curled in a smile, then her breath quickened. "For pity sakes! Will you look at that!" The hawk made such a straight dive that it looked as though he would hit the ground for sure. Pulling out of the nosedive, he spread the long wings, flapping back up to his circling mate. "After the wedding's over he'll quit showing off," Beth said and, with a flush, wished she had not made that statement for it sounded as though she had referred to what her own husband had done. The hawks receded to another playground, and the two children decided it would be fun to roll down the hill through all the soft clover.

"So," John turned toward his sister-in-law and asked, "What do you think of our meadow?"

"Frankly, I can't describe what I think, other than it is heavenly. And heaven is to be even more beautiful than this. It would be hard to imagine, don't you think?"

"I wouldn't even try, but did you know that this is the spot that Charles keeps nagging Papa to let him have now?" And before she could make an answer he added, "As well as acreage of the woods, too."

"No!" Beth exclaimed. "He wouldn't ruin this place with a lot of silly people running away from their city troubles and tramping down this heavenly . . . why, it's almost sacred—untouched by human hands from the day God made it!" She hesitated and remembering his telling her a few months ago about an idea he had to build a resort, she said further, "I had no idea he was talking about this land!"

"I'm afraid this is just what he had in mind, Beth. He even got some of the men at the Thompsons' barbecue riled up because he asked some of them to agree with his idea. He's brought it up to Papa several times."

"You won't let him do it, John, will you? Please promise me you won't." She placed a hand on his arm that was crossed over his knees and looked at him for assurance.

"Of course I won't let him do any such thing. You know I'd promise you the world and most certainly this. I'd take him to court if it came to that, but as long as Papa lives, there'd be no need for that. After he's gone, it might come to that. You know he will get a third of the property . . . unless Papa wills it to the school, and I really don't think he'd leave Teresa and also the grandchildren out. We'll come up with something, you can bet I'll see to that."

Mollified, Beth said softly, "Then I won't have to worry about it anymore."

"I hesitate to tell you this," he looked worried and even wished he had not spoken so quickly. "I'd rather you not mention this to Charles, please, and I do hope you won't think I have acted hastily or under-handed, but then it may make you feel better to know that Doc Harris called me to come up to his house. Really, I was thinking that he or Kate may not be feeling well, but what he wanted shocked me to no end."

Beth was wishing he would just come out with it. "What did he want, Johnny?"

"He asked me if I would buy his property . . . and I did. Said he and Kate were going to move into an assisted living building near Matt's place."

"It looks to me like he would have sold the property either to Matt or Dan," Beth said.

"Kate broke in then and said that neither of their boys wanted the land, and they could take the money they would get from selling to buy the apartment in the building that he had already looked into for them." John looked down at his hands and then to Beth. "I know a wife is not supposed to keep things from her husband, but, well . . . I just didn't want to rock the boat with Charles, so to speak."

"I understand, and really, I think this is the best thing after all. That old couple should not keep on living way back up there alone."

A short silence ensued. They both were watching the children chasing one another, then Beth asked, bluntly, "John, why did you never marry? Weren't you ever in love?" She felt guilty and glanced at him with an embarrassed look on her face for even asking such a question.

This blunt, personal question caught him quite by surprise. He was an inward person, always doctoring others and giving sound advice but never speaking of himself and his personal desires to anyone, not even his dad. "Just like his papa," Ophelia had told Beth one day as they were stringing beans in the kitchen. "That one so much like his papa a body'd think he done spit 'im out. He run affer his papa ever since he was knee high to a grasshopper. Foller him 'bout 'til he done got to actin' thu same and talk thu same. One day I seen 'em comin' acrost thu pasture down younder pas' thu barn and Misser Alyn he had his thumbs stuck under his belt all thinking-like and right behind 'im was that youngun with his thumbs fixed jes' like his papa's. I called to his mama to come an' look at that. She jes' smiled her sweet angel-like smile and shook her head." At that time when Ophelia was telling Beth about this, and Beth had asked about Charles, Ophelia just shook her head and pursed her lips. "Dat one . . . he was diffrunt. He never was clos' to his papa. He couldn't reach him a' tall. Dat youngun, he got more spankins 'fore he's six year old dan mos kids eben oldter."

John finally answered Beth's question. "I think you know I was in love, Beth . . . a long time ago."

She skirted his answer. When they had dated during school days, he never told her that he loved her, although she had assumed that he did. She reached down and picked a "clock." Blowing the thistles off and watching them scatter in the air, she asked further, "What I'm getting at, Johnny, and I don't mean to be prying into your personal life . . . but, are you happy here with your work and no outside interest? Are you ever bored? Don't you ever want to go away and see the world . . . have a life of your own? You live for your patients and for Papa and Teresa. I'm just concerned for you."

He felt pleased that she was concerned for him and that she cared. "Of course I'm happy here, I don't know anything else. You aren't about to play cupid and try to marry me off to one of your city friends, are you? You'd have me move to the city, nearly kill myself working hard, like Charles, so I'd be able to come back to the country to retire?"

She smiled at his humor and recognized that he'd gotten her off track, maybe deliberately. They heard the children laughing and turned from one another to see them throwing stones into the creek. "You are adding to the memories of Knollwood, Beth," John told her.

"Me?" she laughed. "The children, maybe. I think the old house has memories of its own that could not be burned down. They were just transferred to the one your dad and mother built. I think Papa looks upon it as the same old house he grew up in . . . like . . . just a continuation."

"Yes, he does. He even placed the furniture in the exact spots as the old one, so Mama told me. That's for sure, the place is chock-full of happy memories; oh, and a few sad, but you and the children have added new ones. The kids will be telling their own children about the snipe hunt and about coming up here today, such things as that." He looked at her thoughtfully.

Beth felt a strange magnetic pull when he looked at her. On the surface, he was the kind, gentle uncle to her children and her devoted brother-in-law, but underneath all the quiet secret shell, she failed to know what to make of him. He was family and she loved him for that, but it seemed almost as though John understood the battle she was having within herself. She also knew that his true feelings for her went much deeper than family. She'd always heard that a person's first love is never erased, and she had been in love with him too, long ago.

"Oh, I meant to tell you that my mother is coming to visit us soon, and I was wondering . . . do you think Teresa and Papa would mind if I bring her up for a visit?"

"Of course they wouldn't. They'd be happy to see her again. When is she coming?"

"Probably next week, she said. I may not have told you that she has moved back to Mobile recently. Since Daddy died two years ago she felt that she didn't want to be alone out there in California. There are relatives in Mobile other than her two sisters you may remember," and he nodded. "She sold all her things out there and moved in with my two old maid aunts. It's been working out great, even though we offered for her to come stay with us in Atlanta."

"I remember when your Dad died. I was so sorry I didn't make it to the funeral, but I'm sure you got my card explaining that I could not leave a gravely ill patient here."

"Yes, yes I did get it, and I knew you'd be there if you could." She looked down at her hands, twisted her ring, and then looked over at John who was reclined back on an elbow with a blade of grass in his mouth. "Life is certainly fragile, isn't it? We just don't know from one day to the next if that will be our last."

"That's so true and all the more reason we should live life to the fullest and enjoy every minute of it, too . . . so you bring Miss Ester up any time and we'll have a big dinner party!" Beth smiled and then they were quiet for a bit until he said further, "I remember your folks coming up to visit you at the school, and I liked them very much. Both of them were so pleasant and your mother . . . she was a lot of fun, always laughing and having a good time." He grew serious, wondering if he should make the next statement but jumped into it without any more thought. "I remember one time when I was standing behind her in the food line in the cafeteria, she turned to me and leaned over and whispered in my ear that she'd be very disappointed if her daughter let me get away."

Beth was surprised, and it showed on her face. She tried to treat it as a joke and punched John on the shoulder, saying, "Dr. John Russell, it was not my fault. I did not even know you cared other than having someone to hold hands with and sit out front of the school on the courting benches!"

Wanting to change the subject, he stood stretching and said, "Let's put out the lunch." He looked toward the sky that now had gathered a few dark clouds. He whistled loudly with fingers stuck in the corners of his mouth. The horses lifted their heads and then continued their eating, but the children came racing one another up the hill. Of course the boy's legs were longer and about halfway up the hill, he was way ahead when Susan stumbled over a rock and hurt her big toe. She went sprawling to the ground crying. Peter stopped and called her a big crybaby. "Get up and come on." But she lay there crying, mostly because Peter was winning the race and not because she was hurt, until John came to her, gathered her in his arms, and held her affectionately. He wiped her glistening cheeks and said, "Come on, Princess Tagalong. We'll both race ole Peter," and they all ran up the hill with John coming in last . . . on purpose, of course, to the delight of both children.

After what was left of the picnic lunch had been packed back in the basket, the group mounted their horses. Before they were halfway home, however, the rain began falling from a blackened sky, drenching four riders along the trail.

The next day, Beth left for home with a happy heart that the Kendell Mountain School board of directors had appointed her to do two large oil paintings that were to hang in the entrance hallway—one of Joyce Abernathy Kelly and one of Anson Kelly. Anson's daughter, Kate Harris, supplied her with the photographs that she'd had for years.

As John was carrying suitcases down the steps with Beth following behind carrying her makeup case, she was asking about Papa's bum leg, stating that he seemed to be limping much more than the last time they were here.

"Your observation is correct, and I've already made an appointment for him with an orthopedic doctor at Emory. He's about the best in the business so he should find the problem even if it is arthritis, like I've thought, and we can't do much about that other than prescribe pain medicine."

"Let me know when you are coming and be sure and spend a weekend with us," Beth said, "or a night if the appointment happens to be during the week."

Chapter Thirty–nine

THE DAYS SEEMED TO BE FLYING! BETH FELT THAT AT THE rate they were going, she may wake up some morning and discover that the children had finished school, married, and left her nest to make nests of their own. She glanced in the mirror over the bathroom sink to check for gray hairs or any sign of a dreaded wrinkle. No. There were none as yet visible, but inside she had a let-down feeling . . . fagged out. "Christmas does that to people," her friend Connie Roland told her later that same morning sitting in the Russells' living room. "You furiously work up to that big day getting ready for the event and then all of a sudden, boom! It's come and gone and what have you accomplished?" Connie answered her own question before Beth could say anything. "Just a lot of bills and headaches is all I can see."

Beth smiled at her logic and agreed. She had gone over to the fireplace and put another log on the smoldering fire, picking up the poker and stirring around in the ashes. "The aftermath always brings a deflated feeling," her friend continued.

"But you and Gregg have no children so you really don't understand what I've been through lately," Beth complained.

"Oh, I think I have an idea. My sister and her family go through the same rat race that you do . . . kinda makes me glad I never had kids."

"Frankly, I think Christmas would not be Christmas without the kids and all the hurley-burley of shopping and the church Christmas affairs and carols. It's after it is all over that I feel rather blue. It takes awhile to get back in the swing and the kids back into their school routine. Winter just gives me the blahs in general." She placed the poker back where it belonged and went to pour them both a cup of coffee.

"No milk," Connie called after her as she left the room. "Just one spoon of sugar, please." Beth could not imagine Connie with children. She did not know if Connie was self-centered because she never had children or if she'd always been that way. She dressed "to the nines" (whatever that meant) and her hair was always perfect, every hair in place. What could the woman possibly do with her time everyday? Beth had wondered. Gregg played golf at the club where they belonged. That was his only outside interest, but as far as Beth knew, Connie had no other interest except going to the beauty parlor to have her hair and nails done and visiting the spa twice a week. Now that would be a boring life! The only other interest that was evident at all was gossiping. Connie accepted the cup gratefully, saying that was what she really needed to warm her up after being out in the cold. She had only stopped by for a short visit, she said, on her way home from the grocery store and could only stop for a few minutes as she had things in the car that needed to be in the refrigerator.

"Whew! That is certainly hot coffee," she exclaimed after taking a sip.

"Papa Russell brought these cups. They do hold the heat, don't they? He has always disliked my small cups and decided if he was spending Christmas day here he'd have to do something about the cups."

This Christmas, that was now a month behind them, was the first time in quite a while that Beth and Charles had his family at their house for the occasion, as well as her mother, since she'd moved back south. Her mother, Ester Langford, stayed for two days, but the north Georgia Russells only came for the day. They arrived early in the morning and left late in the afternoon, loaded down with gifts and feeling stuffed from the Christmas meal. It was a joyous day of festivity, one that would long live in the memory of Charles and Beth's children. The visitors all inspected Beth's painting with awe, Papa Russell exclaiming at the likeness of Joyce Abernathy Kelley, "Like she could just step down from that canvas." As soon as she finished with this one, she would start on the one of Anson Kelly to match. Teresa commented that she could hardly wait to hang them in the entrance lobby of the school. That would be a proud day indeed. As she was saying that, Alyn Russell stepped back in time to the day the school first opened. He was thinking how proud and excited he had been to get there that early morning now so long ago. That feeling could never ever be duplicated.

Beth had spent the better part of the week before Christmas cooking so she had someone come in to do the cleaning and dared the children to leave a thing out of its proper place. She was pleased to note that Penny was also a great help readying the house while Al cleaned up around the yard, both front and back with the dog, Sally, right on his heels.

Sometime during the day, Charles commented to his brother that Papa seemed to be limping more, and he'd noticed that he rubbed the place more often than he had seen him do before. John replied that he intended to get to the bottom of this problem after Christmas. Papa Russell, still a good-looking man for his age, had not a wrinkle on his face nor were his shoulders stooped, as most tall men's were prone to do. Even with the aggravating pain in his leg, the twinkle in his eyes and the ready smile were still there. He had always been a hard worker and walked with a fast gait, until the pain set in a few years ago.

Now, Christmas had come and gone, and January was now blowing in with full force. Susan and Peter came racing through the room hurrying to get outside to their new bicycles with Sally right behind them barking full force. "Come back here, Peter, and get your coat," Beth said loud enough for him to know she meant business. "The very idea! Do you want to catch a cold and then not be able to go outside and ride the bicycle at all for awhile?" Susan, with her coat on, had already gone out and closed the door. The little boy moaned and retraced his steps.

"Where are your men today, Beth?" Connie asked as she took another sip of the coffee.

"I think you know very well where Charles is with all that hulla-baloo going on with all the carpenters!"

"Yes. I understand that, but I was speaking of Mr. Russell and John."

"Oh, them. Papa Russell had a doctor's appointment this after-noon, and this morning they did some school errands that Teresa asked them to do in order to save her a trip down, so they've been gone all day." She glanced up at the clock on the mantel when she said that. "They should be back anytime now. I have supper already done; wouldn't you stay with us for some hot soup and cornbread? It isn't much to offer company, but that's what Papa ordered. I think he was afraid I'd go to a lot of trouble."

"Thanks, but no . . . I've got to get my groceries on home. By the way, what do you think they'll do about the union?" By the "they," Beth knew she was talking about the upheaval. The workforce had come to a halt and were having meetings with union organizers, against the orders of Gregg Roland and Charles Russell. The organizers were ordered off the property so meetings were being held elsewhere. Gregg and Charles met with their foremen and advised them to get the men back on the job or they would be fired. So far, none of the foremen joined in with the laborers. Today, however, things were heating up. Rocks had been hurled through some office windows, and Charles received a threatening phone call.

Connie stood to put on her coat and asked Beth almost as an after-thought, "Did you know about Charles's threatening phone call? I suppose he has told you about it." She saw the astonished look on Beth's face and knew that she was the first to tell.

"No! Well, I was afraid it would all come to this. I wonder why he hasn't called me!" She had stood and set her cup on an end table, walking toward the door as Connie moved that direction.

"Of course I don't know. I'm always in the dark about what goes on around there. Gregg practically lives in that office, and he has complained to me that Charles practically lives in New York at J. P.'s office so it seems that you and I are office widows."

"Yes, he has been there often while they were getting this shopping center all set up and contracts drawn up. I understand there is a lot to it, but it does look to me like that J. P. Thrower would want to come down here and oversee what's going on with all the money he's investing." While Connie was pulling on her gloves, Beth was saying that she would phone the office now and see what she could find out. Then she asked Connie, "Do you think they are in any danger?"

Connie gave a wry grin and answered, "Don't you think a rock thrown through a window hitting someone on the head would hurt just a little bit?" There were a few seconds of silence, and with her hand on the doorknob, she said, "I always made fun of Gregg keeping a baseball bat beside his desk . . . he said that with his working late hours, he might need it sometime. I told him a forty-four would be better."

When Connie went out the door, Beth turned to telephone Charles's office. Connie had told her the last time she dropped by that Gregg had commented that he felt like Charles was spending an awful lot of money on his trips which was uncalled for, and Connie felt the two partners had not been getting along very well lately. This worried Beth, but after mulling it over, she decided to say nothing and let them work it out by themselves.

In his own capricious way, Charles made up his own rules, side-stepping anything that might pin him down. All through college, Charles had been tagged as the bright young man who would soar to heights unknown in the business world. No one knew the actual truth, which was that without the level head of his partner, Gregg Roland, the business would have succumbed to disaster because of two main factors. One being Charles's impatience with office conformity and the other the law of organization.

No one answered the phone at Roland and Russell Company, and Beth placed the receiver back on the cradle just as she heard a light rap on the door, bringing her back to her senses. "Hello, Rusty," she said to the young man standing on the stoop with his hands in pockets and his shoulders hunched up against the cold.

"Good afternoon, Mrs. Russell. I just saw Susan and Peter down the block, and I thought you wouldn't want them down that far. So I told them to come on home, but they told me to mind my own business. It sure is cold out here. Is Penny at home?"

"Yes, Rusty, she's upstairs doing her homework. Just come on in." She had opened a coat closet door and was taking out her coat when he brushed past her and started to mount the stairs. "No, Rusty. That's a no-no. You just go on in the kitchen and call her on the intercom. I'll be right back."

"Yessum," he answered, turning toward the kitchen with the refrigerator in mind. After calling Penny, he helped himself to a can of Coca-Cola and placed the cookie jar in the middle of the kitchen table.

"Your mom is sure a great cookie maker," he told Penny as she entered with a disgusted look on her face and sat down in the chair across from him.

"All you think about is eating," she sighed. "Don't you ever have anything else on your mind?"

He gulped a mouthful of Coke and wiping a hand across his mouth, said, "What's the matter with you, Pen? Eat a sour grape or a lemon maybe?"

"Good grief, won't you ever grow up?" she asked in reply. Sometimes you act so wonderful and then you revert back to like you were ten years old. When you called on the phone up to the Thompsons' when the kids were lost, I thought you were so sweet and I did appreciate that, Rusty, but remember before that I told you it is over between us. Completely over; that's spelled o-v-e-r. Over, get the message?"

"Yeah. I thought that was what you said. Al told me that you flipped over a country hick up there. Man! A redneck even!"

"I'll thank you to mind your own business, Russell Morgan."

"You know, I always thought when we get married and have a kid, we'd name him 'Russell' after my first name and your last name. Don't you think that would be kinda cute?"

"We won't ever have a kid . . . child, Rusty. Now, will you please go, that is, if you've had enough to eat!"

"Okay, I'll go, but you'll come crawling back. All the guys say their girls usually do after they break up." He finished his last bite of cookie, got up, and threw away his Coke can.

Penny stood up, her expression still unchanged. Just as Rusty turned around, their eyes met, and as serious as someone much older than his years, he said, "You know I love you, Pen . . . you can't just shake me off like this. We've been going together for two whole years." He looked straight into her beautiful eyes, and she knew that he was hurting. He was not the only one, though, for she felt it, too. "It won't be long and we'll be eighteen . . . you'll forget this other guy. Please wait for me, Penny." His expression was very serious as he poured his heart out to her.

"I . . . I don't know, Rusty. It's all so confusing right now. Sometimes I think, I just think . . . well, frankly, I don't know what I do think at this moment. It's very confusing." Then shrugging her shoulders and spreading her hands, she added, "We'll see; just give me time."

"All the time you need, babe. I'll call you in the morning." He kissed her on the forehead and went out the kitchen door to the carport. Penny stood in the doorway as he drove off with tires squealing. Just as he rounded the corner, Beth and the children came in the carport where they left the bicycles. Penny said she was glad they did not come up as Rusty was pulling out of the driveway or he could have hit them.

Chapter Forty

"LET'S GO BY CHARLES'S OFFICE, DAD. IT ISN'T MUCH OUT OF the way from where we are now," John told his father as he turned on to Peachtree Street and headed north. "We'll surprise Charles with the good news about your leg."

"He's probably gone on home by now or he should've been, anyway, don't you think? It's about dark now and look at that sky! Man! It looks like we're in for some bad weather." Papa was gazing out the window, wishing he were at home right this minute and in his own bed.

"Well, it won't be but only a few more minutes to get there and even if he's already gone, I'd like to talk with Gregg . . . haven't seen him in awhile. Maybe Mo will be around, too." John headed on in the direction he'd started and found the traffic to be more than he'd bargained for. "Drat! I wouldn't live in this mess and fight traffic every day for anything!" John said with disgust when a traffic light turned red just as he approached. "I think that light saw me coming and said, 'Here comes a country bumpkin, I think I'll get 'im.'"

Alyn Russell smiled even though he'd rather be getting back to Charles and Beth's house on Howell Mill Road. "You'll have us lost for good, son, and they'll have to call in a posse to find us."

It was 6:00 and nearly dark when John's Buick pulled into the parking lot of Russell and Roland Company. The lot was empty except for Charles's car and another that he assumed belonged to Gregg. At this time of day the other office help would have already left. "Ah, see, I told you, Papa, Charles is still here. That other car must belong to Gregg. So Charles can lead us on home without any problem at all, but I do know how to get there myself." The two got out and headed toward the office door that was left ajar. "It's kinda cold to be leaving the door open," Papa Russell said as they went in. In the front office, the secretary's desk and the bookkeeper's desk had been left neat and clean. No one was in sight nor was there any talking, but John mentioned that a light was on in the office with Gregg Roland painted on the glass door. "Let's just peek inside," John said, and his father answered that he'd better call out before entering so as not to catch him unawares.

"Hello, Gregg. Are you in there?" John called walking toward the door feeling like an intruder. There was no answer. He took hold of the knob, pushing the door open, and discovered an overturned chair and a trash can with litter strewn about. "Oh, no!" John exclaimed, "something is definitely wrong here."

"What is it, son?" Papa Russell asked, walking in behind John, who had already gone around behind the desk and found Gregg Roland lying on the floor in a pool of blood. He had been hit on the head with his baseball bat that was left on the floor beside him.

When Papa also saw him, John had already stooped down, feeling Gregg's wrist for a pulse. "He's alive, Papa. Move back and let me get at the phone. Whatever you do, don't touch a thing. The police will want fingerprints.

"Somebody's mighty dumb. They were bound to leave fingerprints on that bat." Papa Russell's own pulse quickened when he wondered where Charles was at this moment and also wondered if they'd gotten into an argument and maybe Charles had done this to his partner. "May heaven have mercy," he said as John dialed the police.

"Please send an ambulance and tell them to hurry," John said into the phone after he'd given a report of what had happened. Then he dialed Beth to see if she'd heard from Charles. "Oh, dear Lord," John said. "The line's busy. It'll be Penny yapping to Rusty."

"Well, have the operator butt in!"

John followed his father's advice and dialed 0 for the operator. When he was connected and told Beth what had happened and asked about Charles, she exclaimed that she had not heard from him and couldn't understand why his car was parked there in the lot. "Oh, John! What should I do?"

"Not anything, Beth. There's nothing you can do except call Gregg's wife. I don't know which hospital they'll take him to so tell her just to wait and I'll call you back."

"John, look around the office and go into Charles's office to see if anything is amiss. Tell them to take Gregg to Georgia Baptist Hospital. That's where their doctor goes."

"Okay, but hold on the phone, Beth, and let me look. When I saw Gregg on the floor I didn't even think to go in Charles's office."

Beth's heart was beating fast. Why Charles could be lying on the floor in his office as well! She felt so helpless standing there waiting. Al came up behind her when he heard the upset tone in her voice and asked, "What's wrong, Mom? What is it? John and Papa haven't had a wreck, have they?"

"No, son, but someone's hit Gregg Roland on the head, and the police and ambulance are on the way to the office!"

"My stars! Who would do that!" Then Penny came into the room asking what all the loud talking was about and why she was cut off the phone by the operator.

"Hush, both of you . . . yes, John, what did you say?"

"I said that there is no sign of Charles, but I found a note on his desk the secretary left there. It says that he's to catch the next plane he can get to J. P. Thrower's office. I won't take time to read it all, but it seems they are threatening to cancel their contract if Russell and Roland can't get the union mess straightened out down here and the men back on the job at once. Oh, I hear a siren. I'll call you back in a few minutes." Then he hung up abruptly.

BETH PLACED THE PHONE BACK IN THE CRADLE WONDERING how Charles got to the airport. Penny suggested that she telephone Mo's wife or his mother and ask if he knew how and when her dad had left to catch a plane. Immediately, she dialed Mo's apartment downstairs at his mother's house where no one answered so she dialed upstairs to Belle Jackson. After two rings, a pleasant voice said "Hello."

"Oh, Miss Belle, I'm so glad you're at home. This is Beth Russell calling. Is Moses by any chance at your place? There's no answer at his apartment."

"No, Beth. He isn't here. His wife and Scooter went with him to take your husband to the airport."

"Okay then. That's just what I wanted to inquire about. Something terrible happened at the office, and Mr. Roland is on the way to the hospital in an ambulance. We don't know who attacked him. It had to be shortly after they left for the airport. Please tell Moses to call me when he returns."

"I certainly will, and I hope they won't go anywhere else. That is awful news. I've been afraid things would get worse around there. He's been telling us about the upheaval, and he's got us all worried about their safety and Mo's, too. It's sprinkling rain on our side of town and with it turning so cold, it just might turn to ice so I sure hope they get right back on home, honey. I'll tell him to call you the minute they get home."

"Thanks, Miss Belle." Then she hung up hating not knowing anything at all and hating having to wait. She hoped John and Papa would be in soon.

Chapter Forty-one

AFTER THE AMBULANCE PULLED OFF THE PROPERTY WITH Gregg Roland, the police detained John and his father for more than an hour asking question after question. They had sat in the outer office waiting for a Detective Lewis, one of the policemen called him, to arrive. He came in shaking water off his hat and hanging it on a hat rack by the door. The rain was now coming down hard. "We're in for a bad night, Jim," he told the police officer who came from Gregg's office when he heard the front door close.

"Yep, and we always have something like this when we need to check the lot for tire tracks and all, don't you know? This here is the brother and father of Mr. Roland's business partner, Dr. John Russell and Mr. Alyn Russell."

"Nice tu meet cha' gentlemen," the detective said and brushed past them without a handshake toward Gregg's office. "Just wait out here for a few minutes," he continued, following the officer back inside the office where his partner was still combing every inch of the place.

"Wait some more," Alyn Russell grumbled. He had remained seated when John stood to greet the detective. "You don't think they'd suspect that we would've done this to Gregg, do you?"

"Papa, they suspect any and everyone when they are searching for clues. We don't have to worry about that because Gregg will be coming around soon and tell us what happened to him." He sat down again beside Papa Russell with his elbows resting on his knees and wishing he had gone on back to the house like Papa wanted to. Then there was a guilt feeling when it dawned on him that Gregg could have lain there all night and possibly died before help came.

They could see reflections dancing on the milky glass door as the men moved about inside the office. John was tired. He rubbed his hands over his hair as he gazed at the floor between his legs. Then he jumped when the telephone on a desk rang loudly. He stood to answer but hesitated and glanced toward Gregg's office when he heard one of the men answer and heard the talking, not making out what was being said.

"I betcha that'll be Beth calling back after she talked with Sassy Belle," Papa supplied.

"She's been long enough in calling back, but then, she had to call Gregg's wife, too, so I suppose she got tied up. I hope they let me talk with her."

Just then an officer poked his head out the door and told John that Mrs. Russell was on the phone and he could take the call on the desk out there. He jumped to his feet and went hurriedly over to the desk. "Yes, Beth, what did you find out?" he asked at once . . . and to Papa it was a one-sided conversation. "Oh, so he did take him . . . I see . . . when did she say . . . oh, and they still haven't come back? . . . Well, it could take awhile but at least they live somewhere on that side of town so it wouldn't take as long as if he had to come back here . . . I know that . . . Just don't worry, Beth . . . I would like to go to the hospital to check on Gregg, but I'd like to come on back there first and leave Papa because he's worn out . . . Did Gregg's wife say she'd leave at once? . . . I'm glad she did . . . Yes, I know and I do, too . . . But at least we do know where Charles is and evidently he doesn't know a thing about what happened to Gregg because if he did, he wouldn't have gone on, you know . . . No, I don't know how much longer we'll be but you just go on to bed . . . You don't have to do that. I'm sure we couldn't eat a thing right now . . . Tell you what, I'll phone you back when we start to go out the door here, if we get to leave before you call back. Alright, then . . . Let's hang up so Mo could call you and not get a busy signal. We'll see you soon."

Beth hung up, but before he got the phone replaced on the hook, he heard a click. Someone in Gregg's office had been listening in on the conversation. John walked by a water cooler, took a drink, and handed Papa Russell a paper cup of the cool water. Then, with hands in pockets, he turned to look at pictures on the wall.

Before much longer, Detective Lewis made an appearance, throwing questions to John. In all appearances he did not suspect these two at all, mainly because John was the one who had telephoned the discovery to the police station in the first place. Lewis raised his bushy gray eyebrows when John said that Charles had taken a plane to New York just a couple of hours ago.

"My brother would not have done this; what would he have to gain?" Then he explained to the detective about their business financial connection in the big city that entailed frequent trips, especially now since they had been threatened that the contract could be broken due to the workers striking.

Lewis commented that everything hinged on Gregg Roland being able to tell him who had whacked him on the head, maybe intending to kill him. The detective rubbed his chin, squinted his eyes, and said he would put a guard by his hospital room door tonight. "I'll just go on over there and have a talk with his wife now and you two may leave but stay in town, just in case . . ." he never finished his sentence.

John handed his father the walking cane and assisted him to his feet, with Detective Lewis turning back to John asking for the telephone number of his brother's house, saying he'd be in touch.

THE ELEVEN O'CLOCK NEWS WAS ON WHEN JOHN AND PAPA Russell parked in the carport beside Beth's station wagon where Charles usually parked. Beth had just heard the report of Gregg's attack when she heard the car drive up. Papa said as he was getting out of John's car that he was tired to the bone. "Wait a minute, Papa," John said hurrying around to the open door, "let me give you a pull. Don't put any more pressure on that leg than you have to."

"I don't have to worry about that," Papa answered, "because it doesn't want to cooperate much anyway." He grunted when John pulled him up by the arm, feeling totally disgusted with himself. Beth, hearing the car doors slam, came to the carport door, holding it open for them.

"Hi," John said cheerfully even though he was certainly not feeling too cheerful.

"Come in this house, you two. I know you must be simply worn out. I was beginning to worry about you." Sally had heard the door open and the talking and came bounding down the steps from Al and Peter's room, sliding across the linoleum and giving a few barks with her tail doing double time.

"You've got that right, daughter-in-law . . . Man! What a day. Even the weather didn't want to cooperate." Papa Russell came into the kitchen, propped his cane in a corner, hung his hat on a wall hanger, and unbuttoned his coat.

"Go back, Sally," Beth told the little dog and pointed out the kitchen door to the hall. "Go back upstairs." The little terrier tucked its tail and left the room.

John didn't wait until he got his coat off to ask if Mo had called.

"Yes, he called shortly after you left the office," Beth told him. "Let's sit here at the kitchen table and have a cup of coffee and what about a bowl of that soup?"

John sniffed the air and said, "That's just what I need right now. How about you, Papa?" And he nodded in agreement, sitting down at the round table in front of a picture window.

Beth went to the stove and came back with the coffeepot she already had heating and poured each of them and herself a cup of the good-smelling brew. "There's milk and sugar on the table if you need either." Then she went to the cabinet and took out bowls for the soup and opened a drawer for spoons. "Oh, the crackers." She went back for the box of saltines and set them in front of the men.

"I don't suppose you'd want cornbread this late, would you?" They did not.

"Mo did take Charles to the airport, and they had known nothing of what had happened. He said when they left the office, Gregg was sitting behind his desk with a bunch of paperwork in front of him. Mo said the three of them talked there in the office about the striking men. Mo's crew of black guys refused to strike, each saying they needed the pay and couldn't get along without it. He said they all agreed that they had been treated fairly and had no quarrel with the company, but they had been threatened by some of the others that if they went back in to work, they'd regret it. Gregg didn't want Charles to leave so they argued a little bit about that, but Mo said Charles wanted to get to Thrower's office before Thrower's lawyer took steps to break the contract. Gregg said there was bound to be trouble over the weekend."

John swallowed a sip of the coffee and said, "Beth, I really feel concerned for you and the kids here in the house."

"What! Do you actually think any of them would come here?"

He frowned, thinking. "You just can't tell what a bunch of hot heads would do."

Papa set his cup down not believing that this was happening and turning to John asked, "How would a stupid thing like that benefit the men? Any harm they might do would certainly not help them to get a union. If anything, it would harm the effort more. No. I don't think they will have the nerve to come here at all."

Beth was worried—actually more frightened than worried. What should they do? The kids were all upstairs in their beds asleep. Now she feared for their safety.

John saw the anxious expression on her face and was sorry he'd even mentioned that someone may try to come to the house and use some scare tactics. But the police had been concerned enough to have a guard put at the door of Gregg's room at the hospital. "Have you phoned the hospital to inquire about the extent of Gregg's injury, or if he's come to?"

"Yes, of course I did. At the time he was in emergency, and I couldn't find out anything. I asked to speak with his wife, but she had not arrived. I called again later and spoke with her, but of course she didn't know a thing to tell me and said her sister and her sister's husband were there with her."

John got up and poured himself another cup of coffee. "I should go down there myself, but I think maybe I'd better stay here with you and the children. I could do nothing there at all and at least Gregg's wife has her family to be with her."

Beth felt better knowing John would not leave. "Well, I don't understand any of this at all," she said with some asperity. "Things were going well as they were. I wonder who started this anyway. . . . To think that they may lose the whole company because of some meddling . . ." Her words died in the air; the sentence went unfinished. Charles had worked so hard to bring the contracts in! Sure, he'd been away most of the time, but that's what it took to get the ball rolling. And now this! She was mad as fire and it showed.

John took the last of his soup and laid the spoon down. After he dabbed at his mouth with the napkin, he said thoughtfully, "When a company employs a lot of laborers, the unions come in and demand that they form a union to look out for the welfare of the men. The company is growing and it was to be expected."

"I still think if a company treats its employees right, it is all so unnecessary!" Beth said, and then abruptly changing the subject, she turned to Papa and said, "Oh, Papa, I know you must be awfully tired and we haven't even considered you. You must get to bed at once. I've turned down your bed in the guest room and John can sleep on the couch in the den. Oh, but what did the doctor say about your leg, for crying out loud! I didn't even think to ask."

Papa Russell pushed back his chair and stood with some effort. "At least we do have some good news," he grinned. Turning toward John, he said, "Tell 'er, son."

"Nope. You tell 'er."

"Sakes alive! Will one of you please tell me?"

"You won't believe it. This is one for the books," Papa told her. "That blasted piece of steel in my leg has moved, and no wonder it has been hurting more lately. I saw the thing in the X ray! Just looks like a little tiny piece but it's there—been there for all these years. Can you feature that!"

Beth's mouth flew open. "Well, of all things! If that doesn't beat all!" Then she turned to John and asked, "But, can it be removed?"

"Yes, of course, and that's the good news. He'll be as good as new and be dancing a jig before long. In fact, it's all set up with the hospital to take it out next week."

Beth's eyes were radiant. She looked pleased and went around and hugged her father-in-law. Alyn Russell was beaming and already feeling like a young man again. He placed his hand over his daughter-in-law's that was on his shoulder and, looking up at her, said, "John told me you'd bring your mother up when she comes to visit so maybe she won't see an old crippled man by then."

He'd even be ready to walk down the mountain to his old fishing hole by spring.

After Papa had gone to bed and John and Beth were left sitting in the living room before the fire that leapt invitingly, Beth confronted John that she felt he did not seem very happy about his dad's operation.

"Ah, it's not that I'm not happy. Of course I am. Very much so. And I hope Papa doesn't think I'm not happy, but you see . . . now don't think for one minute that I have any jealousy at all, but the thing is . . . well, frankly, I'm just upset because I was not the one who caught this problem before, and I certainly should have. Here I am a doctor, supposed to be a good one at that, and did not detect the problem. I've let Papa suffer with his leg hurting all these years! Really, I'm hurt and I'm mad as an old turkey."

"Now, Johnny, you can't blame yourself! After all, it didn't show up in your X rays, did it?"

"No. I didn't see anything, but I should've let someone else look at them besides myself."

"If you didn't see anything then they wouldn't have seen anything either. It looks to me like the sliver of steel may have surfaced somehow or moved around where it could be seen when he had that bad fall not too long ago."

"That's possible. I forgot about the fall. After that is when I talked him into using the cane. I hope you are right. I'm going to go on that anyway so I can feel a little better about myself.

"Beth, I'm completely bushed. I think I'll hit the hay. I don't think we have to worry about anyone coming here to throw rocks or anything at all tonight in this weather. Nobody in their right mind would be out on a night like this. In the morning I want to get to the hospital and check on Gregg."

"If the police want to talk with us, they may come here before you have time to even get to the hospital."

"You could be right about that. We'll see. Right now I'm calling it a night."

He stood, yawned, and then turned back to Beth. "If it's all the same with you, I think I'll just sleep here on this couch, and if I wake up, I'll toss some more wood on the fire."

"May be a good idea. I put a pillow, a sheet, and a couple of blankets on the couch in the den so just help yourself, brother. No alarm clock, so we'll get up when we wake up. Good night." He returned the "good night" and left the room.

Chapter Forty-two

BETH TURNED OFF THE BEDSIDE LAMP AND GOT INTO BED. The sheets smelled clean, like they'd been hanging out in a summer sun all day long. She stretched out her hand and found that the expanse of the smooth sheet across the king-size bed to the other pillow was like an ocean away. She wished Charles were there. How many times had she been to bed alone in the last few years? Many. She had come to accept this as their way of life. Closing her eyes and giving way to her tiredness, she remembered the old saying that "Life begins at forty," and decided that she had something to look forward to in a couple of years.

She felt cold and reached over to the end table and switched on the electric blanket that Charles had given her for Christmas. "Maybe he thought that this would take his place," she smiled. She had thought that this practical gift was not like previous gifts he had given her. Then after she'd put this one aside, he handed her the diamond heart on a gold chain that she now wore around her neck.

It was still raining when they went to bed, and by not finishing up with the eleven o'clock news, they had not heard the weather prediction of icy conditions by morning. As a thin predawn light began to streak the sky, John rapped softly on Beth's door. Peeking his head inside, he awakened Beth and told her that the electricity and heat were off so she'd need to find more blankets for everyone and asked where he could find a flashlight.

She came out of the bedroom pulling on a robe and smoothing her tousled hair. In the dining room buffet, she pulled out several candles, searched a kitchen pantry and found a lamp, and John found matches and a flashlight in a drawer. He pulled back the curtain from a window that looked out across the backyard exclaiming, "Oh, no! Come here and look at this!" He held the curtain aside for her to look out and see icicles dangling from trees and bushes everywhere, a complete winter wonderland. Pine trees bowed over nearly to the ground.

"Oh, we won't be able to go anywhere!" she said with disgust. "Let me see if the phone will work." She walked into the hallway between the kitchen and den and lifted the receiver. "Dead as a door-nail. Wouldn't you know it."

"Can't even have a cup of coffee," John grumbled. "I suppose we are like prisoners."

Beth smiled. "At least there is a barrel at the back door that will be full of rain water we can use for the toilets! And there is a big pitcher of water in the fridge. I'm thankful we have cereal and plenty of milk for breakfast."

"Well, Al and I will walk somewhere later on and see what we can find. Maybe everyone's electricity isn't off. And thanks to Al, there is some wood beside the fireplace, so I'll start up the fire and you just get out some blankets. Lay one out for me and one for Papa and go on back to bed for now."

"About the wood," she looked sheepishly at John. "Charles told me last week to be sure and order another load and I forgot about it. What we have there beside the fireplace is the last of it."

"And to think of all the wood we have up home . . . and for free, too."

"Too bad we aren't there right now. I do hope the kids will sleep late . . . but, oh, we won't be able to check on Gregg. And I hope the telephones will be back on soon. After the last ice storm we had, the lines were down for several days."

"Yep. And I'll bet the airport will be at a standstill, too."

"John, if the roads aren't iced over so bad and we could get the car out, maybe we should go to the Royal Coach Inn up on the other end of Howell Mill Road."

"They may not have any electricity either. The downtown area would be the only possibility of electricity since there aren't tall trees to fall on the lines, and I don't know if we should try to make it that far or not. There'd be a lot of wrecks and that would be worse than a cold house. We don't want to be stranded in a wrecked automobile."

"You're right. That's true," Beth sighed heavyhearted and conceded with a shrug of her shoulders.

DUE TO THE FORCE OF HABIT, THE CHILDREN WOKE UP AT the usual time to get ready for school and bounded down the steps with Sally in the lead, barking louder than their laughing and chatter. "This house is cold!" Peter complained when his bare feet hit the kitchen floor. He opened the carport door to let Sally out to visit the hedge and a gust of icy wind blew in. "Close that door!" several voices piped up at once.

"Mom!" Penny exclaimed, pulling the kitchen curtain aside to peer out. "Look at the trees bending over! Everything's full of ice!"

"Okay, kids . . . shoo. Go on back to bed. We don't have any heat and there'll be no school today." Beth opened the door to let the dog back in, and she went straight to her bowl and lapped up water. Al poured dry dog food in the other bowl, petting Sally's head as she ate with tail wagging. "You hear that, girl! We won't have to go to school today." They all made beelines back to their warm beds.

"I suppose that's settled for another couple of hours," Beth breathed, glad for the reprieve. She had just decided to go back to bed also when John entered the kitchen.

"Oh, what wouldn't I give for a cup of coffee right now," he said. "And I hate to shave with cold water." He rubbed the stubble on his chin.

"Good morning," she answered cheerily as though it were any ordinary morning.

"That's what I love about you, Beth. You can always be so dang cheery over nothing. Can't you be grumpy once in awhile?"

"If I were down in the dumps with all the woes that pop up I'd turn into an old witch . . . speaking of coffee, I was just thinking . . . Al has some camping stuff in the basement. We should be able to find something there to work with."

"Ah, I'll just wait until he gets up again. Is there orange juice by any chance?" Hoping so, he was looking inside a cabinet for a glass and took down two placing them on the table when he saw she took a pitcher from the refrigerator. "Isn't this just the pits?"

"Happens every January, but even so, we're never prepared for it," she answered with her head in a cabinet where she found some date nut bread and placed it on the table with a knife. "Want some butter on this?" He did not but accepted the piece of bread on a napkin that she put before him.

"Humm, this is good. You bake it?"

"Yes, an old recipe from Mama."

John glanced at his watch that showed seven forty-five on the dot when they heard a car drive up in the driveway and then a rap on the carport door. It was a policeman. Another officer waited in the car with the motor running.

"Good morning," Beth said, inviting him in with a wave of the hand, and he stepped inside the kitchen when he saw John sitting at the table.

"Would you have a glass of juice and some date nut bread with us?" Beth offered.

John stood when the officer refused with thanks for the kind offer and stood beside the closed door. "Since the telephones aren't working, Dr. Russell, I was asked to come by and inform you that Mr. Gregg Roland did not recover. He passed away last night during the operation."

Beth drew in her breath with a long, shocked sigh, her hand flying to her mouth. "Oh, no! How awful! And I can't even get in touch with his wife. Oh, John, what will we do?"

"Beth, there's nothing we can do at all except wait."

"Will we ever know who did this to Gregg?" she said in a soft whisper.

"Ma'am," the police officer said, "he didn't come out of the operation, but he did come around enough before he was taken in to say one word. The word was 'holdup.'"

"Holdup!" John exclaimed. "Then it wasn't any of the employees."

"Can't be too sure but prob'ly not, Dr. Russell. The detective said that the papers on his desk showed that he had been preparing a bank deposit and was no doubt going to drop it in the bank's drop box on the way home. He said to tell you that they have found fingerprints and wants you and your father to come down to the station with us to have your fingerprints taken."

"Of course, we'll be glad to. I'll just get my father up. It will take a little bit for him to get dressed."

As they were going out the door to get in the police car, he told his sister-in-law not to worry for they had touched nothing at all except the chairs in the front office and the telephone on that desk. The police could easily get Charles's prints from his office and there also, Papa Russell and John had touched nothing.

The officer turned to Beth and told her it would be best if she stay in and not try to drive her car for the roads were treacherous and there had been lots of accidents all over the place. If he could get permission from headquarters, he would take Dr. Russell and his father by Mrs. Roland's house on the way home. She and her relatives had been sent home from the hospital in a police car.

"And to think, she was by here only a few hours ago and nothing was wrong. How the world can be turned upside down in a short matter of time."

"Yes, Ma'am," the officer said, "it sure can."

Chapter Forty–three

THANKFULLY, AND TO EVERYONE'S RELIEF, THE TEMPERATURE rose a few degrees, and the electricity came back on Saturday. Enough of "camping out" inside the house with a funeral to be held, a leg operation to be performed, and Charles . . . Charles what? Surely they would hear from him today. The telephone rang with several people running to answer it. "I have it in the kitchen," Beth called to everyone. "Don't touch it, kids."

Yes. It was Charles. "Hello, Beth. What's going on down there? The news report said that the South is covered with an ice storm. Are you and the kids alright?"

"We're okay . . . and we are not okay, Charles. There is plenty going on down here. Are you sitting down?"

"Yes. I'm on the hotel bed; I'm just about to leave out and thought I'd better call in. Sorry I didn't get you before I left, but I did leave word with . . ."

"Just listen, please. Oh, Charles, you won't believe what has happened! It's Gregg. He's dead. Somebody came in his office and smacked him on the head, and he died after they got him to the hospital."

"Oh, my word. What in thu . . . I just can't believe what you are saying! When did this happen?"

"Either while you were on the way to the airport or after you got on the plane, and the police are wanting to question you. Tell me, the two of you did not get in a fuss, did you? Just tell me that you did not hit him, Charles!"

"Don't be absurd! Of course I wouldn't do anything like that. We are always having a few disagreements, but they don't get this out of hand. I can't understand who would . . ."

She cut him off; his words were going nowhere. "John and Papa are here. The heat just came on, and the house is freezing. The police came earlier and took John and Papa to be fingerprinted . . ."

"Why them?"

"Just listen, will you . . . they went by the office after they got out of the Emory doctor's office, and it was them who found Gregg lying on the floor. John said they didn't touch anything but the phone and the chairs they were sitting in while the police inspected the office, but they say they have to be fingerprinted anyway."

"I'm very sorry about Gregg, but on the other side of the coin, this is going to throw a monkey wrench in things up here, too. If I leave now, I'll have to come right back. This lawyer I'm to see was tied up on a case 'til yesterday late and rather than come back on Monday morning, I was just going to stay the weekend. He won't be doing any business on Saturday after the week in court."

"If the office up there knew he was on a case, then why in the name of common sense did you go there in the first place, tell me that!"

"They didn't know here that the case would be held over. I don't know what happened, Beth, and don't crawl all over me. I've got a lot of thinking to do. How's the situation down there with the men; has anything else developed? No more rocks being thrown, are there?"

"No, but John says we may not be safe here in our house. He has suggested that we go up home with them after the roads are passable, but we'll have to wait until after the funeral, Charles. We have to stay here."

"John could be right, but surely nobody would do anything else now until after the funeral. Just stay put there for now, and what did the doctor say about Papa's leg?"

She was surprised that in the face of the news she had just thrown at him that he remembered to ask about Papa. "He's going to be alright with an operation to remove a piece of steel. It's scheduled for next week. I was hoping they'd go ahead and do it now. Seems stupid to me he has to be in pain a few more days."

"I'm glad they can fix him up." A short silence and then he said, "I just can't get over Gregg being gone. This is unreal!" Another short silence and then, "Something else to think about is what will Connie want to do with the business? I hope I won't have to contend with her as a partner . . . well, I'll come on as soon as I can make the flight arrangement, but I'll have to come back right after the funeral. And I hope J. P. can be talked into not being so hasty in breaking our contract."

THE NEWS WAS SPREAD ALL OVER THE NEWSPAPERS AND the TV news that Gregg Roland, Atlanta businessman, had been murdered, and the murderer was still at large. The funeral, which was held on Sunday at Patterson's on Spring Street, was a large one. The children were to stay at home, with Penny in charge, and they were warned of the consequences if they did not mind her. Charles, John, Papa, and Beth all rode together on the cold, blustery day, with the winter sun promising clear weather. The ice had delayed any funerals until now.

After the short cemetery service, people gathered at the deceased's home to offer their condolences to the widow (and his business partner), and to partake of food that had been brought in by friends and family. Connie, stunned over losing her husband, stood quietly shaking hands and feeling grateful for the arms around her shoulders, not hearing what friends were saying, but going through the motions like a robot. As usual, she looked stunning, even dressed in her dark outfit—her hair perfect with not one strand out of place, dark shadows under her eyes powdered away. She looked completely in control. Inside, she was not.

Charles stood beside Connie, his usual handsome self, smiling a "thank you" to everyone that shook his hand and mumbled some words to him. In the little groups of people standing around, the opinion floating through the air was that, of course, Connie Roland would pick up the gauntlet and carry on with her husband's work. Just give her a little time. She and Charles would make a good team. Connie, much more outgoing than her husband had been, would be good for business. She would not back down to anyone.

When everyone had left except for Connie's sister and her husband, and the Russells, Connie kicked off her shoes and announced that it was time for her to let down her guard and fall apart. They all sat down to the dining room table with cups of coffee. The hired woman came in with a pound cake that she had put away to save for this time. Connie waved it away saying she could not possibly eat a bite; the others obliged the maid's kind offer.

After his second cup of coffee, Charles broke the conversation of small talk and said to Connie, who was seated at the head of the table,

"Connie, I know this is not the time nor place to talk business. But you know it is inevitable that we must talk very soon about what you want to do. Tomorrow night I have to go back to New York and talk with the lawyer. If he allows Thrower to break our contract, we will be bankrupt."

"I fully understand all of that, Charles. The whole thing is one big mess. But right now I can't even think straight, so let's let it wait until tomorrow morning."

"Certainly. About eleven alright?"

"Yes, of course, and now, if you all will please excuse me, I'm going to crash in the bed until then." She needed the good cry that had been held in for too long. Possibly a running, throwing fit would help.

Chapter Forty-four

ON THE SOUTH SIDE OF TOWN, MOSES AND HIS WIFE AND child were having dinner upstairs with his mother, Belle Jackson. They, too, had attended the funeral. All the time the service was going on, Moses was wondering what would happen with the business. Would Charles buy Connie's half or would she demand to buy his half? Gregg had been so adamant about not having a union among their workers, so now would Charles or Connie allow it? If Charles would be out of the picture, then would his own job be safe? There was a lot to be considered. He may wind up back on Kendell Mountain picking apples and crating them for shipping. This had been the only job he'd ever known and was completely satisfied with it, until he came to the big city where life was lived completely different, like he was in a foreign country. And he liked it. Here he could make more money for his family and now another child was on the way. The children would go to college, this Moses would demand as well as their grandmother. Being an educator, she would not stand by and watch her grandchildren fail to receive a good education. When Moses was younger, she did not have the means, but now she did. Even if her son could not save for this future investment, she could and considered little Scooter and the unborn child a precious investment.

"Moses," his mother said, "Why don't you call Charles and ask him what they are going to do instead of just worrying about it?"

He put his fork down and pushed his plate away. "Ah, Mama, it's still too soon to go pushing him for answers. And besides, it won't be all his decision, you know. Gregg's wife will have as much say-so now as Charles."

"Well, maybe you are right, of course, but you'd better call in the morning early or you'll let Charles get away. You know how he's always on the move."

Chapter Forty-five

PAPA RUSSELL'S OPERATION WAS SET FOR TUESDAY MORNING at 8:30. John decided that it would be of no use to go back to north Georgia on Sunday, just to come back again so quickly. He phoned Teresa to tell her that the operation would be a simple one and not take very long, so she was not to take off from school to come down. He assured her that Papa would be in no danger and he would call her after it was over. Then he called Emily to have her cancel his appointments for Monday through Wednesday and to ask if there had been any emergencies. No, there were none, and the only sicknesses had been mainly winter colds and congestion, except for Eli Whitfield, who had let his blood sugar get out of hand over Christmas. She had called Dr. Weston in Clayton who would handle it. Emily said she had gotten behind with the posting and billing and would do that today and then go on home.

"Has the school had any sicknesses?"

"None to speak of. Only for some colds and the nurse there has handled them."

So with this news, John felt better in staying over. He would be glad to talk with Charles about his business and see if he could be of any help to him.

When John hung up the phone, it rang again and he answered to the greeting of Moses Jackson. "No, Mo, Charles has already left. He said he was going by his office and then on over to Connie Roland's house to discuss things with her."

"Oh, I was hoping to catch him before he left. You have to be in a hurry to catch that man's coat tail."

"I guess you do, Mo, do you want to speak with Beth?"

"No, Dr. Johnny, I'll just wait until I can catch Charles."

Then just as he hung up, the phone rang with his hand still on the receiver. "Looks like I'll be secretary of the day," he thought as he answered again. This time it was Connie Roland.

"Hello, John is Charles still there?" she asked in a whispery voice.

"No, Connie, he's already gone. Would you like to speak with Beth?"

"No. Did he say where he was going? Oh, I'm sure he'd be going by the office so I'll call over there. I just want some more time before we make any plans."

"I think I heard him say that he would be going back to New York tomorrow, Connie. Are you planning on going with him?"

"Oh, no. I couldn't do that. I just don't want to jump into anything, so I'd rather wait until he gets back to decide on what I want to do. I'll call him at the office, and thanks, John." Then she hung up with her hand lingering on the phone while she pondered the telephone call she had just received from Moses Jackson, a trusted employee. She'd heard Gregg praise his faithfulness before.

LATER IN THE AFTERNOON JOHN DROVE HIS FATHER TO THE hospital to be checked in and sat with him until eight o'clock. "I'll see you before they take you in the operating room tomorrow morning, Papa. You get a good night's sleep and by this time tomorrow, you'll be ready to kick butt with that leg."

"Well, Johnny, I've never heard you talk like that before," Papa grinned, "but I'm glad to know you are so sure that I can get my life back. I would like to go hunting and fishing again."

"Let's make a date to do just that then, say, this time next month?"

"It's a date, son." He made a V for Victory sign in the air as John waved and walked out.

When he arrived back at his brother's house and opened the door, he heard a lot of talking, speckled with laughter coming from the living room. "Come on in here, John," he heard Beth call when she heard the door close. "Look who's here." He walked through the kitchen and dining room to the living room where they were seated around the fireplace with flames leaping invitingly. It was Ester Langford, Beth's mother, and she was playfully teasing Peter and Susan who were hanging on to her.

"We have a surprise, John! My mother came earlier than she said she would and decided to surprise us instead of calling. I'm sure you do remember my mother?"

He walked over to Beth's mother and accepted her extended hand. "Of course I remember Mrs. Langford. It's so good to see you again, Ma'am. Beth had told me you were planning a visit with her and the family." While speaking, he was wondering where she would sleep.

"John Russell, you are still such a charming man. You must have scores of women fighting over you."

"Well, now, I wouldn't go so far as to say . . ."

"Oh, come on, you must have them eating out of your hand with your doctor's bedside manner!"

"Maybe you are right," he laughed. "And you are the same flatterer that I remember and just as pretty, too. I know where your daughter gets her good looks."

Beth broke in, "That's enough of the admiration society! Did you get Papa Russell all settled?"

"Yep. And he is looking forward to getting this operation over so he can go fishing. He's always loved to tromp through the woods and has missed it a lot, so I promised him that we'd go to the old fishing hole in one month." Looking around and not seeing Penny or Al, he asked where they were.

"Doing homework. Penny has a book report to turn in tomorrow and Al is working on a science project. Now, it is time for these two rambunctious animals to go up to bed."

"Ah, Mom, just a little longer," Susan pleaded, and Peter added a "Pleaseee."

"No. This is it so let's have a goodnight kiss for everybody and both of you be off. And tell Al to take Sally for a trip outside before he turns in."

John was tired and would like to go on to bed himself. He would need to be out very early tomorrow morning and had hoped that Beth would go sit with him while Papa's operation was taking place. "Did Charles call and let you know what Connie had to say?"

"Yes, but she didn't have anything to say because she wanted to wait until he got back from New York . . . said she wanted time to think about the situation and didn't want to jump into anything too fast."

"She may be smarter than I had her pegged," John said and after a short pause, said he was going on to his couch in the den. "Do you have an alarm clock I could borrow, Beth?"

She answered that she did, but she had to get up early also in order to get the kids to school and would be glad to wake him at six o'clock or whatever time he wanted to get up. They said their "good nights," and as John went out the door to the hallway, he heard Beth tell her mother that she could sleep with her and he knew they would talk and giggle until the wee hours.

He wished Ester Langford had called before she came up from Mobile. There was enough to contend with without more being added to the confusion. She was a nice lady and he liked her, but it was like adding fuel to the fire.

Chapter Forty-six

TWO DAYS LATER, THE DOCTOR TOLD ALYN RUSSELL THAT his operation had gone so well and the leg was doing fine that he could go home. Since he had a fine doctor to watch over him, all would go well; in fact, he might even surprise them and come up before long to go fishing with him. "I'd be pleased as peas to have you," Alyn told the doctor, who was about John's age. "And I may just not pay the bill if you don't give me your word that you will come! You could even expect a fine dinner to boot."

"In that event, gentlemen, it's a done deal," Dr. Harper told Alyn as he extended his hand to him and then shook hands with John. He put the other on John's shoulder saying he was pleased that Dr. Russell had such faith in his work to entrust his father to him.

On the way back to Charles and Beth's house, Papa Russell insisted that he was feeling fine and the trip home would certainly not be too much for him. John had wanted him to wait another day at least to leave. He could call Emily and extend his absence from the office, but Papa was adamant. He wanted to go home. Dr. Harper had prescribed crutches so John had gone that morning to the hospital pharmacy while the operation was going on and got a pair. "Let's just have lunch with Beth and her mother and then hit the road for the hills," Alyn told his son.

Chapter Forty–seven

EACH PASSENGER FILING THROUGH THE GATE, BOARDING Northeastern flight 233, received a cordial greeting from the senior stewardess, Janet Elderman. She had made it a habit from her first day on the job to evaluate personalities of the passengers who walked past her. In fact, she had done this since her college days when she majored in psychology. Now, smiling sweetly at each passenger, she welcomed them aboard and turned occasionally after one passed, for a more analytical view of an interesting face. Some may have taken this as flirtation.

Today, she observed each as usual, checking them off her list and finding that this load of passengers was the same as any other; oh, there were a few whom she found to be more interesting than on some flights. Sometimes she wondered if she was becoming too intro- spective; if her instincts were too keen perhaps. More often than not, her instincts proved correct. Today's group, for instance, soon proved to be more unusual than she first observed. One particular character bothered her . . . so much that later she mentioned it to Captain Davenport. He never before discounted her views. The man she described to him was rather elderly; he wore a thick black beard and was well-dressed in a suit that revealed to Janet that he had come in to New York aboard a European flight. His small beady eyes had met hers hesitantly in passing but only for an instant as he reverted them when she looked straight at him. He nodded his head and hurried to a seat in the aft section of the Lockheed L-1011.

"What do you make of him?" the captain asked when Janet mentioned this to him.

"I duno . . . name's Albert Roth," she said checking off his name after he had gone past her. "But I do know he is not an honest person."

"I s'pose a lot of dishonest folks have ridden on our planes," Captain Davenport grinned.

"Of course, but he has something to hide, and someone like this man worries me. When he went by, I felt vibrations like crazy, and I'd feel a lot better if you'd alert tower management."

The last passenger had entered and now they turned to do their usual duties. "Honey, I've felt your vibrations before and . . ."

She did not give him time to finish but turned on her heels and left the flight deck with Captain Syd Davenport smiling to himself, remembering her vibrations. "He'd be an utter fool," he thought, "if he alerted the tower about each dishonest jerk that boarded his plane."

Albert Roth shuffled on back in the tourist section and took his seat on the row with a pretty young girl. The girl, Leisa Harding, smiled, being her usual friendly self, as he took his seat, leaving an empty one between them with Roth on the outside next to the aisle.

The wealthy Mrs. Vern Brawnstein occupied a seat in the center aisle across from Albert Roth with the aisle between them. Mrs. Brawnstein, a resident of Cushing, New York, was en route to her granddaughter's wedding in Atlanta. She held a box on her lap, neatly wrapped, containing a precious set of crystal given to her by the late Mr. Brawnstein many years ago. This gift (that a stewardess would surely insist she put overhead) would be prized by the granddaughter for years to come, and Mrs. Brawnstein would be proud for giving the treasured gift. The box perched on her lap, would be coddled as if it were a lap poodle, too precious to entrust to the baggage crew.

Beside the bejeweled old lady reeking with perfume sat a little six-year-old colored girl, with her mother on the far side of the center aisle. The child kept her oversized brown eyes glued to the beautifully wrapped package from the moment she took her seat. Her suspense was building up moment by moment as they sat waiting for the plane to taxi out to the runway. Presents with pretty fluffy bows were a wonder to the child and sensing this, Mrs. Brawnstein permitted a stiff smile on her wrinkled face.

"It's a wedding present for my granddaughter," she said affably. "Someday you may be a bride, too, and receive lots of presents."

"Oh," was the faint answer, her curiosity settled.

Filing up the aisle now was Charles Russell holding his carry-on case with one hand. "Hi, Charles," he heard a voice call to him, "Back here." He saw the young girl waving to him, the astonished look on his face clearly evident.

"Leisa! What in the world are you doing on this plane?" He placed the briefcase overhead. Noting the numbered seat and with an "excuse me," slid past Albert Roth into the middle seat beside the smiling girl.

"Why are you here, Leisa? Does your mother know about this or are you running away?"

"To your first question," she said in her fast New York accent, "I am here to get to Atlanta, and, yes, my mother does know. As for the last question, since my mother does know then I am obviously not running away." She hooked her arm in his. He looked down and promptly removed it.

"When the secretary made your reservation, I asked her to make mine with our seats together. Now, isn't that nice? You can drop me at my hotel, or better still, stay awhile, and I expect you to show me around the town and treat me to dinner."

"You've got it all planned out, haven't you little Leisa. You don't plan my itinerary, little one, and I have a family to go home to, you know."

"Well, the least you could do is invite me home to dinner. I thought all southerners were known for their impeccable hospitality."

"I just lost mine." He leaned over and whispered in her ear, "Now tell me truthfully, what is it you have up your sleeve this time? Are you going to join the flower children on the streets of Atlanta?"

"Charles! You are not complimentary in the least. You know I don't do that anymore. I can see right through my mother . . . she's sending me down there to go to school. And I know she's just trying to get me away from my friends. She has her head in the sand, you see, because she still thinks the South is way behind the goings-on up here."

"Okay, I'll buy your story, but just remember this. If you so much as show your face around my house or my family, I'll pack you back on a plane so quick it will make your head swim, and that's a fact, Leisa."

She frowned and pouted her lips. Then she brightened and smiled saying confidently, "Charles, I think it is I who have the upper hand here. I could tell your wife a few things about you and my darling mother."

At once Charles thought about his beautiful wife and children. They had been through a lot of hard knocks together—business hardships when he first started the business, all the kids' childhood sicknesses, his heart attack, nearly losing the kids in the woods not long ago. No! This girl was not going to damage his life. He had done a lot of thinking these past few days while he was in New York. He loved Beth, and he wanted to make a change. The way his life was heading, it could plunge to rock bottom where he could never get it all back again.

He also decided he'd go to Papa and tell him that he was sorry for being so arrogant and insistent about the property. He really didn't need it, and if his dad wanted to continue living in the back-woods, that was his decision. And about Connie Roland . . . he did not know what she would want to do, but he had a few sugges-tions that may please her. Brad Lyles and Mo Jackson were his right-hand men whom he could depend on, and they would go along with him whatever was decided. If all the men wanted a union, then they could have it. What difference could it make? He and Gregg had always treated them fairly so what more could a union ask for except retirement and actually he'd pondered that lately, too.

So, all things considered, this trip to New York had done wonders for Charles Russell, and this upstart of a girl was not going to spoil it for him. People passing up the aisles looking for their seats were only hurrying faces instead of individuals. A stewardess leaned over Roth and inquired to all seated in that section, "Would any of you care for a pillow?" The couple did not, they replied, and Roth only shook his head.

Across the aisle, Mrs. Brawnstein noticed Albert Roth. Their eyes met only briefly, then the old man turned toward the window to escape her inquisitive eyes. The lady wrinkled her forehead thought-fully, continuing to stare at the back of his head that was still turned aside from her. Something about him was reviving old memories . . . old hurts. Roth lit a cigar. Its strong odor caused several glances from people close by, even a wave of the hand in the air by Charles.

"Mama, dat ole ceegar stinks!" the little girl between her mother and Mrs. Brawnstein loudly pronounced.

Just then stewardess Jane Morrison asked Albert Roth to please observe the "No Smoking" light. "After we are airborne, sir. Thank you."

"I can't see out, Mama," the child proclaimed and stood on the floor to stretch up on her toes for a better view. "I wanna sit where you are, Mama." The mother obliged by changing seats with her daughter as Mrs. Brawnstein quickly grasped her package, giving the little seat partner a worried look.

Even though Charles had made some commitments to himself, he still had misgivings about Leisa confronting Beth. His misgivings became profound when Leisa continued her threats.

"Maybe your wife isn't aware there has been someone else. I assume she isn't a dummy because she landed you, and that's exactly what I intend to do, Charles."

"Shh, Leisa . . . please."

"I won't shh," she said angrily. Then just as quickly as she became angry, she softened and again linked her arm through his and leaned her head against his shoulder. "Oh, Charles," she whispered to appease him, "she's too old; I'll love you like you've never been loved before."

He was embarrassed and turned to each side to see if anyone had been listening. They had not, he decided, because she had been whispering. "Stop it now, Leisa, or I'll ask the stewardess to give me another seat. And don't you ever think of talking to my wife."

The distraught girl withdrew her arm from his and sat back with tears streaming down her face. This girl, only a couple of years older than his own daughter, could truly be a thorn in his side. How did he ever get mixed up with either her mother or this girl? If Beth ever found out, would she ever be forgiving? Maybe it would be best to be completely truthful . . . no . . . the truth would only hurt her. Beth, mother of his children . . . how sweet and innocent. It would be good to get home again. He'd put the girl in a taxi and warn her to never set foot on his doorstep. Penny would be in college in another year, out and gone from them, and sooner than one could blink an eye, they would all be scattered. How the children had grown just this past year. Oh, the years do slip by without even as much as a warning.

THE L-1011 WAS TAXIING ALONG TO THE RUNWAY NOW. IT pulled to a stop where the East-West runway crossed its path for a Delta jet to clear the runway. On the way to their take-off point, Janet Elderman, speaking distinctly and clearly in her New England accent, gave her usual welcome aboard to passengers, via the P.A. system. She knew the welcome passage by heart. Two other stewardesses demonstrated while Janet made the essential announcements about oxygen masks and emergency exits.

The impending storm caused Leisa to wonder if they would need these emergency exits! She cringed each time lightning flashed about them and felt the urge to hold Charles's arm again. She looked over at him hesitantly before doing so. It would sustain her until they were airborne. A splattering of wind-driven rain could be heard hitting against the side, and she saw the reflection of lightning on the wing of the silver plane. "Only a crazy fool would fly in weather like this," she moaned.

"Then we have a load of crazy people," Charles grinned, allowing the arm to remain through his.

Leisa felt the hard masculine arm she clung to. There were so many things she loved about this man. He was so vibrant, somewhat self-centered, and totally dedicated to his work. She must have him for herself . . . not his wife . . . nor her mother . . . but herself alone. The difference in age would not matter; it would only make him feel younger.

The man on the other side of Charles became aware that someone was staring at him, which made him extremely uncomfortable. He cleared his throat, which did not need clearing, and at the same time rested an elbow on the chair arm and placed his fingers over his mouth and the thumb under his chin.

The lights ahead of the Delta 747 disappeared in the distance, and now it was their turn. The stewardesses strapped themselves in as the big jets blasted to take-off speed, and at eleven o'clock P.M., eastern standard time, Northeastern flight number 233 disappeared into the storm. Now climbing, they hit air pockets and lunged as if going over a bump. Leisa gasped, still clinging to Charles's arm. The seat-belt light stayed on. "What's to keep us from being struck by the lightning?" she asked peering out the window.

"We'll be above it shortly. You'll see." Then he thought, "Then you can turn loose of my arm." The big jet surged upward, still climbing. In a moment the heavens would swallow them up in their escape from the storm. Charles Russell was going home. With his mission completed, he felt like a new man with a load of bricks lifted off his shoulders. His father would be proud of him after he got over the actual shock of seeing the change in his son. His brother, the doctor, may be the one with sound sense and stability, but Charles was now willing to bridge the gap that had separated his father and himself.

The old man in the outside seat next to Charles was tired to the bone from three days of continuous strain. He listened impatiently to the conversation going on between the man and the silly girl, wishing he could nap. Then, there was that jabbering child on the inside aisle and that old woman next to her that kept staring a hole through him. He did not know why for he'd never laid eyes on the old bag. Only a few hours more, and he would be free, free, free. If only he could sleep for just a little while, but never mind, there would be plenty of time to sleep later. Still, he would like to kick that old hag out at 15,000 feet and listen to her scream all the way down. And another thing, that stewardess—the older one who seemed to be in charge—kept glancing back at him like she suspected him of something. He decided that he was feeling unduly guilty and told himself that the stewardess was not looking at him at all but at everyone in the cabin in general. It was her duty.

Breaking through a bank of angry, dark clouds, the plane suddenly appeared in the midst of millions of stars and a moon so bright that it looked as though it had been hung out to dry after having been washed clean by rainwater and New Improved Tide. Leisa dropped Charles's arm and staring out the window gasped, "Oh, how beautiful! How simply gorgeous!"

He leaned over to gaze out the window at the spectacle she'd described. "It makes a person feel so infinite and useless . . . like we are only a speck of dust in the whole universe." Then he added, "Didn't I tell you we'd be out of the storm in a few minutes."

The girl smiled, feeling much better, and sat back relaxed.

"You know," Charles said honestly, "there are times when I quite like you."

"I know. I grow on people. Just you wait."

He decided to leave well enough alone and closed his eyes to shut her out.

Captain Syd Davenport pushed the button for the forward galley phone. To the stewardess who answered, he said, "Anne, tell Janet she's wanted on the double."

The second officer, Theo Beckman, now had the controls. Both pilots' headsets were pushed upward over one ear, enabling them to converse and at the same time listen to flight patterns and radio calls. As the flight patterns were announced, they filed in their memory bank the altitudes of different aircraft close by.

Janet Elderman entered the darkened flight deck shortly. "Want some coffee?" she asked.

"You guessed it," Davenport told her, "but I also wanted to ask you about our friend you were feeling the vibrations for." He smiled, still making a joke of it.

"I did not feel vibrations 'for' him but strange vibrations, like he has something to hide . . . and he hasn't jumped out. He's there and quiet as a mouse. He hasn't even asked for a drink or anything. I think he's afraid to speak."

"Probably a harmless ole coot. I think you've been watching too many TV shows."

"Janet watching TV shows in her hotel room, that's a laugh." This came bluntly from Theo Beckman.

"That was certainly uncalled for, Theo, and may I ask what you do on your layovers? Don't be casting stones!" Davenport said. "And how about that coffee?"

"Okay, I'm going," she said but stopped when she saw a flashing light on the intricate instrument panel signifying a radio call. Each aircraft had its own private code. "That's us," Syd Davenport said as he switched from the radio to which he had been listening.

"This is U.S.N.E. Two-Three-Three," he acknowledged.

"Flight Two-Three-Three, this is U.S.N.E. Dispatcher, Kennedy. I have a message for the captain from Tower Management. Advise when ready to copy."

"Go ahead, Kennedy. We're ready," Davenport said pulling a note pad toward him.

"We have reason to believe a dangerous criminal is aboard your flight. His name is Albert Von Rothstein, alias Albert Roth. Please check and advise Ground Control."

Janet Elderman had turned to leave the cabin when she heard the message. "We don't have to check, do we Captain Davenport?" she said emphatically. Davenport reported back to the Kennedy dispatcher and asked what their instructions were.

"Don't do a thing. He will be apprehended upon disembarking in Atlanta. Repeat . . . do nothing."

Janet left the cabin in a huff. Had her intuitions ever failed her? Never. She wondered what the old man had done.

In the seat directly in front of Roth was a Methodist minister. Janet made her way agilely back to the minister to inquire if he would mind moving three rows forward to comfort a blind girl, by the name of Ruth Amsley, who had never before flown. Stewardess Ann Tyson had reported to Janet just before she was summoned to the flight deck that the girl appeared to be upset and was traveling alone. Of course the reverend would be delighted to sit with the girl and moved forward. Janet then cast a furtive glance toward Roth, who returned a cold stare. "If I turn my head each time," he thought, "she may become suspicious."

Syd Davenport was now making another radio check to Air Route Control. As he spoke, he gazed out into the bright night sky that was illuminated by the millions of stars winking at the moon, while far below the lights of some large city blinked back at them.

Beckman pushed his headset up and spoke to the senior pilot. "Well, I guess it's about time we had some excitement, don'cha think? The flights have been rather routine for awhile."

"That's the way I like 'em," Captain Davenport answered. "The more routine, the better. I always like to know that I'll land a load of safe passengers. And I'm due for retirement in another year, so I hope the flights will all be downright boring, until then anyway."

"You've put in a lot of years flying so what will you do with yourself then? Go to pot I imagine . . . or will you and your lovely wife fly [he emphasized the word "fly"] to some remote island for a long vacation?"

"Oh, a short vacation, maybe, but in an automobile. My wife won't fly."

Beckman laughed. "But vacations can't last forever."

"Well, then I'm going into business with her father. He'll be retiring in about five years so then the business will be ours. He started this auto parts business and it's really taking off."

Beckman wished he were close to retirement time as well.

The presence of Albert Roth had been recorded in the flight records and now Beckman recorded their position that had been reported. "I wonder what that old duck did," he said casually knowing that neither of them knew.

"Whatever it is, I'll never hear the end of it from our senior stewardess. But I'd bet you he's headed to South America."

"With a name like that, he must be German."

BACK IN THE CABIN, ROTH HAD GIVEN IN AND ACCEPTED A drink from a stewardess. It relaxed him and eased his earlier tension. Now, he closed his tired eyes and smiled, thinking of the free days that lay ahead. All would be a bed of roses from now on . . . clear sailing . . . maybe those terrible dreams would subside . . . all those marching people moving toward him, shouting, pushing, shoving, screaming! Oh, that nightmarish screaming was the most terrible of all! His head would nearly split apart. When all this happened, he generally shot upright in bed and awoke to find his clammy hands clasped over his ears, sweat rolling off his ashen face in beads.

Now, here was this soothing relaxed feeling. He felt assured there would be no more dreams . . . no more. Then he asked for another drink and threw it down almost immediately. In all the previous dreams, Roth could not visualize the people's faces. There were blurs where faces were suppose to be, and the clothes were all dark, drab, with no shape at all . . . if the figures would just not scream, he maybe could have stood the rest.

Almost from the moment Reverend Vick Bradberry sat down beside the attractive brunette, she felt a calmness sweep over her body that built from her toes and flowed upward. He touched her hand, letting her know he was gentle and kind. She smiled and drew a mental picture of him, and when she described his features, he laughed a melodious laugh, saying, "You are absolutely correct. How could you know I am so handsome!"

"It's a gift," the girl said. "I read voices. They can tell me every-thing."

He knew all about the gifts of the Spirit, but not knowing about such a gift as she described, he changed the subject. "Are you traveling alone?"

"Yes, someone is to meet me at the Atlanta Airport."

"I see," he replied and then bit his underlip for saying that.

She sensed it and said, "It's alright. That is just a phrase that people use all the time. We blind say it also when we understand something. Tell me, Reverend, why was I afraid until you sat down beside me?"

"Actually, that is pretty simple. It's like knowing someone is there . . . faith that there is someone to lean on, like when I was learning to swim. I remember the pool was not over my head at any spot, and I had the assurance that I could stop anywhere to rest if need be. Gave me confidence I suppose." There was a silence and then he continued. "I know a person can feel alone even in a crowd, but we all can have the assurance that God is always with us." This reminded him of last Sunday's sermon. The agnostic man would not believe because he had no tangible object to see or touch. If he would be still and anticipate, he too would feel the presence of the

Holy One. So it was with this one without sight; she knew someone was there.

"I'm going away to school," Ruth told the preacher happily. "And I will major in music. They say I have a gifted voice."

"Then I am sure you have. I would love to hear you sing. Well, Ruth, maybe I will hear you someday when you become famous, and when I do, I will stand up and cheer and then put my fingers between my lips and whistle." His statement made her chuckle happily, and he felt a great satisfaction in meeting this remarkable girl. "Where are you going to school, in Atlanta?"

"Oh, no. The school is in New York, but I'm going home for the weekend. I've always dreamed of going to this school, and now I can't really believe that it is actually happening to me."

"I see," he said again unexpectedly and smiled. "I did it again."

"Never mind. I see more than most people see in an entire life-time." There was expression in her eyes as she spoke, and he noticed that the beauty of them had not been marred by her blindness. Nor could one detect a downcast look, which was often a trait of most blind. "And how did you guess my name?"

"Oh, I didn't guess at all; the stewardess told me. It's a very pretty name, and it is such a pleasure to meet someone as pleasant as you. All the people at my church call me 'Vick.'"

"Then I will call you 'Vick.' Are you getting off in Atlanta or going on to Miami?"

"Atlanta is my home, and I'm glad that I will be able to escort you up the concourse to the rotunda and your waiting folks. By the way, sometime when you are home from school, I'd like it very much if you would come to our church and sing for us."

"Oh, of course, and I'll have my mother give you her name and phone number."

Vick told Ruth that he would be looking forward to the occasion and hoped it would be very soon.

THE LITTLE COLORED CHILD, AGAIN SITTING BETWEEN MRS. Brawnstein and her mother, stood down on the floor and looked at the package and then up into Mrs. Brawnstein's watchful eyes. "I'm goin'

tu my Granny's," she told the woman, "An' I bets she will have a present fo' me."

"I'm sure she will. Grandmothers always have presents for little grandchildren."

"I know. She always give me a present. Last time it was a baby doll but it was white and my Pap wouldn't leme keep it. He give it away. He say I couldn't . . ."

"Lessie, don' you talk so much," her mother interrupted and jerked her back on the seat. "You bother that lady with all that jabber. Let her be, now, baby."

"But, Mama," little Lessie loudly protested, "I gotta go boo-boo!"

"Hush up, chile. I tolt you tu whisper that. . . . 'Scuse her, please, Ma'am." She pushed the child out into the aisle. "Go on back there in the back. The toilet's back there." Then she called her back. "Here, Lessie, come back here and pick up that hair ribbon you just dropped." Lessie hurriedly picked up the bright red ribbon and scampered down the aisle to the toilet.

Mrs. Brawnstein turned to observe the little girl. "Her mother should have gone with her," she thought. Then her eyes met those of Albert Roth. He lowered his eyes, immediately turning toward the window.

"Drat that old fool . . . was she trying to start a conversation? Maybe she likes my looks," he thought. He had heard about these American widows. She would not get a peep out of him. He was too close now to spoil anything. All of these long years had gone by without being detected. He'd dyed his hair and the beard, but even then, there had been too many narrow escapes for comfort. The last straw was that woman who moved next door to him. Snooping old biddie who had come too close to the truth. There had come the dreadful day she knocked upon his door, and when he answered it, she called him by name! He had slammed the door and left from the rear without any personal belongings. What's with these old bags with minds of elephants?

Mrs. Brawnstein's mind drifted on a cloud back many years ago to the time she was a woman of thirty-five. Whenever she was tense or nervous, she felt as though this thought returned to haunt her. She saw a man hovering over her, smirking at her, talking to her in foul language. His strong hands held her arms tightly pinned back. His mouth searched frantically for hers as she flailed her head from side to side. She was a good-looking woman in those days with a full figure and fiery red hair. Her fighting spirit only made him more adamant. He had fought another officer for her, at the risk of losing his rank. "This one is mine!" he said with determination not to be outdone and now he'd have her. They were both strong and handsome; they would have a fine son for the state who would grow up to be a Nazi like his father . . . one to make the Führer proud. He slapped the fräulein's face to still her.

"Himmel! Fräulein! Be silent. Had you rather go to the Auschwitz ovens? Yes?" Then he smiled his most fetching smile into her eyes, revealing a front gold tooth that she found most repulsive.

Oh, why did these memories bother the old woman still? Why? Couldn't the years of tears erase even the worst thing? She had had a good life with her husband these past years since the war, and he had given her a fine daughter. But the son she lost to the Nazis. . . . She heard later that this Von Rothstein was put in charge of Auschwitz. Her parents had been there. They were old . . . the ovens. . . . As these terrible thoughts pounded through her head gathering momentum, causing her breath to quicken, for some reason she glanced back toward the man across the aisle. He had smiled at the little colored child's remark! His front gold tooth was revealed . . . those eyes . . . yes . . . without the presence of the beard . . . yes! Yes! It was Von Rothstein!

Jumping to her feet with the package of crystal crashing to the floor, she screamed a bloodcurdling scream that could be heard over the entire plane, except the flight deck. She threw herself across the aisle with all the force a sixty-five-year-old woman could muster. Her purse handle in hand, she pounded Roth unmercifully, screaming all the time.

Surprised passengers jumped to their feet, each freezing, trying to figure out what had happened and just what should be done. Roth, as surprised as anyone else, raised his hand over his head for protection. With sudden savagery, all pretense of kindness on Mrs. Brawnstein's face was gone.

From the first-class section, Janet Elderman came rushing along the aisle with another stewardess and a male passenger following along behind. "What is this! What is this!" Janet Elderman exclaimed. "Madam! Get back to your seat!" The aisle was blocked, and she and the man could not get through.

Roth was caught off guard just as Mrs. Brawnstein gave him a shove that landed him in the lap of Charles Russell, preventing himself and Leisa from moving from their seats. Behind them, a man and woman scrambled to the back for safety, while in front, passengers now stood, blocking the aisle. The preacher and the blind girl were now moving further toward the front with others.

Before Roth could get up, Charles clasped both arms around the man, subduing him. Mrs. Brawnstein was yelling, "He's a Nazi war criminal! For God's sake! Don't let him loose. He may be armed!" The woman then raised her hand and lowered her purse across the bridge of Roth's nose cutting a wide gap from which blood poured freely. It ran down his face and dripped on Charles's hands and pant leg. At the sight of blood, Lessie's mother pulled the woman away. Her strong hands twisted the purse away from Mrs. Brawnstein.

It was then that little Lessie emerged from the toilet and pushed her way through the standing passengers, the hair ribbon that she had not been able to tie, still in her hand. "Mama!" she called. "Mama! What's going on out here. What's all that racket?" She darted quickly past people to reach her mother, distracting attention from Roth, who quickly took advantage of the moment's detraction and broke free from Charles's hold just in time to grab Lessie before the little girl could get to her mother. He stood in the aisle with the child in his arms oblivious to her bites and kicks, blood still dripping from his nose onto the squirming child.

"Put me down you white trash! Put me down . . . Mama!"

"Shut up, brat, or I'll kill you!"

"Lessie!" the child's mother wailed. "Please, please be quiet for Mama! Don't say a word." Then to the man who was holding her daughter, she pleaded, "Please, misser, don't hurt her." The colored woman began to cry. "She's just a little girl. Please don't."

"Shut up!" Roth spoke loudly. He jerked the ribbon that the child clutched in her hand and twisted it around her neck, holding her arm tightly now with one hand to prevent her escape.

Charles Russell knew that Roth possessed no weapon or he would have already used it. He shook Leisa free from his arm and leaped to the aisle, about to make a lunge for the child when he caught his chest with his hands. A stabbing pain, like a ton of bricks had fallen on him, shot through his chest. He fell helplessly to the floor. Roth was still holding Lessie when Leisa Harding stood up in the seat to get past Roth, and she jumped down to Charles on the floor. "Charles! Oh, please, someone help him!" She hovered over him, rubbing a hand. He was lying on the other one.

"Stay back!" Roth warned emphatically. "Come near me and I will choke the child." It seemed like an eternity of silence that Charles lay in the aisle between the people and Roth.

All this happened so quickly! Janet Elderman turned and hurried to first class to alert a doctor there and to call the captain. Passengers in first class were all on their feet, and already the doctor had observed what was happening and had taken his bag down from the overhead rack and was pushing his way through the crowd. The three minutes during which all of this transpired seemed like an eternity to Vern Brawnstein, who had been subdued by the man who had been seated directly in front of her.

Reverend Vick Bradbury helped the blind girl back to her seat and, in his loud voice, asked everyone to please be seated. "Kindly clear the aisle for the doctor to get through." They obeyed like little lambs obey their shepherd. The doctor looked at Roth still standing in the rear of the plane next to the toilet door, with the ribbon tightly around Lessie's throat. "For the love of God, man! I must attend the man on the floor." Roth said nothing but gave a half-nod. The doctor dropped to his knees over Charles, his stethoscope suddenly appearing around his neck almost like the work of a magician.

Captain Syd Davenport had pushed his way through to the tourist section, instructing passengers to be seated as he progressed along. Then as he appeared through the doorway, Roth loudly proclaimed, "That is far enough, Captain. One more step and this child dies." His thick accent boomed, and he tightened the ribbon. Lessie squealed, and little fingers pulled against the ribbon.

Reverend Bradbury spoke softly to Roth. "You cannot succeed. They will get you when we land. Use your head, man. What will harming the little girl prove?" He sensed that it was of utmost importance to keep talking.

"I am afraid of no one." Roth told him in hostile words.

Dr. Minzetti, general practitioner, worked over Charles Russell. He pumped his chest over the heart area to no avail. There was no pulse. Charles Russell was dead!

Someone with kind gentle hands pulled Leisa Harding back in a seat away from the group around Charles. At first she had screamed without hearing herself and then clapping her hands over her mouth, she emitted little sobs. Now she lay back in the seat unconscious, ominously white. The one thing she ever really wanted out of life vanished in an instant. She did not even know when Mr.

Pinkerton emerged from the other toilet, white from being sick, and surprised Albert Roth, who dropped his hold on Lessie as the toilet door hit him on the backside. The little girl's mother saw what happened instantly. "Run, Lessie! Run to Mama!" The child obeyed her mother quicker than she had ever before obeyed anyone, and Roth locked himself in the toilet, not coming out until officials at the Atlanta airport prized him out. Like a cornered wild animal, Roth crouched on the seat, with his mind a total blur, able only to realize one thing . . . that he would never make South America now. All these years of concealing his identity now lost. He had come so close, and now the thousands of marching people came at him from out of thin air. They yelled, pushed, shoved, pointed fingers at him. At last they had him cornered with no way out.

Chapter Forty–eight

THE JANUARY DAY WAS EXTREMELY COLD. A WIND WHIPPING through bare branches caused people to hunch down into coats and hold onto hats. As the boughs dipped and swayed in the wind, they made music all their own that sounded mournful and carried across the mountain, down the deep sides, and into the valleys. The cold could be felt clear to the bone, enough to cause shivers no matter how thick a fur coat one had on.

Alyn Russell had many memories of standing at this spot on the mountain from childhood until now. They say memories tend to fade, and deep hurts become bearable; but this day would wring his heart out so greatly that it would take years to recover his joy, or so he felt at this moment. As the reverend was intoning some words of comfort he did not hear, the memories did a replay in his mind like a movie film on fast run. He was thinking how fast one's life goes by. It was just like he was a little boy running through the woods with his friend Luther and walking the sweet little Cynthee home from school. Cynthia—the love of his life. What a wonderful wife and mother she was. It took a number of years to turn the memories of her into sweet ones instead of sorrow. And then there were Aunt Joyce and Uncle Anson who had meant the world to him! After all the years that had flown by, things and people dear to his heart were still alive in his memory as though they only happened yesterday or last week perhaps.

Now Charles. Does one ever get over losing a child? Oh, he was now no child, but in Alyn's mind, he would always be the little headstrong boy, with the crooked mischievous smile, who required such a firm hand to rear. "Oh, Cynthee, did I go wrong with him?" he'd asked over her grave many times. "Is there something more I could have done?"

After the service inside the church on Kendell Mountain, Alyn Russell stood here now in the cemetery with bowed head as last farewells were being said to Charles Anson Russell. His loving family and friends were gathered around. Teresa had an arm around her father. On the other side stood John with an arm around Beth; her younger children stood in front of them, with Penny and Al next to her.

Before the church service, Teresa had asked John if he knew who the attractive lady was that came in late and took a seat. Instead of stopping at the back, she made no bones about coming down the left-side aisle during a song. She took a seat on the end of the third pew that someone had vacated to take out a fussing baby. John only shook his head that he did not know her, leaving Teresa to assume she was an acquaintance from Atlanta.

As people were filing past the family offering their condolences, this well-dressed, attractive woman approached and extended a gloved hand to Beth. She was the last person in line. "Please accept my condolence, Mrs. Russell," she said in a husky voice. Turning to Penny and Al she said, "These must be Charles's beautiful children." She placed a hand on Peter's head, which he loathed. Beth had shaken many hands this day, and this face looking at her now was just another in a sea of faces.

The woman reached over to John with her hand out saying, "And this handsome man must be Charles's brother, John, whom I've heard so much about." She smiled, flashing a mouth full of beautiful teeth.

"Yes," he answered, "John Russell . . . and your name is?" he asked, not caring if she were the president's wife or the Queen of England.

"Oh, forgive me, please. I thought everyone would know that I am J. P. Thrower. Everyone just calls me J. P. I don't know why I was stuck with the obtrusive name of Jacquilyn Patricia. I assumed that Charles had told you that I am his financial backer."

"Yes. Well, we just assumed that . . ."

She laughed, which Beth thought was absolutely inappropriate. "I know, Dr. Russell . . . may I call you John? Charles told me his brother is a doctor." Without waiting for an answer she continued. "I know this is not the place or time to discuss business, but as there will be no other time available, I'd just like to say that this project Charles has started needs completing." She should have been speaking to Beth about this matter. "He had a fabulous idea," J. P. continued, "that would be a real moneymaker. Why don't you step in and finish it, John?" Teresa and Papa had turned aside to speak with others and did not hear this suggestion or Papa would have said a few words to this Thrower woman. "Together, you and I would make a great team." She looked smug and sure of herself. He had noticed her Mercedes when she had pulled up to a stop at the cemetery blocking several other cars. No doubt the vehicle was a rented one, for she would have had to immediately come from New York City by plane to get here for the funeral. Connie Roland was standing close by. As far as looks, she could lay J. P. Thrower in the shade any day and no doubt her quick tongue could, too. But this sophisticated New York woman would be needed by the persons who would take over the business and complete Charles and Gregg's project, so she would have to be handled with kid gloves.

"Don't be too hasty to say no. We would make a great team, and I would make you a wealthy man, John Russell," J. P.'s eyes gazed deep into his own.

With his arm already around Beth, he smiled into her face, saying both to Beth and to J. P. Thrower, "Thanks, but I am already a very wealthy man. Yes. A very wealthy man."